FamilyCircle®

Healthy Home-Style Cooking

Meredith® Books
Des Moines, Iowa

Des Moines, Iowa.
First Edition.
Printed in the United States of America.
ISSN: 1944-6926
ISBN: 978-0-696-24225-0

All of us at Meredith® Books are dedicated to providing you with information and ideas to enhance your home. We welcome your comments and suggestions. Write to us at: Meredith Special Interest Media, 1716 Locust St., Des Moines, IA 50309-3023.

Pictured on the front cover:
Apple Puffed Oven Pancake, page 290

Ahh... don't you just love the smell of roasting beef?

Or the sight of mashed potatoes heaped in a bowl? Or the sweet flavor of a fruity dessert crowned with crumb topping? And then, don't you just cringe at the thought of unwanted calories that comes with eating so many of those favored family-made classics—the ones steeped in rich and indulgent ingredients that typify the tradition of homemade goodness?

Stop right there. You don't have to give up those treasured time-honored recipes. *Healthy Home-Style Cooking* is loaded with hundreds of cherished recipes from yesteryear, all re-created with fewer calories for families of today. You'll also find new creations (some designed just for kids) that are sure to become classic recipes for the next generation.

You ask, how is it done? It's easy: the old-fashioned way. Begin with fresh foods that naturally abound with all the good-for-you stuff, use less fat (or substitute a more healthful fat when appropriate), and choose lower-fat and/or reduced-sodium products when possible.

Not only are these heartwarming recipes better for you, you'll discover they suit your busy schedule as well. Whether you have 15 minutes or two hours until dinnertime, there's an entrée, soup, or sandwich that will quiet your family's ready-to-eat-now demand. There are also those long-simmered recipes that you can toss into the slow cooker in the morning and not think about until it's time to put dinner on the table.

And that's just the beginning. More than main dishes, you'll also find tasty snacks to satisfy rumbling tummies between meals, delicious morning foods to jump-start your day, and fabulous desserts to indulge your sweet tooth. If menu planning is not your forte, try one of the tasty menu ideas designed to make putting a balanced meal on the table easier for you. It's all here. Everything you need to enjoy old classics and new favorites—and your good health too.

Because meal planning for a busy family can be challenging, look for these helpful icons throughout the book:

Any recipe that can be made from start to finish in 30 minutes or less.

This symbol denotes recipes approved by kids.

Contents

page 15
page 31
Smart

Snacks & Starters

Wasabi Party Mix

Wasabi Party Mix

MAKES 80 (¼-cup) servings
PREP 15 minutes

- 5 cups wasabi peas*
- 4 cups bite-size toasted rice cracker mix
- 4 cups sesame sticks
- 4 cups honey-roasted peanuts
- 2 cups shredded coconut

1 In a very large bowl stir together all ingredients. Store in an airtight container at room temperature for up to 2 weeks or in the freezer for up to 4 months.
***Note:** To make wasabi peas, place 5 cups dehydrated peas in a large bowl. Lightly coat peas with nonstick cooking spray. Sprinkle with 2 to 3 teaspoons wasabi powder; toss to coat.

PER SERVING 99 calories; 6 g fat (2 g sat.); 3 g protein; 9 g carbohydrate; 1 g fiber; 134 mg sodium; 0 mg cholesterol

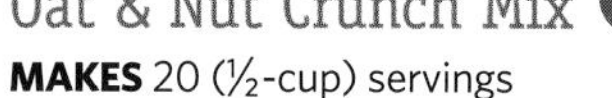

Oat & Nut Crunch Mix

MAKES 20 (½-cup) servings
PREP 10 minutes **BAKE** 20 minutes **COOL** 30 minutes
OVEN 300°F

- 4 cups sweetened oat square cereal or brown sugar-flavored oat biscuit cereal
- ½ cup sliced almonds
- 2 tablespoons butter, melted
- ½ teaspoon apple pie spice
- Dash salt
- 1 cup dried cherries and/or golden raisins

1 In a 15×10×1-inch baking pan combine cereal and almonds. In a small bowl stir together melted butter, apple pie spice, and salt. Drizzle butter mixture over cereal mixture; toss to coat.
2 Bake in a 300°F oven about 20 minutes or until almonds are toasted, stirring once halfway through baking. Cool in pan on a wire rack for 20 minutes. Stir in dried cherries. Cool completely. Store in an airtight container at room temperature for up to 1 week.

PER SERVING 83 calories; 3 g fat (1 g sat.); 2 g protein; 12 g carbohydrate; 1 g fiber; 63 mg sodium; 3 mg cholesterol

Apple Crunch Mix 

MAKES 6 (½-cup) servings
PREP 5 minutes

- 2 cups cinnamon-flavored oat square cereal
- ⅔ cup original or cinnamon-flavored crisp baked apple pieces
- ½ cup shelled, lightly salted pistachio nuts or coarsely chopped toasted pecans
- ¼ cup golden raisins

1 In a medium bowl stir together cereal, apple pieces, nuts, and raisins. Store in an airtight container at room temperature for up to 1 week.

PER SERVING 164 calories; 6 g fat (1 g sat.); 5 g protein; 25 g carbohydrate; 3 g fiber; 94 mg sodium; 0 mg cholesterol

Cheesy Chili Popcorn 

MAKES 10 (¾-cup) servings
START TO FINISH 10 minutes

- 8 cups popped popcorn
- 2 tablespoons butter, melted
- 1 teaspoon chili powder
- ⅛ teaspoon garlic powder
- 2 tablespoons grated Parmesan cheese

1 Place popcorn in a large bowl. In a small bowl stir together butter, chili powder, and garlic powder. Drizzle over popcorn; toss to coat. Sprinkle with Parmesan cheese; toss to coat. Store in an airtight container at room temperature for up to 3 days.

PER SERVING 51 calories; 3 g fat (2 g sat.); 1 g protein; 5 g carbohydrate; 1 g fiber; 46 mg sodium; 7 mg cholesterol

Apple Crunch Mix

Frozen Yogurt Pops

Frozen Yogurt Pops 

MAKES 8 pops
PREP 20 minutes **FREEZE** overnight

- 2 **cups low-fat vanilla yogurt**
- 1 **12-ounce can frozen juice concentrate, thawed***
- ½ **teaspoon vanilla**
- 8 **5-ounce paper cups**
- 8 **wooden popsicle sticks**

1 In a large bowl stir together yogurt, juice concentrate, and vanilla. Pour yogurt mixture evenly into paper cups. Cover cups with foil; cut a slit in the center of the foil on each cup and insert a wooden stick. Freeze overnight or until firm.

2 To serve, remove foil and peel away the paper cup.

***Note:** For sweet, fruity pops, try grape, raspberry, or a fruit-blend juice concentrate. For milder pops or for tart juices like orange or lemonade, make 6 pops using a 6-ounce can of fruit juice concentrate rather than a 12-ounce can. You also can make 2 or 3 different batches using different juices and swirl them together or layer them by freezing after each layer.

PER POP 165 calories; 1 g fat (0 g sat.); 3 g protein; 36 g carbohydrate; 0 g fiber; 63 mg sodium; 3 mg cholesterol

Fruit Sundae Cones 

MAKES 6 cones
START TO FINISH 5 minutes

- **¾ cup cut-up strawberries**
- **3 cups assorted cut-up fruit (such as apples, bananas, cherries, seedless red grapes, kiwifruit, plums, and/or peaches)**
- **6 large waffle cones**
- **¼ cup toasted coconut (optional)**

1 Place strawberries in a blender; cover and blend until smooth. Place assorted fruit in a large bowl; gently toss together. Spoon fruit into cones. Drizzle with the strawberry puree. If desired, top with coconut. Serve immediately.

PER CONE 105 calories; 1 g fat (0 g sat.); 1 g protein; 24 g carbohydrate; 2 g fiber; 25 mg sodium; 0 mg cholesterol

Tropical Dip with Jicama Chips

MAKES 8 (¼-cup) servings
PREP 25 minutes **CHILL** up to 4 hours

- **1 cup finely chopped, pitted, and peeled mango (2 medium)**
- **1 kiwifruit, peeled and finely chopped**
- **¼ cup finely chopped red sweet pepper**
- **2 tablespoons thinly sliced green onion (1)**
- **1 tablespoon lime juice**
- **1 tablespoon snipped fresh cilantro, parsley, or basil**
- **1 tablespoon packed brown sugar**
- **1 teaspoon grated fresh ginger**
- **Dash cayenne pepper**
- **1 medium jicama**

1 For dip, in a serving bowl combine mango, kiwifruit, sweet pepper, green onion, lime juice, cilantro, brown sugar, ginger, and cayenne pepper. Toss to coat. Cover and chill for up to 4 hours.
2 Meanwhile, for jicama chips, use a sharp knife to peel and halve jicama; cut jicama into ¼-inch slices. Serve jicama chips with dip.

PER SERVING 61 calories; 0 g fat; 1 g protein; 15 g carbohydrate; 1 g fiber; 2 mg sodium; 0 mg cholesterol

Double Dippin' Fruit 

MAKES 6 servings
START TO FINISH 15 minutes

- **1 4-ounce container vanilla pudding (prepared pudding cup)**
- **3 tablespoons caramel ice cream topping**
- **½ teaspoon vanilla**
- **¼ of an 8-ounce container frozen light whipped dessert topping, thawed**
- **¾ cup low-fat granola**
- **Assorted fresh fruit dippers (such as sliced apples, banana chunks, or strawberries)**

1 For caramel dip, in a medium bowl combine pudding, caramel topping, and vanilla; stir until smooth. Fold in whipped topping.
2 To serve, spoon caramel dip into a serving bowl. Place granola in another serving bowl. Serve with fruit. Dip fruit in caramel dip then in granola.

PER SERVING 129 calories; 3 g fat (2 g sat.); 1 g protein; 24 g carbohydrate; 1 g fiber; 86 mg sodium; 0 mg cholesterol

Double Dippin' Fruit

Very Veggie Dip 

MAKES 2 cups dip
START TO FINISH 20 minutes

- **1** **8-ounce carton light dairy sour cream**
- **½** **of an 8-ounce package reduced-fat cream cheese (Neufchâtel)**
- **1** **tablespoon fat-free milk**
- **¼** **cup finely chopped red or yellow sweet pepper**
- **¼** **cup finely chopped zucchini**
- **2** **tablespoons shredded carrot**
- **1** **tablespoon snipped fresh chives or green onion tops**
- **¼** **teaspoon salt**
- **¼** **teaspoon black pepper**
- **Assorted vegetable dippers, whole grain crackers, and/or multigrain tortilla chips**

1 In a medium bowl combine sour cream, cream cheese, and milk. Beat with an electric mixer on low to medium speed until smooth. Stir in sweet pepper, zucchini, carrot, and chives. Stir in salt and black pepper. Cover and chill for up to 3 days. Serve with vegetables, crackers, and/or tortilla chips.

PER 2 TABLESPOONS DIP 39 calories; 3 g fat (2 g sat.); 1 g protein; 2 g carbohydrate; 0 g fiber; 76 mg sodium; 10 mg cholesterol

Thai Spinach Dip

MAKES about 2½ cups dip
PREP 15 minutes **CHILL** 2 to 24 hours

- **1** **cup chopped fresh spinach**
- **1** **8-ounce carton dairy sour cream**
- **1** **8-ounce carton plain fat-free yogurt**
- **¼** **cup snipped fresh mint**
- **¼** **cup finely chopped peanuts**
- **¼** **cup peanut butter**
- **1** **tablespoon honey**
- **1** **tablespoon soy sauce**
- **1** **to 2 teaspoons crushed red pepper**
- **Assorted vegetable dippers (such as baby carrots, sliced zucchini, and/or cucumber sticks)**

1 Stir together spinach, sour cream, and yogurt. Stir in mint, peanuts, peanut butter, honey, soy sauce, and crushed red pepper. Cover; chill 2 to 24 hours. Serve with vegetables.

PER 1 TABLESPOON DIP WITH 3 BABY CARROTS 44 calories; 3 g fat (1 g sat.); 1 g protein; 4 g carbohydrate; 1 g fiber; 61 mg sodium; 3 mg cholesterol

Very Veggie Dip

Pine Nut-White Bean Dip

MAKES 1½ cups dip
PREP 15 minutes **STAND** 5 minutes **CHILL** 2 to 24 hours

- **¼** **cup soft bread crumbs**
- **2** **tablespoons fat-free milk**
- **1** **15-ounce can cannellini (white kidney) beans or Great Northern beans, rinsed and drained**
- **¼** **cup fat-free or light dairy sour cream**
- **3** **tablespoons pine nuts, toasted**
- **¼** **teaspoon salt-free garlic and herb seasoning blend or other salt-free seasoning blend**
- **⅛** **teaspoon cayenne pepper**
- **2** **teaspoons chopped fresh oregano or basil, or ½ teaspoon dried oregano or basil, crushed**
- **Pine nuts, toasted (optional)**
- **Fresh oregano or basil leaves (optional)**
- **Assorted vegetable dippers (such as baby carrots, radishes, broccoli florets, sweet pepper strips, sliced zucchini, and/or cucumber sticks)**

1 In a small bowl combine bread crumbs and milk. Cover and let stand for 5 minutes.
2 Meanwhile, in a blender or food processor combine beans, sour cream, the 3 tablespoons pine nuts, the seasoning blend, and cayenne pepper. Cover and blend until nearly smooth. Add bread crumb mixture. Cover and blend until smooth. Stir in oregano. Cover and chill for 2 to 24 hours.
3 If desired, sprinkle dip with additional pine nuts and garnish with oregano leaves. Serve with vegetables.

PER 2 TABLESPOONS DIP 40 calories; 1 g fat (0 g sat.); 3 g protein; 7 g carbohydrate; 2 g fiber; 70 mg sodium; 1 mg cholesterol

Quick to make. Great to take.

Walnut-Feta Yogurt Dip

MAKES 2 cups dip
PREP 25 minutes **CHILL** 24 to 48 hours + 1 hour

- **4 cups plain low-fat or fat-free yogurt***
- **½ cup crumbled feta cheese (2 ounces)**
- **¼ cup chopped walnuts or pine nuts, toasted**
- **2 tablespoons snipped dried tomatoes (not oil-packed)**
- **2 teaspoons snipped fresh oregano or marjoram, or 1 teaspoon dried oregano or marjoram, crushed**
- **¼ teaspoon salt**
- **⅛ teaspoon freshly ground black pepper**
- **Walnut halves (optional)**
- **Assorted vegetable dippers (such as baby carrots, broccoli florets, steamed and chilled asparagus spears, sweet pepper strips, sliced zucchini, and/or cucumber sticks)**

1 For yogurt cheese, line a yogurt strainer, sieve, or small colander with three layers of 100-percent-cotton cheesecloth or a clean paper coffee filter. Suspend lined strainer over a bowl. Spoon yogurt into strainer. Cover with plastic wrap. Chill for 24 to 48 hours. Discard liquid in bowl.

2 Transfer yogurt cheese to a medium bowl. Stir in feta cheese, chopped walnuts, dried tomatoes, oregano, salt, and pepper. Cover and chill for 1 to 24 hours. If desired, garnish with walnut halves. Serve with vegetables.

***Note:** Be sure to use yogurt that contains no gums, gelatin, or fillers. These ingredients may prevent the curd and whey from separating to make the yogurt cheese.

PER 2 TABLESPOONS DIP 68 calories; 4 g fat (1 g sat.); 4 g protein; 5 g carbohydrate; 0 g fiber; 140 mg sodium; 8 mg cholesterol

Walnut-Feta Yogurt Dip (top)
Pine Nut-White Bean Dip (bottom)

Spinach-Roasted
Red Pepper Dip

Creamy dip that's loaded with spinach, sweet peppers, and cheese always qualifies as sensible party fare. Crisp sweet pepper strips make good dippers, and so do crispy baked pita chips or crunchy low-fat crackers.

Spinach-Roasted Red Pepper Dip 

MAKES 2¼ cups dip
PREP 15 minutes **BAKE** 15 minutes **OVEN** 350°F

- **½ cup shredded part-skim mozzarella cheese**
- **½ cup plain low-fat or fat-free yogurt**
- **½ cup light mayonnaise dressing or salad dressing**
- **4 tablespoons grated Parmesan cheese**
- **1 tablespoon all-purpose flour**
- **1 teaspoon Dijon-style mustard**
- **1 cup loosely packed fresh spinach leaves, coarsely chopped**
- **¾ cup bottled roasted red sweet peppers, drained and chopped**
- **3 tablespoons thinly sliced green onion (2)**
- **3 red and/or yellow sweet peppers, seeded and cut into strips**

1 In a large bowl stir together mozzarella cheese, yogurt, mayonnaise dressing, 2 tablespoons of the Parmesan cheese, the flour, and mustard. Stir in spinach, roasted red peppers, and 2 tablespoons of the green onion. Spread mixture evenly in a shallow oven-going 1-quart dish or a 9-inch pie plate. Sprinkle with the remaining 2 tablespoons Parmesan cheese.
2 Bake in a 350°F oven for 15 to 20 minutes or until edges are bubbly and mixture is heated through. Sprinkle with remaining 2 tablespoons green onion. Serve with sweet pepper strips.

PER 1 TABLESPOON DIP 21 calories; 2 g fat (0 g sat.); 1 g protein; 1 g carbohydrate; 0 g fiber; 47 mg sodium; 3 mg cholesterol

Creamy Shrimp Dip

MAKES 3 cups dip
PREP 10 minutes **CHILL** 2 to 24 hours

- **1 pound cooked small, peeled, and deveined shrimp**
- **1 8-ounce carton reduced-fat dairy sour cream**
- **4 teaspoons prepared horseradish (or more to taste)**
- **¼ cup ketchup**
- **¼ cup light mayonnaise dressing**
- **½ teaspoon salt**
- **2 tablespoons snipped fresh dill or 2 teaspoons dried dill**
- **¼ teaspoon hot pepper sauce**
- **¼ teaspoon black pepper**
- **3 heads endive**
- **Fresh dill**

1 Finely chop shrimp; set aside. In a medium bowl stir together sour cream, horseradish, ketchup, mayonnaise dressing, salt, snipped fresh dill, hot pepper sauce, and black pepper. Stir in shrimp. Cover and chill for 2 to 24 hours.
2 Trim bottoms off endive and remove leaves, cutting ends as needed. Remove dip from refrigerator 30 minutes before serving; garnish with dill. Serve with endive.

PER 2 TABLESPOONS DIP 21 calories; 1 g fat (0 g sat.); 2 g protein; 1 g carbohydrate; 0 g fiber; 77 mg sodium; 20 mg cholesterol

Double Cranberry Crostini

MAKES about 30 appetizers
PREP 45 minutes **COOL** 1 hour **BAKE** 6 minutes
OVEN 375°F

- **1 recipe Cranberry-Ginger Chutney**
- **⅓ cup dried cranberries**
- **2 3-ounce packages cream cheese, softened**
- **2 tablespoons chopped pecans, toasted**
- **1 teaspoon peeled and finely chopped fresh ginger**
- **1 teaspoon lime juice**
- **1 16-ounce loaf baguette-style French bread**
- **4 ounces thinly sliced smoked turkey or ham**

1 Prepare Cranberry-Ginger Chutney; let cool. Place dried cranberries in a small bowl with enough boiling water to cover; cover and let stand 15 minutes. Drain well.
2 In a medium mixing bowl beat cream cheese with an electric mixer on medium speed until smooth. Beat in drained cranberries, pecans, ginger, and lime juice; set aside.
3 Slice bread diagonally into ½-inch slices. Arrange bread slices on a very large baking sheet. Bake in a 375°F oven for 6 to 8 minutes or until edges are just starting to brown. Cool slightly. Cut smoked turkey into about 30 pieces to fit on top of bread slices. Spread bread with cranberry-cheese mixture. Top each with a piece of turkey. Add a spoonful of Cranberry-Ginger Chutney.

Cranberry-Ginger Chutney: In a medium saucepan combine 1½ cups cranberries; ¾ cup packed brown sugar; ⅓ cup dried apricot halves, chopped; ⅓ cup golden raisins; 2 tablespoons peeled and finely chopped fresh ginger; 2 tablespoons cranberry juice; ¾ teaspoon ground cardamom; and ¼ teaspoon cayenne pepper. Cook over medium heat, stirring constantly, until brown sugar is dissolved. Cook, uncovered, for 3 to 4 minutes more or until cranberries pop, stirring occasionally. Transfer to a medium bowl; let stand about 1 hour or until completely cool. Cover and chill up to 1 week.

PER APPETIZER 107 calories; 3 g fat (1 g sat.); 3 g protein; 18 g carbohydrate; 1 g fiber; 150 mg sodium; 8 mg cholesterol

Easy Olive Focaccia 

MAKES 32 servings
PREP 20 minutes **BAKE** 20 minutes **COOL** 10 minutes
OVEN 375°F

- **1 16-ounce package hot roll mix**
- **3 tablespoons olive oil**
- **2 cloves garlic, minced**
- **1 tablespoon snipped fresh rosemary**
- **½ to 1 teaspoon kosher salt**
- **¼ teaspoon black pepper**
- **½ cup crumbled blue cheese (2 ounces)**
- **½ cup chopped, pitted ripe olives**

1 Lightly grease a 15×10×1-inch baking pan; set aside.
2 Prepare hot roll mix according to package directions, except substitute 2 tablespoons of the olive oil for the butter or margarine called for on the package. Knead dough and allow to rest as directed.
3 On a lightly floured surface, roll dough into a 15×10-inch rectangle. Carefully transfer dough to prepared baking pan; use your fingers to push dough into corners and sides of pan. Using your fingertips, press indentations randomly into dough.
4 In a small bowl stir together the remaining 1 tablespoon oil and the garlic; brush over dough. In another small bowl stir together the rosemary, salt, and pepper; sprinkle over dough. Sprinkle dough with cheese and olives; press cheese and olives gently into the dough.
5 Bake in a 375°F oven about 20 minutes or until golden. Cool in pan on a wire rack for 10 minutes. Using a wide spatula, lift focaccia from baking pan; place on a wire rack and cool completely. Serve within 2 hours.
Make-Ahead Directions: Place cooled focaccia in an airtight container or freezer bag; seal. Freeze for up to 3 months.

PER SERVING 75 calories; 2 g fat (1 g sat.); 3 g protein; 11 g carbohydrate; 0 g fiber; 158 mg sodium; 8 mg cholesterol

Spanish Potato Omelet Bites

MAKES about 4 dozen bites
PREP 35 minutes **BAKE** 15 minutes **STAND** 5 minutes
OVEN 450°F

- **6 eggs**
- **2 tablespoons half-and-half, light cream, or milk**
- **½ teaspoon salt**
- **¼ teaspoon black pepper**
- **Dash powdered saffron**
- **1 tablespoon olive oil**
- **1 tablespoon butter**
- **1 cup coarsely chopped fresh mushrooms**
- **2 cloves garlic, minced**
- **2 cups frozen diced hash brown potatoes with onions and peppers**
- **¼ cup snipped fresh chives or 2 tablespoons snipped fresh Italian parsley**

1 Grease an 8×8×2-inch baking pan; set aside. In a medium bowl whisk together eggs, half-and-half, salt, pepper, and saffron. Set aside.

2 In a large skillet heat oil and butter over medium heat until butter melts. Add mushrooms and garlic; cook and stir for 1 minute. Stir in potatoes. Cook, covered, over medium-low heat about 10 minutes or until potatoes are light brown and tender, stirring occasionally. Remove from heat; stir in chives.

3 Spread potato mixture evenly in prepared baking pan. Pour egg mixture evenly over potato mixture, pressing down lightly with the back of a spoon to completely cover potatoes. Bake, uncovered, in a 450°F oven about 15 minutes or until set and top is golden (center may puff during baking, but will fall during standing time). Let stand for 5 minutes. Cut into 1-inch squares. Serve warm.

Make-Ahead Directions: Bake and cut omelet bites as directed; place on an oven-going platter or baking sheet. Cover and chill for up to 24 hours. Reheat, uncovered, in a 350°F oven about 10 minutes or until heated through.

PER BITE 19 calories; 1 g fat (0 g sat.); 1 g protein; 1 g carbohydrate; 0 g fiber; 36 mg sodium; 27 mg cholesterol

Spanish Potato Omelet Bites

Veggie-Filled Quesadillas 

MAKES 20 wedges
PREP 20 minutes **BAKE** 5 minutes **OVEN** 425°F

- **2 small green and/or red sweet peppers, cut into thin strips**
- **1 small red onion, cut into thin 1-inch-long strips**
- **1 teaspoon olive oil or cooking oil**
- **½ teaspoon ground cumin**
- **½ teaspoon chili powder**
- **2 tablespoons snipped fresh parsley or cilantro**
- **⅓ cup tub-style reduced-fat cream cheese**
- **5 6- to 7-inch flour tortillas**
- **1 teaspoon olive oil or cooking oil**
- **Salsa (optional)**

1 In a large nonstick skillet cook sweet peppers and onion in 1 teaspoon hot oil over medium heat for 3 to 5 minutes or until crisp-tender. Stir in cumin and chili powder. Cook and stir for 1 minute more. Stir in parsley. Set aside.

2 Spread cream cheese over half of 1 side of each tortilla. Top with sweet pepper mixture. Fold tortilla in half over sweet peppers, pressing gently.

3 Place tortillas on an ungreased large baking sheet. Brush tortillas evenly with 1 teaspoon oil. Bake, uncovered, in a 425°F oven for 5 minutes. Cut each quesadilla into four wedges. If desired, serve warm with salsa.

PER 2 WEDGES 85 calories; 3 g fat (1 g sat.); 2 g protein; 11 g carbohydrate; 1 g fiber; 118 mg sodium; 4 mg cholesterol

Spicy Cheddar Twists

Spicy Cheddar Twists

MAKES 56 (5-inch) or 20 (14-inch) twists
PREP 45 minutes **BAKE** 10 minutes **OVEN** 425°F

- **1 teaspoon paprika**
- **½ teaspoon garlic powder**
- **½ teaspoon onion powder**
- **½ teaspoon ground ginger**
- **½ teaspoon ground cardamom (optional)**
- **⅛ to ¼ teaspoon cayenne pepper**
- **1 egg white**
- **1 tablespoon water**
- **1 17.3-ounce package (2 sheets) frozen puff pastry, thawed**
- **1½ cups shredded smoked or regular cheddar cheese (6 ounces)**

1 In a small bowl stir together paprika, garlic powder, onion powder, ginger, cardamom (if using), and cayenne pepper; set aside. In a small bowl gently beat egg white with the water; set aside. Lightly grease baking sheets; set aside.
2 On a lightly floured surface, unfold pastry sheets. Brush each sheet with some of the egg white mixture; sprinkle each with ¼ cup of the shredded cheese. Fold sheets in half. Using a rolling pin, roll each folded sheet into a 12×8-inch rectangle. Brush tops with more of the egg white mixture; sprinkle each with ½ cup of the remaining cheese. Sprinkle evenly with paprika mixture. Fold in half; roll each sheet into a 14×5-inch rectangle, pressing edges together to seal.
3 Cut each rectangle crosswise into ½-inch-wide strips (or cut lengthwise for longer twists). Twist ends of each strip in opposite directions several times. Place twists on prepared baking sheets, pressing down ends of strips onto the baking sheet. Brush twists lightly with remaining egg white mixture. Bake in a 425°F oven for 10 to 12 minutes or until brown. Serve warm or cooled to room temperature.*
***Note:** You can make these twists an hour or two ahead. To reheat, place twists in a single layer on a baking sheet. Bake in a 350°F oven about 5 minutes or until heated through.

PER 5-INCH TWIST 51 calories; 4 g fat (1 g sat.); 1 g protein; 3 g carbohydrate; 0 g fiber; 53 mg sodium; 3 mg cholesterol

Mushroom Bruschetta

Mushroom Bruschetta 

MAKES about 16 servings
PREP 20 minutes **BAKE** 5 minutes **OVEN** 425°F

- **1 8-ounce loaf baguette-style French bread**
- **Olive oil**
- **3 cups thinly sliced fresh mushrooms (shiitake, oyster, morel, porcini, portobello, cremini, and/or button) (8 ounces)**
- **4 cloves garlic, minced**
- **2 tablespoons olive oil**
- **½ cup dry white wine**
- **¼ teaspoon salt**
- **¼ cup snipped fresh parsley**

1 For toasted bread, slice bread into ¼- to ½-inch slices. Arrange bread slices on a large baking sheet. Brush one side of each slice lightly with the oil. Bake in a 425°F oven for 5 to 7 minutes or until crisp and light brown, turning once.
2 Meanwhile, in a large skillet cook the mushrooms and garlic in the 2 tablespoons hot oil over medium heat until mushrooms are tender, stirring occasionally. Add wine. Bring to boiling; reduce heat. Simmer, uncovered, about 5 minutes or until liquid is almost evaporated. Stir in salt. Remove from heat; cool slightly.
3 To serve, spoon mushroom mixture onto the oiled side of each bread slice. Sprinkle with parsley. Serve immediately.

PER SERVING 72 calories; 3 g fat (0 g sat.); 2 g protein; 8 g carbohydrate; 1 g fiber; 124 mg sodium; 0 mg cholesterol

Potato Skins with Roasted Peppers 

MAKES 12 appetizers
PREP 15 minutes **BAKE** 40 minutes + 8 minutes
OVEN 425°F/450°F

- **6 medium baking potatoes (about 2 pounds total)**
- **¼ teaspoon salt**
- **⅛ teaspoon black pepper**
- **1 7-ounce jar roasted red sweet peppers, drained and chopped**
- **3 tablespoons thinly sliced green onion (2)**
- **1 cup shredded reduced-fat mozzarella cheese (4 ounces)**
- **½ cup light dairy sour cream**
- **¼ teaspoon dried Italian seasoning, crushed**
- **1 clove garlic, minced**
- **Sliced green onion tops (optional)**

1 Scrub potatoes; prick with a fork. Bake in a 425°F oven for 40 to 45 minutes or until tender. Let stand until cool enough to handle.
2 Increase oven temperature to 450°F. Halve each potato lengthwise. Scoop out the insides of potato halves, leaving about ¼-inch shells. Cover and chill scooped-out potato for another use.
3 Line a 15×10×1-inch baking pan with foil. Arrange potato shells, cut sides up, on the prepared baking sheet. Lightly sprinkle shells with salt and black pepper. Sprinkle with roasted sweet peppers and the 3 tablespoons green onion. Top evenly with cheese. Bake for 8 to 10 minutes or until cheese melts and potato skins are heated through.
4 Meanwhile, in a small bowl stir together sour cream, Italian seasoning, and garlic. If desired, sprinkle potato skins with green onion tops. Serve warm with sour cream mixture.

PER APPETIZER 79 calories; 3 g fat (2 g sat.); 4 g protein; 11 g carbohydrate; 1 g fiber; 110 mg sodium; 8 mg cholesterol

Pesto Chicken Salad in Mini Peppers

MAKES 20 servings
START TO FINISH 35 minutes

- **20 mini sweet peppers (1½ to 2 inches long)**
- **1 cup chopped cooked chicken**
- **2 tablespoons finely chopped onion**
- **2 tablespoons finely chopped yellow or red sweet pepper**
- **3 tablespoons purchased pesto**
- **2 tablespoons mayonnaise**
- **⅛ teaspoon ground black pepper**

1 To make pepper shells, cut sweet peppers lengthwise, removing the top one-third of sweet peppers and leaving stems on the other portion. Finely chop some of the removed sweet pepper and use for the salad (reserve remaining sweet pepper for another use). Remove seeds and membranes from sweet pepper shells.

2 For salad, in a small bowl combine chicken, onion, and chopped sweet pepper. In another small bowl stir together pesto, mayonnaise, and black pepper. Add pesto mixture to chicken mixture, stirring to combine.

3 To serve, spoon some chicken mixture into each pepper portion. Arrange on a platter.

Make-Ahead Directions: Prepare filled peppers as directed. Arrange on a serving platter. Cover with plastic wrap; chill peppers in the refrigerator for up to 2 hours.

PER SERVING 45 calories; 3 g fat (0 g sat.); 3 g protein; 2 g carbohydrate; 0 g fiber; 32 mg sodium; 8 mg cholesterol

Pesto Chicken Salad in Mini Peppers

Fiesta Rolls

MAKES 8 to 10 servings
PREP 20 minutes **ROAST** 20 minutes **STAND** 15 minutes
CHILL up to 6 hours **OVEN** 425°F

- **2 large fresh poblano chile peppers***
- **2 medium red sweet peppers**
- **½ of an 8-ounce tub plain fat-free cream cheese (½ cup)**
- **1 tablespoon snipped fresh cilantro**
- **2 teaspoons lime juice**
- **⅛ teaspoon cayenne pepper**
- **2 cloves garlic, minced**
- **4 7- or 8-inch flour tortillas**

1 To roast poblano and sweet peppers, halve peppers and remove stems, membranes, and seeds. Place peppers, cut sides down, on a baking sheet lined with foil. Roast in a 425°F oven for 20 to 25 minutes or until skin is bubbly and brown. Wrap the peppers in the foil; let stand for 15 to 20 minutes or until cool enough to handle. Using a paring knife, gently pull off the skin; discard skin. Cut peppers into thin strips.
2 Meanwhile, in a small bowl stir together cream cheese, cilantro, lime juice, cayenne pepper, and garlic. Spread cream cheese mixture over tortillas. Lay poblano and sweet pepper strips over cream cheese mixture. Roll up tortillas. Wrap with plastic wrap; refrigerate for up to 6 hours. Unwrap and bias-slice rolls into 1¼-inch slices.
***Note:** Because chile peppers contain volatile oils that can burn your skin and eyes, avoid direct contact with them as much as possible. When working with chile peppers, wear plastic or rubber gloves. If your bare hands do touch the chile peppers, wash your hands and nails well with soap and warm water.

PER SERVING 67 calories; 1 g fat (0 g sat.); 3 g protein; 11 g carbohydrate; 1 g fiber; 61 mg sodium; 2 mg cholesterol

Chili Chicken Appeteasers

Chili Chicken Appeteasers 

MAKES 16 appetizers
START TO FINISH 15 minutes

- **4 medium nectarines or peaches**
- **½ cup shredded cooked chicken (about 3 ounces)**
- **2 teaspoons bottled Thai garlic-chili sauce or chili sauce**
- **2 teaspoons snipped fresh cilantro**
- **Fresh cilantro leaves (optional)**

1 Cut the nectarines into quarters and remove the pits. Carefully scoop out some of the fruit, leaving a ¼-inch shell inside the peel. Chop the scooped-out portion of the nectarines.
2 In a medium bowl stir together chopped nectarines, shredded chicken, garlic-chili sauce, and snipped cilantro. Spoon about 1 rounded teaspoon of the chicken mixture into each nectarine shell. If desired, garnish each filled shell with a cilantro leaf.

PER APPETIZER 26 calories; 1 g fat (0 g sat.); 2 g protein; 4 g carbohydrate; 0 g fiber; 12 mg sodium; 4 mg cholesterol

One, two, or a few—beware, these

Sweet, Hot, & Sour Meatballs

spunky little balls are addictive.

Sweet, Hot & Sour Meatballs

MAKES about 48
PREP 20 minutes **BAKE** 30 minutes **OVEN** 375°F

- 2 eggs
- ½ cup fine dry bread crumbs
- ½ cup finely chopped onion (1 small)
- ¼ cup milk
- ½ teaspoon salt
- ½ teaspoon black pepper
- 1 pound bulk pork sausage
- 1 pound ground beef
- ¾ cup apple jelly
- ⅓ cup spicy brown mustard
- ⅓ cup whiskey or apple juice
- 1½ teaspoons Worcestershire sauce
- Few dashes bottled hot pepper sauce

1 In a large bowl beat eggs with a fork. Add bread crumbs, onion, milk, salt, and pepper. Add sausage and beef; mix well. Shape into about forty-eight 1¼- to 1½-inch meatballs. Place in a shallow baking pan. Bake, uncovered, in a 375°F oven about 30 minutes or until cooked through (160°F). Drain.

2 Meanwhile, in a large saucepan stir together jelly, mustard, whiskey, Worcestershire sauce, and bottled hot pepper sauce; heat and stir until jelly melts and mixture bubbles. Add meatballs, stirring gently to coat. Cook for 3 to 5 minutes or until sauce thickens slightly and meatballs are coated.

PER MEATBALL 78 calories; 4 g fat (2 g sat.); 3 g protein; 5 g carbohydrate; 0 g fiber; 115 mg sodium; 20 mg cholesterol

Couscous-Stuffed Pork Spirals

MAKES about 36 slices
PREP 35 minutes **ROAST** 45 minutes **STAND** 5 minutes
OVEN 375°F

- 1 cup chicken broth
- ¾ cup dried couscous
- 1½ cups shredded fresh baby spinach leaves
- ½ cup sliced green onion (4)
- ½ cup tropical-blend mixed dried fruit bits
- ⅓ cup pine nuts, toasted
- 1 teaspoon finely shredded orange peel
- ¼ teaspoon salt
- ¼ teaspoon ground cinnamon
- ⅛ teaspoon cayenne pepper
- ⅛ teaspoon black pepper
- ¼ cup orange juice
- 2 12- to 16-ounce pork tenderloins, trimmed
- Salt and black pepper
- Mango chutney (optional)

1 In a small saucepan bring broth to boiling. Stir in couscous. Remove from heat and cover. Let stand for 5 minutes. Transfer couscous to a medium bowl and fluff with a fork. Stir in spinach, green onion, fruit bits, pine nuts, orange peel, the ¼ teaspoon salt, the cinnamon, cayenne pepper, and the ⅛ teaspoon black pepper. Stir in orange juice.

2 Working with 1 tenderloin at a time, use a sharp knife to make a lengthwise cut down the center of the tenderloin, cutting to within ½ inch of the other side. Open tenderloin like a book. Place knife in the V of the first cut. Cut parallel to the first cut to within ½ inch of the other side of tenderloin. Repeat on opposite side of V. Spread these sections open to lay tenderloin flat. Place opened tenderloin between two pieces of plastic wrap. Working from the center to the edges, pound lightly with the flat side of a tenderloin mallet to form a 10×8-inch rectangle. Fold in the narrow ends as necessary to make an even rectangle. Remove plastic wrap.

3 Spoon half of the couscous mixture over one of the tenderloins to within 1 inch of the edges. Roll tenderloin into a spiral, starting from a long side. Tie tenderloin spiral every 2 inches with 100-percent-cotton kitchen string. Place tenderloin, seam side down, in a shallow roasting pan lined with foil. Repeat with remaining tenderloin and couscous mixture, placing the second tenderloin next to the first in the roasting pan. Season with additional salt and black pepper.

4 Roast, uncovered, in a 375°F oven for 45 to 50 minutes or until an instant-read thermometer inserted in the stuffing registers 160°F. Loosely cover tenderloins with foil and let stand for 5 minutes. Remove kitchen string. Cut tenderloins into ½-inch slices. If desired, serve warm with mango chutney.

Make-Ahead Directions: Prepare as directed through Step 4, except do not slice the tenderloins. After roasting, cool tenderloins for 20 minutes; wrap each in foil. Chill for up to 24 hours. Remove kitchen string; slice. Serve chilled with chutney, if desired.

PER SLICE 58 calories; 2 g fat (0 g sat.); 5 g protein; 5 g carbohydrate; 0 g fiber; 64 mg sodium; 12 mg cholesterol

Fiesta Shrimp Skewers

MAKES 10 to 12 servings
PREP 25 minutes **MARINATE** 30 minutes to 1 hour
GRILL 8 minutes

- **1 recipe Cool Cilantro Dip**
- **1 pound fresh or frozen large shrimp in shells (about 32 shrimp)**
- **½ cup amber ale or other ale**
- **½ teaspoon finely shredded lime peel**
- **¼ cup lime juice**
- **2 tablespoons snipped fresh cilantro**
- **1 small fresh jalapeño chile pepper, seeded and finely chopped***
- **¼ teaspoon ground cumin**
- **⅛ teaspoon cayenne pepper**
- **1 clove garlic, minced**
- **2 fresh poblano chile peppers, seeded and cut into 1-inch pieces***
- **2 limes, cut into wedges**

1 Prepare Cool Cilantro Dip. Cover and chill until ready to serve. Thaw shrimp, if frozen. Peel and devein shrimp. Rinse shrimp; pat dry with paper towels. Place shrimp in a resealable plastic bag.
2 For marinade, in a small bowl stir together ale, lime peel, lime juice, cilantro, jalapeño pepper, cumin, cayenne pepper, and garlic. Pour marinade over shrimp. Seal bag; turn to coat shrimp. Marinate in the refrigerator for at least 30 minutes or up to 1 hour, turning bag occasionally.
3 Drain shrimp, reserving marinade. Alternately thread shrimp and poblano pieces onto ten to twelve 6-inch skewers,** leaving a ¼-inch space between pieces. Brush with the reserved marinade; discard any remaining marinade.
4 For a charcoal grill, place skewers on the grill rack directly over medium coals. Grill, uncovered, for 8 to 10 minutes or until shrimp are opaque, turning once halfway through grilling. (For a gas grill, preheat grill. Reduce heat to medium. Place skewers on grill rack over heat. Cover and grill as above.) Add a lime wedge to the end of each skewer. Serve the skewers with Cool Cilantro Dip.
Cool Cilantro Dip: In a small bowl stir together one 8-ounce carton light dairy sour cream, 2 tablespoons snipped fresh cilantro, 1 tablespoon bottled salsa, ½ teaspoon finely shredded lime peel, and 1 garlic clove, minced.

***Note:** Because chile peppers contain volatile oils that can burn your skin and eyes, avoid direct contact with them as much as possible. When working with chile peppers, wear plastic or rubber gloves. If your bare hands do touch the chile peppers, wash your hands and nails well with soap and warm water.
****Note:** If using wooden skewers, soak skewers in water for 30 minutes before using.

PER SERVING 81 calories; 3 g fat (1 g sat.); 9 g protein; 5 g carbohydrate; 1 g fiber; 71 mg sodium; 59 mg cholesterol

Crab-Vegetable Roll-Ups

MAKES 16 appetizers
START TO FINISH 40 minutes

- **2 medium zucchini and/or yellow summer squash**
- **½ cup cooked crabmeat, flaked and cartilage removed**
- **1 tablespoon mayonnaise or salad dressing**
- **1 teaspoon wasabi paste**
- **⅛ teaspoon salt**
- **½ of a medium avocado**
- **2 tablespoons coarsely shredded carrot**
- **16 small fresh basil leaves**

1 Trim ends of zucchini and squash. Using a sharp vegetable peeler, cut zucchini and squash lengthwise into wide, flat "ribbons." Discard first and last slices, and the seedy portions in the middle. (You will need 32 ribbons.) Set ribbons aside.
2 Drain crabmeat well in a colander, pressing with the back of a spoon to remove most of the liquid. Pat dry with paper towels. In a small bowl stir together crabmeat, mayonnaise, wasabi paste, and salt. Pit and peel the avocado; cut into thin strips.
3 For each roll-up, place one zucchini ribbon on top of one squash ribbon. Place 1 slightly rounded teaspoon of the crab mixture at one end of a doubled squash ribbon. Top with avocado strips, a few shreds of carrot, and a basil leaf; roll up. Place roll-ups, seam sides down, on a serving platter. If desired, cover and chill for up to 30 minutes.

PER APPETIZER 23 calories; 2 g fat (0 g sat.); 1 g protein; 1 g carbohydrate; 1 g fiber; 37 mg sodium; 4 mg cholesterol

Greek Salad Bites

MAKES 30 bites
PREP 15 minutes **CHILL** 2 to 24 hours

- 1 cup crumbled feta cheese (4 ounces)
- ½ cup dairy sour cream
- ¼ cup snipped fresh parsley
- 2 tablespoons oil-packed dried tomatoes, drained and finely chopped
- 2 cloves garlic, minced
- ½ teaspoon cracked black pepper
- 1½ medium cucumbers
- ¼ cup sliced pitted kalamata olives
- Tiny fresh basil leaves (optional)

1 In a small bowl stir together feta cheese, sour cream, parsley, dried tomatoes, garlic, and pepper. Cover and chill for 2 to 24 hours.

2 Using a sharp knife, trim the ends from cucumbers; discard ends. Bias-slice the cucumbers into ¼-inch slices. Spoon about 1½ teaspoons of the cheese mixture onto each cucumber slice. Arrange cucumber slices on a serving platter. Top slices with olives. If desired, garnish with basil leaves. Serve immediately.

PER BITE 22 calories; 2 g fat (1 g sat.); 1 g protein; 1 g carbohydrate; 0 g fiber; 58 mg sodium; 5 mg cholesterol

Fiesta Shrimp Skewers (top),
Crab-Vegetable Roll-Ups (above left), Greek Salad Bites (above right)

Fresh Spring Rolls

Fresh Spring Rolls

MAKES 24 rolls
START TO FINISH 50 minutes

- **24 fresh or frozen medium shrimp in shells**
- **2 ounces dried rice vermicelli noodles**
- **2 cups shredded napa cabbage**
- **1 cup shredded carrot (2 medium)**
- **½ cup fresh cilantro leaves**
- **½ cup fresh mint leaves or Italian parsley**
- **24 round rice-paper wrappers (8½-inch diameter)**
- **1 recipe Dipping Sauce**

1 Thaw shrimp, if frozen. Peel and devein shrimp, removing tails. Rinse shrimp; pat dry with paper towels. In a large saucepan cook the shrimp in lightly salted boiling water for 1 to 2 minutes or until shrimp are opaque; drain. Rinse with cold water; drain again. Halve shrimp lengthwise; set aside.
2 In a medium saucepan cook noodles in lightly salted boiling water for 3 minutes; drain. Rinse under cold water; drain well. Use kitchen shears to snip the noodles into small pieces; set aside.
3 In a large bowl combine cooked noodles, cabbage, carrot, cilantro, and mint; set aside.
4 Pour 1 cup *warm water* into a shallow dish. Dip rice papers, one at a time, into water; gently shake off excess water. Place the wet rice papers between clean, damp, 100-percent-cotton kitchen towels; let stand for 10 minutes. Brush any dry edges with a little additional water. Place a well-rounded tablespoon of cabbage mixture across lower third of one softened rice paper (keep others covered). Fold bottom of rice paper over filling; arrange 2 shrimp halves across filling; fold in rice paper sides. Tightly roll up the rice paper and filling. Place seam side down on a large plate. Repeat with remaining rice paper, filling, and shrimp. Cover and chill for up to 6 hours.

Dipping Sauce: In a small saucepan combine ½ cup water and 2 tablespoons sugar. Bring to boiling over medium heat, stirring occasionally until sugar is dissolved. Remove from heat and stir in 2 tablespoons rice wine vinegar, 1 tablespoon fish sauce (nuoc nam or nam pla,* and 1 tablespoon shredded carrot.

***Note:** Fish sauce and coconut milk are available in Asian markets and the specialty sections of large supermarkets.

PER ROLL 65 calories; 0 g fat (0 g sat.); 2 g protein; 13 g carbohydrate; 1 g fiber; 55 mg sodium; 10 mg cholesterol

Smoked Trout Mousse on Cucumber 

MAKES about 36 appetizers
START TO FINISH 25 minutes

- **3 large cucumbers (each about 8 inches long)**
- **1 8-ounce package cream cheese, softened**
- **4 ounces soft goat cheese (chèvre)**
- **¼ cup chopped green onion (2)**
- **3 tablespoons snipped fresh dill**
- **2 tablespoons snipped fresh Italian parsley**
- **8 ounces smoked trout fillets, skin and bones removed**
- **Fresh dill sprigs (optional)**

1 Cut cucumbers into ½-inch-thick slices. Pat slices dry with paper towels. Set aside.
2 In a medium bowl combine cream cheese and goat cheese; beat with an electric mixer on medium speed until smooth. Stir in green onion, snipped dill, and parsley. Flake trout and stir into cream cheese mixture. If desired, cover and chill for up to 4 hours.
3 Just before serving, spoon trout mixture onto cucumber slices. If desired, garnish with dill sprigs.

PER APPETIZER 45 calories; 3 g fat (2 g sat.); 2 g protein; 2 g carbohydrate; 0 g fiber; 54 mg sodium; 16 mg cholesterol

Seafood Bruschetta 

MAKES 48 servings
START TO FINISH 20 minutes

- **3 tablespoons olive oil**
- **1 tablespoon lemon juice**
- **1 tablespoon snipped fresh chives**
- **1 tablespoon snipped fresh basil**
- **1 tablespoon snipped fresh mint**
- **2 cloves garlic, minced**
- **6 ounces frozen crabmeat, thawed and drained, or one 6.5-ounce can crabmeat, drained, flaked, and cartilage removed**
- **8 ounces cooked, peeled, and deveined shrimp, coarsely chopped**
- **1 cup chopped roma tomato (3 medium)**
- **½ cup finely chopped onion (1 medium)**
- **1 8-ounce loaf baguette-style French bread**
- **Freshly ground black pepper**
- **Fresh mint (optional)**

1 In a large bowl stir together 1 tablespoon of the oil, the lemon juice, chives, basil, mint, and garlic. Add crabmeat, shrimp, tomato, and onion; toss to coat. Set aside.
2 Slice the bread into 48 thin slices. Arrange bread slices on a large baking sheet. Brush one side of each slice evenly with the remaining 2 tablespoons oil; sprinkle lightly with pepper. Broil 4 inches from the heat for 1 to 2 minutes or until toasted. Turn slices and broil other sides until toasted.
3 To serve, spoon seafood mixture onto the oiled side of each slice. If desired, garnish with mint. Serve immediately.

PER SERVING 32 calories; 1 g fat (0 g sat.); 2 g protein; 3 g carbohydrate; 0 g fiber; 48 mg sodium; 13 mg cholesterol

Seafood Bruschetta

Apricot Slush

Coconut Lemonade

MAKES 4 servings
PREP 10 minutes **CHILL** 4 to 24 hours

- **3 cups water**
- **⅔ cup lemon juice**
- **½ cup sugar**
- **2 tablespoons coconut beverage flavoring syrup (such as Monin or Torani) or cream of coconut**
- **½ cup frozen unsweetened blueberries**
- **½ cup frozen red raspberries**
- **1 small fresh star fruit, thinly sliced crosswise**
- **Ice cubes (optional)**

1 In a large bowl combine the water, the lemon juice, sugar, and coconut syrup. Stir until sugar is well dissolved. Cover and chill for 4 to 24 hours.
2 To serve, transfer lemon juice mixture to a serving bowl or pitcher. Add blueberries, raspberries, and star fruit. If desired, serve over ice cubes.

PER SERVING 150 calories; 0 g fat; 1 g protein; 39 g carbohydrate; 2 g fiber; 7 mg sodium; 0 mg cholesterol

Apricot Slush

MAKES about 24 servings
PREP 15 minutes **FREEZE** 24 hours **STAND** 30 minutes

- **1 46-ounce bottle apricot nectar**
- **3 cups pineapple juice**
- **1 12-ounce can frozen orange juice concentrate, thawed**
- **⅓ cup frozen lemonade concentrate, thawed**
- **1 2-liter bottle ginger ale, chilled**
- **Apricot slices (optional)**

1 In a 3-quart plastic freezer container combine apricot nectar, pineapple juice, orange juice concentrate, and lemonade concentrate. Seal and freeze at least 24 hours or up to 1 week.
2 To serve, let frozen mixture stand at room temperature for 30 minutes. Scrape into a slush. For each serving, fill a glass two-thirds full with slush. Carefully add ginger ale, stirring gently to mix. If desired, garnish with an apricot slice.

PER SERVING 115 calories; 0 g fat; 1 g protein; 29 g carbohydrate; 1 g fiber; 9 mg sodium; 0 mg cholesterol

Cranberry-Apple Crush 

MAKES 8 to 10 servings
START TO FINISH 15 minutes

- **5 cups apple cider or apple juice**
- **5 cups cranberry juice**
- **1½ cups guava juice or mango nectar**
- **¼ cup lime juice**
- **1 teaspoon ground ginger**
- **½ teaspoon ground cinnamon**
- **½ teaspoon ground allspice**
- **Honey (optional)**
- **Lime slices (optional)**

1 In a 4-quart Dutch oven combine cider, cranberry juice, guava juice, lime juice, ginger, cinnamon, and allspice. Bring to boiling; reduce heat. Simmer, uncovered, for 5 minutes, stirring occasionally.
2 To serve, pour into mugs. If desired, sweeten to taste with honey and garnish with lime slices.

PER SERVING 182 calories; 0 g fat (0 g sat.); 0 g protein; 46 g carbohydrate; 0 g fiber; 28 mg sodium; 0 mg cholesterol

Be sure some fruit decorates each serving.

Coconut Lemonade

Spiced Fruit Tea

Some drinks go down better with crushed ice, and this cool mint classic is one of them. If your refrigerator-freezer doesn't have an automatic ice crusher, you can purchase a small bag of crushed ice at the grocery store or make your own. Here's how: Place a few cubes in a resealable plastic freezer bag. Then use the flat side of a meat mallet or a rolling pin to crush the cubes into smaller pieces.

Summer Mint Julep

Spiced Fruit Tea

MAKES 8 to 10 servings
PREP 15 minutes **CHILL** 4 hours to 3 days **FREEZE** 4 hours

- **5 cups boiling water**
- **5 bags orange-flavored spiced herb tea**
- **⅓ cup sugar**
- **¼ teaspoon ground cinnamon**
- **1 46-ounce can unsweetened pineapple juice**
- **2 cups cranberry juice cocktail**
- **⅓ cup lime juice**
- **Kumquat slices (optional)**
- **Orange slices, lime slices, fresh pineapple chunks, and/or mint sprigs (optional)**

1 Pour boiling water into a very large bowl. Add the tea bags. Let steep for 5 minutes. Remove and discard tea bags. Stir in sugar and cinnamon until sugar is dissolved. Stir in pineapple juice, cranberry juice, and lime juice. Remove 3 cups of the tea mixture. Cover and chill the remaining tea mixture for at least 4 hours or up to 3 days.
2 Pour the 3 cups tea mixture into two clean ice cube trays, adding kumquat slices, if desired. Cover and freeze tea mixture until firm.
3 To serve, divide prepared ice cubes among glasses. Add chilled tea mixture. If desired, garnish with fruit and/or mint sprigs.

PER SERVING 157 calories; 0 g fat; 1 g protein; 39 g carbohydrate; 0 g fiber; 9 mg sodium; 0 mg cholesterol

Summer Mint Julep

MAKES 2 servings
PREP 15 minutes **CHILL** 4 hours

- **Crushed ice**
- **2 tablespoons Minted Simple Syrup**
- **4 to 8 large fresh mint sprigs**
- **6 to 8 tablespoons bourbon**
- **Fresh mint sprig (optional)**

1 Fill two tall glasses with crushed ice. Pour 1 tablespoon of the Minted Simple Syrup into each glass. (For a sweeter cocktail, add more syrup.)
2 Slightly crush the 4 to 8 mint sprigs; add half to each glass. Pour half of the bourbon into each glass; stir. If desired, garnish with additional mint.
Minted Simple Syrup: In a small bowl pour ½ cup boiling water over ½ cup sugar; stir until sugar dissolves. Stir in ¼ cup lightly packed fresh mint leaves. Cover and chill for at least 4 hours. Strain mixture through sieve. Discard mint leaves. Store syrup, covered, in the refrigerator for up to 3 days.

PER SERVING 140 calories; 0 g fat; 0 g protein; 8 g carbohydrate; 0 g fiber; 1 mg sodium; 0 mg cholesterol

page 48
page 66
Better

Breakfasts & Brunches

Cherry-Berry Smoothies 

MAKES 4 (8-ounce) servings
START TO FINISH 15 minutes

- **1½ cups fresh strawberries, hulled**
- **1 cup pitted fresh dark sweet cherries or 1 cup frozen unsweetened pitted dark sweet cherries***
- **1 cup fresh raspberries**
- **1 cup pomegranate juice, chilled**
- **½ cup fresh blueberries**

1 In a blender combine strawberries, cherries, raspberries, pomegranate juice, and blueberries. Cover and blend until almost smooth. Pour smoothie mixture into glasses.
***Note:** If using fresh cherries, chill all the fruit before making smoothies. Frozen cherries, if using, will make the smoothies cold.

PER SMOOTHIE 104 calories; 0 g fat; 1 g protein; 25 g carbohydrate; 4 g fiber; 3 mg sodium; 0 mg cholesterol

Banana-Berry Smoothies  

MAKES 3 (about 8-ounce) servings
START TO FINISH 10 minutes

- **2 ripe bananas, chilled**
- **1 cup frozen unsweetened whole strawberries**
- **1 8-ounce carton vanilla low-fat yogurt**
- **¾ cup milk**
- **Fresh whole strawberries (optional)**

1 Cut bananas into chunks. In a blender combine bananas, frozen strawberries, yogurt, and milk.
2 Cover and blend until smooth. Pour smoothie mixture into glasses or transfer to a small pitcher and chill for up to 6 hours. If desired, garnish smoothies with whole strawberries.

PER SMOOTHIE 182 calories; 3 g fat (1 g sat.); 7 g protein; 35 g carbohydrate; 3 g fiber; 82 mg sodium; 9 mg cholesterol

Mango Smoothies 

MAKES 6 (6-ounce) servings.
START TO FINISH 10 minutes

- **2 ripe bananas, chilled**
- **⅔ cup peeled mango slices**
- **1 12-ounce can mango, peach, apricot, or other fruit nectar, chilled**
- **1 cup plain fat-free yogurt**
- **1 tablespoon honey (optional)**
- **Cut-up fresh fruit such as bananas, peeled kiwifruit, and/or peeled mango (optional)**

1 Cut bananas into chunks. In a blender combine bananas, mango, mango nectar, yogurt, and, if desired, honey. Cover and blend until smooth. Pour smoothie mixture into glasses. If desired, garnish with cut-up fresh fruit.

PER SMOOTHIE 108 calories; 0 g fat; 3 g protein; 24 g carbohydrate; 1 g fiber; 33 mg sodium; 1 mg cholesterol

Banana-Berry Smoothies (left) and Mango Smoothies (below)

For an extra-frosty treat, place the glasses in the freezer the night before. Once the smoothie mixture is ready to go, pull out the glasses and prepare for a refreshing chill.

Simply superb... sugar-topped fruit.

Warm Citrus Fruit with Brown Sugar

Grilled ham steak

Poached eggs

Warm Citrus Fruit with Brown Sugar [below]

Cinnamon-raisin toast

Warm Citrus Fruit with Brown Sugar

MAKES 4 servings
PREP 15 minutes **BROIL** 5 minutes

- **2 medium red grapefruit, peeled and sectioned or 1½ cups drained refrigerated grapefruit sections**
- **2 medium oranges, peeled and sectioned**
- **1 cup fresh pineapple chunks or one 8-ounce can pineapple chunks, drained**
- **2 tablespoons rum (optional)**
- **¼ cup packed brown sugar**
- **2 tablespoons butter, softened**

1 Preheat broiler. In a medium bowl combine grapefruit, oranges, and pineapple. Transfer to a 1-quart broiler-safe au gratin dish or casserole.*
2 If desired, in a small saucepan heat rum until it almost simmers. Carefully ignite with a long kitchen match and pour over fruit. Stir gently to coat until flames extinguish.
3 In a small bowl stir together brown sugar and butter until well mixed; sprinkle over fruit. Broil about 4 inches from the heat for 5 to 6 minutes until brown sugar is bubbly and fruit is warmed.
***Note:** For individual servings, use four individual au gratin dishes but omit the rum option.

PER SERVING 192 calories; 6 g fat (4 g sat.); 2 g protein; 35 g carbohydrate; 4 g fiber; 68 mg sodium; 16 mg cholesterol

Baked Breakfast Apples 

MAKES 2 servings
PREP 10 minutes **BAKE** 20 minutes **OVEN** 350°F

- **2 medium apples, cut into bite-size pieces**
- **2 tablespoons snipped, pitted dates**
- **¼ teaspoon ground cinnamon**
- **½ cup apple juice**
- **1 tablespoon raspberry spreadable fruit**
- **¼ cup low-fat granola**

1 In two individual casseroles combine apples and dates. Sprinkle with cinnamon. Divide apple juice evenly between casseroles. Bake, covered, in a 350°F oven for 20 to 25 minutes or until apples are slightly tender. Stir spreadable fruit; spoon over apple mixture; sprinkle with granola. Serve warm.
Microwave Directions: In two individual microwave-safe casseroles combine the apples and dates. Sprinkle with the cinnamon. Reduce apple juice to ¼ cup; divide evenly between casseroles. Microwave, covered, on 100-percent power (high) for 3 to 4 minutes or until apples are slightly tender. Stir spreadable fruit; spoon over apple mixture. Sprinkle with granola. Serve warm.

PER SERVING 188 calories; 1 g fat (0 g sat.); 1 g protein; 47 g carbohydrate; 4 g fiber; 15 mg sodium; 0 mg cholesterol

Fresh Fruit Salad with Creamy Lime Topping

MAKES 12 servings
START TO FINISH 35 minutes

- ½ cup light dairy sour cream
- ⅓ cup fat-free or light mayonnaise dressing or salad dressing
- 1 teaspoon finely shredded lime peel
- 2 tablespoons powdered sugar
- 2 tablespoons lime juice
- 1 tablespoon fat-free milk (optional)
- 6 cups assorted fresh fruit (such as clementine segments, cut-up mango, raspberries, star fruit slices, pineapple chunks, cut-up kiwifruit, and/or halved strawberries)
- Lime peel (optional)

1 In a small bowl stir together sour cream, mayonnaise dressing, the 1 teaspoon lime peel, powdered sugar, and lime juice. If desired, stir in milk to make desired consistency.

Fresh Fruit Salad with Creamy Lime Topping

2 Divide fruit among 12 salad or dessert dishes.* Spoon sour cream mixture over fruit. If desired, garnish with additional lime peel.

***Note:** If you aren't serving 12, use ½ cup fruit per serving; top each serving with about 1 tablespoon of the sour cream mixture. Cover and chill remaining sour cream mixture for up to 5 days.

PER SERVING 64 calories; 1 g fat (1 g sat.); 1 g protein; 13 g carbohydrate; 2 g fiber; 61 mg sodium; 3 mg cholesterol

Lemon Breakfast Parfaits

MAKES 6 servings
PREP 25 minutes **COOL** 30 minutes

- ¾ cup fat-free milk
- Dash salt
- ⅓ cup dried couscous
- ½ cup lemon low-fat yogurt
- ½ cup reduced-calorie dairy sour cream
- 1 tablespoon honey
- ¼ teaspoon finely shredded lemon peel
- 3 cups assorted fruit (such as sliced strawberries, kiwifruit, nectarine, or star fruit; and/or blueberries or raspberries)
- Chopped crystallized ginger (optional)
- Fresh mint (optional)

1 In a medium saucepan bring the milk and salt to boiling; stir in the couscous. Simmer, covered, for 1 minute. Remove from heat; let stand for 5 minutes. Fluff couscous with a fork; cool.

2 In a small bowl stir together yogurt, sour cream, honey, and lemon peel; stir into the couscous. In another small bowl place the fruit.

3 To serve, divide half of the fruit mixture among six parfait glasses. Spoon couscous mixture over fruit; top with remaining fruit. If desired, garnish with ginger and mint.

PER SERVING 127 calories; 2 g fat (1 g sat.); 5 g protein; 22 g carbohydrate; 2 g fiber; 70 mg sodium; 6 mg cholesterol

Lemon Breakfast Parfaits

A simple mix of store-bought cereals and chewy dried fruits fashion a crunchy new blend.

Good Morning Cereal Blend

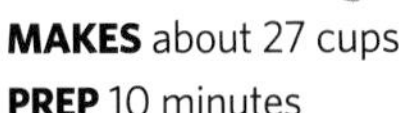

Good Morning Cereal Blend

MAKES about 27 cups
PREP 10 minutes

- **8 cups whole-bran cereal**
- **6 cups low-fat granola**
- **4 cups wheat and barley nugget cereal (such as Grape-Nuts cereal)**
- **7 cups seven-grain-and-sesame medley cereal (such as Kashi Medley cereal)**
- **2 cups dried cranberries and/or raisins**

1 In an airtight container combine cereals and cranberries. Cover and store at room temperature for up to 2 weeks. Or seal in freezer bags; freeze for up to 3 months.

PER ¾ CUP 196 calories; 2 g fat (0 g sat.); 6 g protein; 46 g carbohydrate; 8 g fiber; 140 mg sodium; 0 mg cholesterol

Double-Oat Granola

Double-Oat Granola

MAKES 5 cups
PREP 15 minutes **BAKE** 40 minutes **OVEN** 325°F

- **Nonstick cooking spray**
- **2½ cups rolled oats**
- **1 cup toasted oat bran cereal**
- **½ cup toasted wheat germ**
- **⅓ cup pecans, coarsely chopped**
- **½ cup unsweetened applesauce**
- **2 tablespoons honey**
- **1 tablespoon cooking oil**
- **¼ teaspoon ground cinnamon**
- **⅓ cup snipped dried cranberries, snipped dried tart cherries, and/or dried blueberries**

1 Lightly coat a 15×10×1-inch baking pan with cooking spray; set aside. In a large bowl stir together rolled oats, oat bran cereal, wheat germ, and pecans. In a small bowl stir together applesauce, honey, oil, and cinnamon. Pour applesauce mixture over oats mixture; stir until evenly coated.
2 Spread granola evenly in the prepared pan. Bake, uncovered, in a 325°F oven about 40 minutes or until golden brown, stirring every 10 minutes. Stir in dried fruit. Spread granola on foil to cool. Store in an airtight container at room temperature for up to 2 weeks.

PER ½ CUP 175 calories; 6 g fat (1 g sat.); 5 g protein; 27 g carbohydrate; 4 g fiber; 29 mg sodium; 0 mg cholesterol

Spiced Irish Oatmeal 

MAKES 3 cups
PREP 5 minutes **COOK** 10 minutes

- **3 cups water**
- **1 cup steel-cut oats**
- **1 tablespoon packed brown sugar**
- **¼ teaspoon ground cinnamon**
- **⅛ teaspoon salt**
- **⅛ teaspoon ground allspice**
- **Dash ground cloves or ground nutmeg**
- **3 cups fat-free milk**

1 In a medium saucepan stir together the water, the steel-cut oats, brown sugar, cinnamon, salt, allspice, and cloves. Bring to boiling; reduce heat. Simmer, uncovered, for 10 to 15 minutes or until desired doneness and consistency, stirring occasionally. Serve with milk.

PER ½ CUP 158 calories; 2 g fat (0 g sat.); 9 g protein; 27 g carbohydrate; 3 g fiber; 106 mg sodium; 2 mg cholesterol

Spinach-Cheese Omelet

Spinach-Cheese Omelet 

MAKES 2 servings
START TO FINISH 20 minutes

- **Nonstick cooking spray**
- 4 **eggs or 1 cup refrigerated or frozen egg product, thawed**
- **Dash salt**
- **Dash cayenne pepper**
- ¼ **cup shredded sharp cheddar cheese (1 ounce)**
- 1 **tablespoon snipped fresh chives, Italian parsley, or chervil**
- 1 **cup fresh spinach leaves**
- 1 **recipe Red Pepper Relish**

1 Lightly coat a small nonstick skillet with cooking spray. Heat skillet over medium-high heat.

2 In a medium bowl whisk together eggs, salt, and cayenne pepper until frothy. Pour egg mixture into hot skillet; reduce heat to medium. As egg mixture sets, run a spatula around edge of skillet, lifting egg mixture so uncooked portion flows underneath. Continue cooking and lifting edges until egg mixture is almost set (surface will be moist).

3 Sprinkle omelet with cheese and chives. Top with ¾ cup of the spinach and 2 tablespoons of the Red Pepper Relish. Using the spatula, lift and fold an edge of the omelet partially over filling. Top with the remaining ¼ cup spinach and 1 tablespoon of the remaining Red Pepper Relish. (Reserve the remaining relish for another use.) Cut the omelet in half and transfer to warm plates.

Red Pepper Relish: In a small bowl stir together ⅔ cup chopped red sweet pepper (1 medium), 2 tablespoons finely chopped onion, 1 tablespoon cider vinegar, and ¼ teaspoon black pepper.

PER SERVING 214 calories; 15 g fat (6 g sat.); 17 g protein; 3 g carbohydrate; 2 g fiber; 303 mg sodium; 440 mg cholesterol

Fresh Tomato Omelets with Mozzarella Cheese (30)

MAKES 2 servings
START TO FINISH 20 minutes

- **Nonstick cooking spray**
- **1 cup refrigerated or frozen egg product, thawed, or 4 eggs, beaten**
- **⅛ teaspoon salt**
- **⅛ teaspoon black pepper**
- **1 teaspoon snipped fresh oregano or ¼ teaspoon dried oregano, crushed**
- **4 medium tomato slices**
- **¼ cup shredded mozzarella cheese (1 ounce)**

1 Coat a medium nonstick skillet with cooking spray. Heat skillet over medium-high heat.
2 In a small bowl stir together egg product, salt, and pepper. Pour 1/2 cup of the egg mixture into the hot skillet; reduce heat to medium. Begin stirring egg mixture gently but continuously with a wooden or heat-resistent spatula until egg mixture resembles small pieces of cooked egg surrounded by liquid egg. Stop stirring. Cook for 30 to 60 seconds more or until egg mixture is set but shiny.
3 Sprinkle omelet with 1/2 teaspoon of the fresh oregano or 1/8 teaspoon of the dried oregano. Top with 2 slices of tomato and half of the mozzarella cheese.
4 Using a spatula, lift and fold an edge of the omelet over filling. Transfer omelet to a warm plate. Repeat with remaining egg mixture, oregano, tomato, and cheese to make another omelet.

PER SERVING 103 calories; 2 g fat (1 g sat.); 16 g protein; 4 g carbohydrate; 1 g fiber; 463 mg sodium; 9 mg cholesterol

Italian Baked Eggs

MAKES 4 servings
PREP 20 minutes **BAKE** 15 minutes **STAND** 5 minutes
OVEN 350°F

- **1 small zucchini, halved lengthwise and thinly sliced**
- **½ cup chopped red onion (1 medium)**
- **½ cup chopped red or green sweet pepper (1 small)**
- **2 cloves garlic, minced**
- **2 teaspoons olive oil or cooking oil**
- **6 egg whites**
- **1 egg**
- **1 cup fat-free milk**
- **1 tablespoon shredded fresh basil**
- **¼ cup shredded mozzarella cheese (1 ounce)**
- **Chopped tomato (optional)**

1 In a medium skillet cook zucchini, onion, sweet pepper, and garlic in hot oil over medium heat about 5 minutes or until onion is tender. Set aside.
2 In a medium bowl stir together the egg whites, egg, milk, and basil. Stir in zucchini mixture. Pour egg mixture into four individual quiche dishes or shallow casseroles, about 4½ inches in diameter.
3 Bake, uncovered, in a 350°F oven for 15 to 20 minutes or until set. Sprinkle each serving with mozzarella cheese. Let stand for 5 minutes before serving. If desired, sprinkle with chopped tomato.

PER SERVING 114 calories; 5 g fat (2 g sat.); 11 g protein; 6 g carbohydrate; 1 g fiber; 164 mg sodium; 58 mg cholesterol

Italian Baked Eggs

Poached Eggs with Mustard Vinaigrette 

MAKES 4 servings
START TO FINISH 20 minutes

- **2 tablespoons vinegar**
- **2 tablespoons olive oil**
- **1 tablespoon coarse grain brown mustard**
- **Cooking oil**
- **4 eggs**
- **2 cups mixed salad greens, or 8 cups torn fresh spinach sauteed in 1 tablespoon butter**
- **2 slices dark rye bread, toasted and halved diagonally**
- **Salt**
- **Black pepper**

1 In a small saucepan combine vinegar, olive oil, and mustard. Bring to boiling, stirring to combine. Reduce heat; keep warm, stirring again just before serving.

2 Grease four cups of an egg poaching pan* with cooking oil. Place poacher cups over pan of boiling water (water should not touch bottoms of cups). Reduce heat to simmering. Break one of the eggs into a measuring cup. Carefully slide egg into a poacher cup. Repeat with remaining eggs. Cover and cook for 6 to 9 minutes or until the egg whites are completely set and yolks begin to thicken but are not hard.

3 To serve, place greens evenly on rye bread halves. Loosen poached eggs by running a knife around edge of each poacher cup; invert poacher cups and slip eggs onto greens.

Pour warm mustard mixture over all. Sprinkle with salt and pepper.

***Note:** If you don't have an egg poaching pan, lightly grease a medium skillet. Half fill the skillet with water. Bring the water to boiling; reduce heat to simmering (bubbles should begin to break the surface of the water). Break one of the eggs into a measuring cup. Holding the lip of the cup as close to the water as possible, carefully slide egg into the simmering water. Repeat with remaining eggs, allowing each egg an equal amount of space. Simmer eggs, uncovered, for 3 to 5 minutes or until the whites are completely set and yolks begin to thicken but are not hard. Remove eggs with a slotted spoon. Serve as directed in Step 3.

PER SERVING 183 calories; 13 g fat (3 g sat.); 8 g protein; 10 g carbohydrate; 1 g fiber; 257 mg sodium; 213 mg cholesterol

Tex-Mex Breakfast Pizza 

MAKES 8 servings
PREP 25 minutes **BAKE** 8 minutes **OVEN** 375°F

- **Nonstick cooking spray**
- **1½ cups frozen diced hash brown potatoes, thawed**
- **¼ cup sliced green onion (2)**
- **1 to 2 canned whole green chile peppers, drained, seeded, and chopped**
- **¼ teaspoon ground cumin**
- **1 clove garlic, minced**
- **1 cup refrigerated or frozen egg product, thawed**
- **¼ cup milk**
- **1 tablespoon snipped fresh cilantro**
- **1 16-ounce Italian bread shell (Boboli®)**
- **½ cup shredded reduced-fat Monterey Jack cheese (2 ounces)**
- **⅓ cup chopped seeded tomato (1 small)**

1 Lightly coat a large skillet with cooking spray. Heat skillet over medium heat. Add the potatoes, green onion, chile peppers, cumin, and garlic. Cook and stir about 3 minutes or until the vegetables are tender.

2 In a medium bowl whisk together egg product, milk, and cilantro; add to potato mixture in skillet. Cook over medium heat, without stirring, until egg mixture begins to set on the bottom and around the edge. Using a spatula, lift and fold the partially cooked egg mixture so uncooked portion flows underneath. Continue cooking over medium heat for 2 to 3 minutes or until egg mixture is cooked through but is still glossy and moist. Immediately remove from heat.

Tex-Mex Breakfast Pizza

Get your taste buds going with a slice of this peppery early-morning pizza. Need some more flavor to wake you up? Drizzle salsa or sprinkle bottled hot sauce over the top.

3 To assemble pizza, place the bread shell on a large baking sheet or a 12-inch pizza pan. Sprinkle half of the cheese over the shell. Top with egg mixture, tomato, and remaining cheese. Bake, uncovered, in a 375°F oven for 8 to 10 minutes or until cheese melts.

PER SERVING 227 calories; 5 g fat (1 g sat.); 13 g protein; 33 g carbohydrate; 2 g fiber; 429 mg sodium; 8 mg cholesterol

Quick Salmon Benedict

Quick Salmon Benedict 

MAKES 4 servings
START TO FINISH 20 minutes

- **¼ cup dairy sour cream**
- **1 teaspoon lemon juice**
- **¾ to 1 teaspoon dry mustard**
- **3 to 4 teaspoons milk**
- **Cooking oil**
- **4 eggs**
- **4 ½-inch slices baguette-style French bread, lightly toasted**
- **4 ounces thinly sliced smoked salmon**
- **Diced red sweet pepper (optional)**
- **Salt and black pepper**

1 In a small bowl stir together sour cream, lemon juice, and mustard. Stir in enough of the milk to make sauce of desired consistency. Set aside.
2 Grease four cups of an egg poaching pan (see note, page 47) with oil. Place poacher cups over pan of boiling water (water should not touch bottoms of cups). Reduce heat to simmering. Break one of the eggs into a measuring cup. Carefully slide egg into a poacher cup. Repeat with remaining eggs. Cover and cook for 6 to 9 minutes or until the egg whites are completely set and yolks begin to thicken but are not hard.
3 Top bread slices with smoked salmon. Loosen poached eggs by running a knife around edge of each poacher cup; invert poacher cups and slip eggs onto salmon. Top with sour cream mixture. If desired, sprinkle with sweet pepper. Season to taste with salt and black pepper.

Quick Classic Benedict: Prepare as directed, except substitute 4 slices Canadian-style bacon for the salmon.

PER SERVING 206 calories; 10 g fat (4 g sat.); 14 g protein; 14 g carbohydrate; 1 g fiber; 481 mg sodium; 225 mg cholesterol

Beef Hash with a Spicy Kick

MAKES 6 servings
PREP 30 minutes **MARINATE** 30 minutes **COOK** 20 minutes

- **½ cup orange juice**
- **2 tablespoons lime juice**
- **1 tablespoon adobo sauce (from canned chipotle peppers)**
- **1¼ pounds beef sirloin or top loin steak, finely chopped**
- **2 cups finely chopped onion (2 large)**
- **6 cloves garlic, minced**
- **1 tablespoon chili powder**
- **1 tablespoon cooking oil**
- **1½ pounds Yukon gold potatoes or red-skinned potatoes, cooked* and diced**
- **1 tablespoon chopped chipotle peppers in adobo sauce**
- **⅔ cup chopped, seeded roma tomatoes (2 medium)**
- **¼ cup snipped fresh cilantro**
- **Fried eggs (optional)**
- **Fresh cilantro sprig (optional)**

1 In a resealable plastic bag combine orange juice, lime juice, and adobo sauce; add beef. Seal bag; turn to coat. Marinate in the refrigerator for 30 minutes. Drain and discard marinade. Pat beef dry with paper towels.**
2 In a large heavy skillet cook the onion, garlic, and chili powder in hot oil over medium heat 5 minutes or until onion is tender. Increase heat to medium-high. Add beef to skillet; cook and stir about 2 minutes or until beef is brown. Stir in potatoes and chipotle peppers. Spread beef mixture in an even layer in the skillet. Cook about 8 minutes more or until potatoes are golden brown, turning occasionally. Fold in tomatoes and cilantro; heat through. Season with *salt* and *black pepper.* If desired, serve with fried eggs and garnish with fresh cilantro.
***To Cook Potatoes:** Wash potatoes. Cut into quarters. Cook, covered, in enough boiling lightly salted water to cover for 20 to 25 minutes or until tender. Drain.
****Note:** Removing as much moisture as possible from the beef makes for a crispier hash.

PER SERVING 263 calories; 6 g fat (2 g sat.); 24 g protein; 28 g carbohydrate; 4 g fiber; 189 mg sodium; 45 mg cholesterol

Beef Hash with a Spicy Kick

Menu

Rosemary Potato Frittata
[opposite]

Green and/or red grapes

Orange juice

Rosemary Potato Frittata

Rosemary Potato Frittata 

MAKES 2 servings
START TO FINISH 20 minutes

- **4 ounces tiny new potatoes, cut into ¼-inch slices (1 cup)**
- **¼ cup chopped red or white onion**
- **¼ cup chopped red, green, or yellow sweet pepper**
- **Nonstick cooking spray**
- **1 cup refrigerated or frozen egg product, thawed, or 4 eggs, lightly beaten**
- **½ teaspoon snipped fresh rosemary or ¼ teaspoon dried rosemary, crushed**
- **⅛ teaspoon salt**
- **⅛ teaspoon black pepper**
- **¼ cup shredded Swiss cheese (1 ounce)**
- **Fresh rosemary sprigs (optional)**

1 In a covered 6- to 7-inch nonstick skillet with flared sides, cook potatoes and onion in a small amount of boiling water for 7 minutes. Add sweet pepper. Cook, covered, for 3 to 5 minutes more or until vegetables are tender. Drain vegetables in a colander. Wipe out skillet; lightly coat the skillet with cooking spray. Return vegetables to skillet.
2 In a small bowl whisk together the eggs, rosemary, salt, and black pepper. Pour over vegetables in skillet. Cook over medium heat. As egg mixture sets, run a spatula around edges of skillet, lifting egg mixture so uncooked portion flows underneath. Continue cooking and lifting edges until egg mixture is almost set (surface will be moist).
3 Remove skillet from heat. Sprinkle frittata with cheese. Cover and let stand for 3 to 4 minutes or until top is set and cheese is melted. Loosen edges; transfer to a serving plate. To serve, cut frittata into wedges. If desired, top each serving with a rosemary sprig.

PER SERVING 168 calories; 4 g fat (3 g sat.); 17 g protein; 15 g carbohydrate; 2 g fiber; 407 mg sodium; 13 mg cholesterol

Asparagus-Zucchini Frittata

MAKES 6 servings
PREP 30 minutes **BAKE** 40 minutes **STAND** 10 minutes
OVEN 350°F

- **Nonstick cooking spray**
- **1½ pounds fresh asparagus, trimmed and cut into 1-inch-long pieces**
- **1 medium yellow sweet pepper, cut into strips**
- **⅓ cup chopped onion (1 small)**

Asparagus-Zucchini Frittata

- **¼ cup bottled roasted red sweet peppers, drained and chopped**
- **1 small zucchini, halved lengthwise and cut into ¼-inch slices (about 1 cup)**
- **10 eggs**
- **1 cup fat-free milk**
- **2 tablespoons snipped fresh dill or ½ teaspoon dried dill**
- **1 teaspoon salt**
- **½ teaspoon black pepper**
- **Fresh dill sprigs (optional)**

1 Coat a 3-quart oval or rectangular baking dish with cooking spray; set aside.
2 In a large saucepan bring about 1 inch of water to boiling. Add asparagus, yellow sweet pepper, and onion. Return to boiling; reduce heat. Simmer, covered, about 1 minute or until vegetables are crisp-tender. Drain well. Stir in roasted red sweet peppers. Evenly spread asparagus mixture in the prepared baking dish. Layer zucchini slices on top.
3 In a large bowl beat eggs with a wire whisk until combined. Beat in milk, dill, salt, and black pepper. Pour egg mixture over vegetables in baking dish. Bake, uncovered, in a 350°F oven for 40 to 45 minutes or until a knife inserted near the center comes out clean. Let stand for 10 minutes before serving. If desired, garnish with dill sprigs.

PER SERVING 176 calories; 9 g fat (3 g sat.); 15 g protein; 11 g carbohydrate; 3 g fiber; 527 mg sodium; 353 mg cholesterol

Like a quiche without a crust, the frittata is an Italian-style omelet. The delicious combos of ingredients are mixed with the egg rather than folded inside like a traditional French-style omelet. These easy one-pan meals serve one or a few, and are great for breakfast as well as dinner.

Denver Frittata 

MAKES 8 servings
PREP 15 minutes **BAKE** 15 minutes **COOK** 10 minutes
OVEN 350°F

- **Nonstick cooking spray**
- **1 tablespoon butter**
- **½ cup chopped green sweet pepper (1 small)**
- **½ cup chopped red sweet pepper (1 small)**
- **⅓ cup chopped onion (1 small)**
- **8 eggs**
- **¼ cup milk**
- **¾ cup shredded cheddar cheese (3 ounces)**
- **2 ounces cooked ham, cut into thin ribbons (about ½ cup)**
- **¼ teaspoon salt**
- **¼ teaspoon black pepper**

1 Coat a medium oven-going nonstick skillet with cooking spray. Melt butter in skillet over medium heat. Add sweet peppers and onion; cook for 5 minutes, stirring occasionally.
2 In a large bowl whisk together eggs and milk; whisk in ½ cup of the cheese, the ham, salt, and black pepper. Pour egg mixture into skillet; stir to combine. Cook over medium-low heat for 5 minutes, stirring egg mixture gently halfway through cooking.
3 Sprinkle the remaining ¼ cup cheese on top. Place skillet in a 350°F oven; bake for 15 minutes. Remove skillet from oven. Loosen edges of frittata; transfer to a serving plate. To serve, cut into 8 wedges.

PER SERVING 156 calories; 11 g fat (5 g sat.); 11 g protein; 4 g carbohydrate; 1 g fiber; 309 mg sodium; 232 mg cholesterol

Shrimp-Artichoke Frittata 

MAKES 4 servings
START TO FINISH 30 minutes

- **4 ounces fresh or frozen medium shrimp in shells**
- **½ of a 9-ounce package frozen artichoke hearts**
- **2 cups refrigerated or frozen egg product, thawed**
- **¼ cup fat-free milk**
- **¼ cup thinly sliced green onion (2)**
- **⅛ teaspoon garlic powder**
- **⅛ teaspoon black pepper**
- **Nonstick cooking spray**
- **3 tablespoons finely shredded Parmesan cheese**
- **Cherry tomatoes, quartered (optional)**
- **Italian (flat-leaf) parsley (optional)**

1 Thaw shrimp, if frozen. Peel and devein shrimp. Rinse shrimp; pat dry. Halve shrimp lengthwise; set aside. Meanwhile, cook artichoke hearts according to package directions; drain. Cut artichoke hearts in quarters; set aside.
2 In a medium bowl stir together egg product, milk, green onion, garlic powder, and pepper; set aside.
3 Lightly coat a large nonstick skillet with cooking spray. Heat skillet over medium heat. Add shrimp to skillet; cook and stir for 1 to 3 minutes or until shrimp are opaque.
4 Pour egg mixture into skillet; do not stir. Cook over medium-low heat. As egg mixture sets, run a spatula around edges of skillet, lifting egg mixture so uncooked portion flows underneath. Continue cooking and lifting edges until egg mixture is almost set (surface will be moist).
5 Remove skillet from heat. Sprinkle artichoke pieces and cheese over frittata. Cover and let stand for 3 to 4 minutes or until top is set. Loosen edges of frittata; transfer to a serving plate. To serve, cut into wedges. If desired, garnish with cherry tomatoes and parsley.

PER SERVING 126 calories; 3 g fat (1 g sat.); 19 g protein; 6 g carbohydrate; 2 g fiber; 343 mg sodium; 37 mg cholesterol

Shrimp-Artichoke Frittata

Wait for the tops to bubble

Chocolate Pancakes

Chocolate Pancakes 

MAKES 16 pancakes
PREP 15 minutes **COOK** 4 to 5 minutes per batch

- **1⅔ cups all-purpose flour**
- **⅓ cup unsweetened cocoa powder**
- **¼ cup sugar**
- **1 teaspoon baking soda**
- **¼ teaspoon salt**
- **2¼ cups buttermilk**
- **1 egg, lightly beaten**
- **3 tablespoons cooking oil**

1 In a large bowl stir together flour, cocoa powder, sugar, baking soda, and salt. In medium bowl use a fork to combine buttermilk, egg, and oil. Add buttermilk mixture all at once to flour mixture. Stir just until moistened (batter should be slightly lumpy).
2 For each pancake, pour about ¼ cup batter onto a hot, lightly greased griddle or heavy skillet. Cook over medium-low heat for 1 to 2 minutes on each side or until pancakes are golden brown, turning to second side when pancakes have bubbly surfaces and edges are slightly dry. Serve warm.

PER PANCAKE 104 calories; 4 g fat (1 g sat.); 3 g protein; 16 g carbohydrate; 1 g fiber; 156 mg sodium; 15 mg cholesterol

Orange Buttermilk Pancakes  

MAKES 16 pancakes
PREP 20 minutes **COOK** 2 to 4 minutes per batch

- **2¼ cups all-purpose flour**
- **3 tablespoons sugar**
- **1 tablespoon baking powder**
- **½ teaspoon salt**
- **2 teaspoons finely shredded orange peel**
- **1 cup orange juice**
- **1 cup buttermilk**
- **1 egg, lightly beaten**
- **2 tablespoons cooking oil**

1 In a large bowl stir together the flour, sugar, baking powder, salt, and orange peel. In a medium bowl use a fork to combine orange juice, buttermilk, egg, and oil. Add orange juice mixture all at once to flour mixture. Stir just until moistened (batter should be slightly lumpy).

before turning pancakes.

2 For each pancake, pour about 1/4 cup batter onto a hot, lightly greased griddle or heavy skillet. Cook over medium heat for 1 to 2 minutes on each side or until pancakes are golden brown, turning to second side when pancakes have bubbly surfaces and edges are slightly dry. Serve warm.

PER PANCAKE 101 calories; 2 g fat (0 g sat.); 3 g protein; 17 g carbohydrate; 0 g fiber; 139 mg sodium; 14 mg cholesterol

Crunch-Topped French Toast

MAKES 6 servings
PREP 20 minutes **CHILL** 2 to 24 hours **BAKE** 30 minutes
OVEN 375°F

- **Nonstick cooking spray**
- **1 cup evaporated fat-free milk**
- **¾ cup refrigerated or frozen egg product, thawed, or 3 eggs, lightly beaten**
- **3 tablespoons sugar**
- **2 teaspoons vanilla**
- **½ teaspoon ground cinnamon**
- **¼ teaspoon ground nutmeg**
- **6 1-inch slices Italian bread (3 to 4 inches in diameter)**
- **1 large shredded wheat biscuit, crushed (⅔ cup)**
- **1 tablespoon butter, melted**
- **2 cups sliced strawberries**
- **3 tablespoons sugar**
- **½ teaspoon ground cinnamon**

1 Lightly coat a 2-quart rectangular baking dish with cooking spray; set aside. In a medium bowl whisk together milk, the egg product, 3 tablespoons sugar, the vanilla, 1/2 teaspoon cinnamon, and the nutmeg. Arrange bread slices in a single layer in the prepared baking dish. Pour milk mixture evenly over bread. Cover and chill for 2 to 24 hours, turning bread slices once.
2 In a small bowl combine crushed shredded wheat biscuit and melted butter; sprinkle evenly over the bread slices. Bake, uncovered, in a 375°F oven about 30 minutes or until light brown.
3 Meanwhile, in a small bowl toss together strawberries, the remaining 3 tablespoons sugar, and the remaining 1/2 teaspoon cinnamon. Serve with French toast.

PER SERVING 227 calories; 3 g fat (2 g sat.); 10 g protein; 39 g carbohydrate; 3 g fiber; 296 mg sodium; 7 mg cholesterol

Stuffed French Toast 

MAKES 8 slices
START TO FINISH 25 minutes

- **½ cup fat-free cream cheese (about 5 ounces)**
- **2 tablespoons apricot or strawberry spreadable fruit**
- **8 1-inch slices French bread**
- **2 egg whites, lightly beaten**
- **1 egg, lightly beaten**
- **¾ cup fat-free milk**
- **½ teaspoon vanilla**
- **⅛ teaspoon apple pie spice**
- **Nonstick cooking spray**
- **½ cup apricot or strawberry spreadable fruit**

1 In a small bowl stir together cream cheese and the 2 tablespoons spreadable fruit. Using a serrated knife, cut a pocket in top crust of each bread slice. Fill pockets evenly with cream cheese mixture. In a medium bowl whisk together egg whites, egg, milk, vanilla, and apple pie spice.
2 Lightly coat a nonstick griddle with cooking spray. Heat griddle over medium heat. Dip stuffed bread slices into egg mixture, coating both sides. Place bread slices on hot griddle and cook for 2 to 3 minutes per side or until golden brown.
3 Meanwhile, in a small saucepan heat the 1/2 cup spreadable fruit until melted, stirring frequently. Spoon over French toast.

PER SLICE 150 calories; 1 g fat (0 g sat.); 7 g protein; 29 g carbohydrate; 0 g fiber; 163 mg sodium; 30 mg cholesterol

Crunch-Topped French Toast

Breakfast Bread Pudding [right]

Country-Style Turkey Sausage [page 42]

Mixed fresh berries

Pomegranate or orange juice

Breakfast Bread Pudding 

MAKES 6 servings
PREP 30 minutes **BAKE** 40 minutes **STAND** 15 minutes
OVEN 325°F

- **5 to 6 slices whole wheat cinnamon-swirl bread or cinnamon-raisin bread**
- **Nonstick cooking spray**
- **1½ cups fat-free milk**
- **3 eggs**
- **2 tablespoons sugar**
- **1 teaspoon vanilla**
- **¼ teaspoon ground nutmeg**
- **1 5.5-ounce can apricot nectar or peach nectar (⅔ cup)**
- **2 teaspoons cornstarch**

1 Cut enough of the bread into cubes to make 4 cups. Place bread cubes in a shallow baking pan. Bake in a 325°F oven about 10 minutes or until bread is dry, stirring once. Cool in pan on a wire rack.
2 Lightly coat six 6-ounce soufflé dishes or custard cups with cooking spray. Divide bread cubes evenly among the prepared dishes. In a medium bowl whisk together milk, eggs, sugar, vanilla, and nutmeg. Pour milk mixture evenly over bread cubes. Press lightly with the back of a spoon to thoroughly moisten bread.
3 Place soufflé dishes in a 13×9×2-inch baking pan. Place baking pan on oven rack. Carefully pour hot tap water into the baking pan around dishes to a depth of 1 inch.
4 Bake, uncovered, in the 325°F oven for 30 to 35 minutes or until a knife inserted near centers comes out clean. Transfer dishes to a wire rack. Let stand for 15 minutes.
5 Meanwhile, for sauce, in a small saucepan gradually stir apricot nectar into cornstarch until combined. Cook and stir over medium heat until thickened and bubbly. Reduce heat. Cook and stir for 2 minutes more.
6 If desired, remove puddings from soufflé dishes. Spoon sauce over warm puddings.
Make-Ahead Directions: Prepare as above through Step 2. Place soufflé dishes in a 13×9×2-inch baking pan. Cover with plastic wrap. Refrigerate overnight. Uncover; add hot tap water to pan as directed. Continue with Step 4.

PER SERVING 178 calories; 4 g fat (1 g sat.); 9 g protein; 27 g carbohydrate; 3 g fiber; 179 mg sodium; 107 mg cholesterol

Breakfast Bread Pudding

Reminiscent of cinnamon rolls, but much easier to make.

Spiced Fan Biscuits

Spiced Fan Biscuits 

MAKES 12 biscuits
PREP 20 minutes **BAKE** 10 minutes **OVEN** 450°F

- **2 cups all-purpose flour**
- **4 teaspoons baking powder**
- **½ teaspoon cream of tartar**
- **¼ teaspoon salt**
- **¼ cup shortening**
- **¾ cup fat-free milk**
- **2 tablespoons sugar**
- **1 teaspoon ground cinnamon**

1 Preheat oven to 450°F. Grease twelve 2½-inch muffin cups; set aside. In a large bowl stir together flour, baking powder, cream of tartar, and salt. Using a pastry blender, cut in shortening until flour mixture resembles coarse crumbs. Make a well in the center of the flour mixture. Add milk all at once. Using a fork, stir just until mixture is moistened.
2 Turn dough out onto a lightly floured surface. Knead dough by folding and gently pressing it for 10 to 12 strokes or until dough is nearly smooth. Divide dough in half. Roll each dough half into a 12×10-inch rectangle. In a small bowl stir together sugar and cinnamon. Sprinkle the sugar mixture over the rectangles.
3 Cut each rectangle into five 12×2-inch strips. Stack the strips on top of each other; cut each into six 2-inch-square stacks. Place each stack, cut side down, in a prepared muffin cup. Bake for 10 to 12 minutes or until golden. Serve warm.

PER BISCUIT 121 calories; 4 g fat (1 g sat.); 3 g protein; 18 g carbohydrate; 1 g fiber; 190 mg sodium; 0 mg cholesterol

Blueberry-Oat Scones with Flaxseeds

MAKES 12 scones
PREP 30 minutes **BAKE** 16 minutes **OVEN** 400°F

- **2 tablespoons flaxseeds, toasted***
- **1½ cups all-purpose flour**
- **½ cup rolled oats**
- **¼ cup sugar**
- **2 teaspoons baking powder**
- **¼ teaspoon salt**
- **¼ cup cold butter, cut into pieces**
- **1 6-ounce carton plain fat-free or low-fat yogurt**
- **1 egg white, lightly beaten**
- **1¼ cups fresh blueberries**
- **Fat-free milk**
- **Rolled oats and/or flaxseeds (optional)**

1 Preheat oven to 400°F. Line a baking sheet with foil or parchment paper; set aside. Place toasted flaxseeds in a spice grinder and pulse until ground to a fine powder.
2 In a medium bowl stir together ground flaxseeds, flour, the ½ cup oats, the sugar, baking powder, and salt. Using a pastry blender, cut in butter until mixture resembles coarse crumbs. Make a well in center of the flour mixture; set aside.
3 In a second medium bowl stir together yogurt and egg white. Gently fold in blueberries. Add yogurt mixture all at once to flour mixture. Using a fork, stir just until moistened.
4 Turn dough out onto a lightly floured surface. Knead dough by folding and gently pressing it for 10 to 12 strokes or until dough is nearly smooth. Pat or lightly roll dough into a 10-inch circle. Cut circle into 12 wedges.
5 Place dough wedges 1 inch apart on the prepared baking sheet. Brush wedges with milk. If desired, sprinkle lightly with additional oats and/or flaxseeds. Bake for 16 to 18 minutes or until golden. Remove scones from baking sheet; serve warm.
***Note:** To toast flaxseeds, place in a small dry skillet over medium heat. Cook and stir until flaxseeds are fragrant and begin to pop.

PER SCONE 148 calories; 5 g fat (3 g sat.); 4 g protein; 22 g carbohydrate; 2 g fiber; 133 mg sodium; 11 mg cholesterol

Blueberry-Oat Scones with Flaxseeds

Lemon-Nutmeg Scones

To create delicate layers within, you must gently knead the dough and not overwork it. For best results, count the strokes or stop kneading when the dough is almost smooth.

Lemon-Nutmeg Scones

MAKES 8 scones
PREP 20 minutes **BAKE** 12 minutes **COOL** 5 minutes
OVEN 400°F

- **Nonstick cooking spray**
- **1¼ cups all-purpose flour**
- **¾ cup oat bran**
- **3 tablespoons sugar**
- **2 teaspoons baking powder**
- **¼ teaspoon baking soda**
- **¼ teaspoon ground nutmeg**
- **⅛ teaspoon salt**
- **¼ cup butter**
- **1 6-ounce carton lemon low-fat yogurt with no-calorie sweetener**
- **¼ cup refrigerated or frozen egg product, thawed, or 1 egg**
- **Fruit jam or preserves (optional)**

1 Preheat oven to 400°F. Lightly coat a baking sheet with cooking spray. Set aside.
2 In a medium bowl stir together flour, oat bran, sugar, baking powder, baking soda, nutmeg, and salt. Using a pastry blender, cut in butter until flour mixture resembles coarse crumbs. Make a well in the center of the flour mixture; set aside.
3 In a small bowl stir together yogurt and egg product. Add yogurt mixture all at once to flour mixture. Using a fork, stir just until moistened.
4 Turn dough out onto a floured surface. Knead dough by folding and gently pressing it for 10 to 12 strokes or until dough is nearly smooth. Pat or lightly roll dough into a 6-inch circle. Cut circle into 8 wedges.
5 Place dough wedges about 2 inches apart on the prepared baking sheet. Bake about 12 minutes or until golden. Cool scones on baking sheet on a wire rack for 5 minutes. Serve warm with jam, if desired.

PER SCONE 173 calories; 7 g fat (3 g sat.); 5 g protein; 26 g carbohydrate; 2 g fiber; 206 mg sodium; 16 mg cholesterol

Cranberry Whole Wheat Scones

MAKES 12 scones
PREP 20 minutes **BAKE** 13 minutes **OVEN** 400°F

- **1½ cups all-purpose flour**
- **½ cup whole wheat flour**
- **3 tablespoons sugar**
- **1½ teaspoons baking powder**
- **1 teaspoon ground ginger or cinnamon**
- **¼ teaspoon baking soda**
- **¼ teaspoon salt**
- **⅓ cup butter**
- **½ cup refrigerated or frozen egg product, thawed, or 2 eggs, lightly beaten**
- **⅓ cup buttermilk or sour milk***
- **¾ cup dried cranberries or dried currants**
- **Buttermilk or milk**
- **3 tablespoons rolled oats**

1 Preheat oven to 400°F. In a large bowl stir together all-purpose flour, whole wheat flour, sugar, baking powder, ginger, baking soda, and salt. Using a pastry blender, cut in butter until flour mixture resembles coarse crumbs. Make a well in the center of the flour mixture.

2 In a medium bowl stir together egg product and the ⅓ cup buttermilk. Stir in dried cranberries. Add the egg mixture all at once to the flour mixture. Using a fork, stir just until moistened (some of the dough may look dry).

3 Turn dough out onto a lightly floured surface. Knead dough by gently folding and pressing it for 10 to 12 strokes or until dough is nearly smooth. Pat or lightly roll dough into an 8-inch circle. Cut circle into 12 wedges.

4 Place dough wedges 1 inch apart on an ungreased baking sheet. Brush wedges with additional buttermilk. Sprinkle with oats, pressing gently into dough. Bake for 13 to 15 minutes or until edges are light brown. Remove scones from baking sheet; serve warm.

***Note:** To make ⅓ cup sour milk, place 1 teaspoon lemon juice or vinegar in a glass measuring cup. Add enough milk to make ⅓ cup total liquid; stir. Let stand for 5 minutes before using.

PER SCONE 169 calories; 6 g fat (3 g sat.); 4 g protein; 26 g carbohydrate; 2 g fiber; 172 mg sodium; 15 mg cholesterol

Cranberry Whole Wheat Scones

Crinkled muffin tops kissed

Raisin-Carrot Muffins

Raisin-Carrot Muffins 

MAKES 16 muffins
PREP 20 minutes **BAKE** 18 minutes **COOL** 5 minutes
OVEN 400°F

- **⅔ cup golden raisins or dried currants**
- **1½ cups all-purpose flour**
- **½ cup whole wheat flour**
- **⅓ cup toasted wheat germ**
- **1½ teaspoons baking powder**
- **½ teaspoon baking soda**
- **½ teaspoon salt**
- **½ teaspoon ground cinnamon**
- **1 egg, beaten**
- **1¼ cups buttermilk or sour milk***
- **⅓ cup packed brown sugar**
- **¼ cup cooking oil**
- **1 cup shredded carrot (2 medium)**
- **Ground cinnamon**

1 Preheat oven to 400°F. Lightly grease sixteen 2½-inch muffin cups or line with paper bake cups. In a small bowl pour enough *boiling water* over raisins to cover; set aside.
2 In a medium bowl stir together the flours, wheat germ, baking powder, baking soda, salt, and the ½ teaspoon cinnamon. Make a well in center of flour mixture; set aside.
3 In another medium bowl combine egg, buttermilk, brown sugar, and oil. Add the egg mixture all at once to the flour mixture. Stir just until moistened (batter should be lumpy). Drain raisins. Gently fold raisins and carrot into batter.
4 Spoon batter into prepared muffin cups, filling each about two-thirds full. Sprinkle additional cinnamon over muffin batter in cups. Bake for 18 to 20 minutes or until golden and a wooden toothpick inserted in centers comes out clean. Cool in muffin cups on a wire rack for 5 minutes. Remove from muffin cups; serve warm.
***Note:** To make 1¼ cups sour milk, place 4 teaspoons lemon juice or vinegar in a 2-cup glass measuring cup. Add enough milk to make 1¼ cups total liquid; stir. Let stand for 5 minutes before using.

PER MUFFIN 146 calories; 4 g fat (1 g sat.); 4 g protein; 24 g carbohydrate; 2 g fiber; 167 mg sodium; 14 mg cholesterol

Pumpkin Spice Muffins

MAKES 12 muffins
PREP 20 minutes **BAKE** 18 minutes **COOL** 5 minutes
OVEN 375°F

- **Nonstick cooking spray**
- **1¼ cups all-purpose flour**
- **½ cup whole wheat flour**
- **3 tablespoons toasted wheat germ**
- **1 tablespoon pumpkin pie spice or apple pie spice**
- **2 teaspoons baking powder**
- **¾ teaspoon salt**
- **¼ teaspoon baking soda**
- **2 eggs, beaten**
- **1 cup canned pumpkin**
- **1 cup buttermilk**
- **⅓ cup packed brown sugar**
- **¼ cup cooking oil**
- **¼ cup quick-cooking rolled oats**

1 Preheat oven to 375°F. Lightly coat twelve 2½-inch muffin cups with cooking spray; set aside. In a large bowl stir together the flours, wheat germ, pumpkin pie spice, baking powder, salt, and baking soda. Make a well in center of flour mixture; set aside.
2 In a medium bowl combine eggs, pumpkin, buttermilk, brown sugar, and oil. Add egg mixture all at once to flour mixture. Stir just until moistened (batter should be lumpy).
3 Spoon batter into prepared muffin cups, filling each two-thirds full. Sprinkle oats over muffin batter in cups. Bake for 18 to 20 minutes or until a wooden toothpick inserted in centers comes out clean. Cool in muffin cups on a wire rack for 5 minutes. Remove from muffin cups; serve warm.

PER MUFFIN 167 calories; 6 g fat (1 g sat.); 5 g protein; 24 g carbohydrate; 2 g fiber; 275 mg sodium; 36 mg cholesterol

Chocolate-Cherry Banana Bread

MAKES 1 loaf (16 slices)
PREP 20 minutes **BAKE** 35 minutes **COOL** 10 minutes
OVEN 350°F

- **Nonstick cooking spray**
- **1½ cups all-purpose flour**
- **⅔ cup sugar**
- **2 teaspoons baking powder**
- **¼ teaspoon baking soda**
- **¼ cup fat-free dairy sour cream**
- **¼ cup fat-free milk**
- **¼ cup refrigerated or frozen egg product, thawed, or 1 egg, lightly beaten**
- **2 teaspoons cooking oil**
- **⅔ cup mashed banana (2 medium)**
- **1 teaspoon vanilla**
- **8 maraschino cherries, drained and chopped**
- **¼ cup chopped walnuts**
- **2 tablespoons miniature semisweet chocolate pieces**

1 Preheat oven to 350°F. Lightly coat the bottom and ½ inch up sides of a 9×5×3-inch loaf pan with cooking spray; set aside. In a large bowl stir together flour, sugar, baking powder, and baking soda. Make a well in center of flour mixture; set aside.
2 In a medium bowl stir together sour cream, milk, egg product, and oil. Stir in banana and vanilla. Add sour cream mixture all at once to flour mixture. Stir just until moistened (batter should be lumpy). Fold in cherries, walnuts, and chocolate pieces. Spoon batter into prepared pan.

Chocolate-Cherry Banana Bread

3 Bake for 35 to 40 minutes or until a wooden toothpick inserted near center comes out clean. Cool in pan on a wire rack for 10 minutes. Remove from pan. Cool completely on the wire rack.

PER SLICE 119 calories; 2 g fat (0 g sat.); 2 g protein; 23 g carbohydrate; 1 g fiber; 61 mg sodium; 0 mg cholesterol

Tangerine Puckers ✪

MAKES 18 muffins
PREP 15 minutes **BAKE** 14 minutes **COOL** 5 minutes
OVEN 400°F

- **Nonstick cooking spray**
- **1 cup all-purpose flour**
- **1½ teaspoons baking powder**
- **2 tablespoons sugar**
- **¼ teaspoon salt**
- **½ cup fat-free milk**
- **2 tablespoons refrigerated or frozen egg product, thawed, or 1 egg white, lightly beaten**
- **1 tablespoon cooking oil**
- **1 teaspoon vanilla**
- **½ cup fresh tangerine sections (2 to 3 tangerines), coarsely chopped**

1 Preheat oven to 400°F. Lightly coat eighteen 1¾-inch muffin cups with cooking spray; set aside. In a medium bowl stir together flour, baking powder, sugar, and salt. Make a well in center of flour mixture; set aside.
2 In a small bowl combine milk, egg product, oil, and vanilla. Add egg mixture all at once to the flour mixture. Stir just until moistened (batter should be lumpy). Fold in the tangerine sections.
3 Spoon batter into prepared muffin cups, filling each almost full. Bake about 14 minutes or until golden brown and a wooden toothpick inserted in centers comes out clean. Cool in muffin cups on a wire rack for 5 minutes. Remove from muffin cups; serve warm.

PER MUFFIN 43 calories; 1 g fat (0 g sat.); 1 g protein; 8 g carbohydrate; 0 g fiber; 59 mg sodium; 0 mg cholesterol

Mango Coffee Cake

MAKES 10 servings
PREP 25 minutes **BAKE** 35 minutes **COOL** 30 minutes
OVEN 375°F

- **Nonstick cooking spray**
- **2 mangoes**
- **½ cup sugar**
- **¼ cup cooking oil**
- **¾ cup fat-free milk**
- **⅓ cup refrigerated or frozen egg product, thawed, or 2 egg whites**
- **⅔ cup all-purpose flour**
- **½ cup whole wheat flour**
- **2 teaspoons baking powder**
- **½ teaspoon finely shredded lime peel**
- **¼ teaspoon ground cardamom or ground allspice**
- **1¼ cups quick-cooking rolled oats**

1 Preheat oven to 375°F. Lightly coat a 9×1½-inch round baking pan with cooking spray; set aside. Pit, peel, and chop one of the mangoes; set aside. Pit, peel, and slice the remaining mango; set aside.
2 In a large mixing bowl stir together the sugar and oil. Add milk and egg product. Beat with an electric mixer on medium speed for 1 minute.
3 In a small bowl stir together the flours, baking powder, lime peel, and cardamom. Add flour mixture to milk mixture; beat until combined. Using a wooden spoon, stir in oats and chopped mango. Spoon batter into prepared pan. Arrange sliced mango over batter.
4 Bake for 35 to 40 minutes or until a wooden toothpick inserted near center of cake comes out clean. Cool in pan on a wire rack for 30 minutes. Serve warm.

PER SERVING 208 calories; 6 g fat (1 g sat.); 4 g protein; 35 g carbohydrate; 3 g fiber; 73 mg sodium; 0 mg cholesterol

Menu

Soft-cooked eggs

Steamed asparagus spears

Mango Coffee Cake
[opposite]

Coffee or hot tea

Mango Coffee Cake

Apple Surprise Rolls

Use a serrated

Cranberry Twist

MAKES 18 servings
PREP 30 minutes **RISE** 1 hour + 30 minutes **BAKE** 25 minutes

- **2¾ to 3 cups all-purpose flour**
- **1 package active dry yeast**
- **½ cup milk**
- **2 tablespoons granulated sugar**
- **2 tablespoons butter**
- **1 egg**
- **½ cup finely chopped fresh cranberries**
- **¼ cup packed brown sugar**
- **2 tablespoons finely chopped pecans**
- **1½ teaspoons finely shredded orange peel**
- **¼ teaspoon ground cinnamon**
- **¼ teaspoon ground nutmeg**
- **⅛ teaspoon ground cloves**
- **1½ teaspoons butter, melted**
- **1 recipe Orange Icing (optional)**

1 In a bowl combine 1 cup of the flour and the yeast; set aside. In a saucepan, heat and stir milk, ¼ cup *water,* granulated sugar, the 2 tablespoons butter, and ½ teaspoon *salt* until warm (120°F to 130°F) and butter almost melts. Add milk mixture to flour mixture; add egg. Beat with an electric mixer on medium speed for 30 seconds, scraping sides of bowl. Beat on high speed 3 minutes. Using a wooden spoon, stir in as much of the remaining flour as you can.
2 Turn out dough onto a floured surface. Knead in enough of the remaining flour to make a soft dough that is smooth and elastic (3 to 5 minutes total). Shape into a ball. Place in a lightly greased bowl; turn once. Cover and let rise in a warm place until double in size (1 to 1½ hours).
3 For filling, combine cranberries, brown sugar, pecans, orange peel, cinnamon, nutmeg, and cloves; set aside.
4 Punch down dough. Turn out onto lightly floured surface. Cover; let rest for 10 minutes. Grease a baking sheet. Roll dough into a 14×10-inch rectangle. Brush with the melted butter. Spread filling over dough. Starting from a long side, roll up dough. Seal seam. Cut roll in half lengthwise. Turn cut sides up. Loosely twist halves together, keeping the cut sides up. Pinch ends to seal. Place loaf on the prepared baking sheet. Cover; let rise in a warm place until nearly double in size (about 30 minutes). Preheat oven to 375°F.
5 Bake 25 minutes or until golden. Transfer loaf to a wire rack; cool completely. If desired, drizzle with Orange Icing.
Orange Icing: Combine ½ cup powdered sugar and enough orange juice (1 to 3 teaspoons) to make icing of drizzling consistency.

PER SERVING 116 calories; 3 g fat (1 g sat.); 3 g protein; 20 g carbohydrate; 1 g fiber; 85 mg sodium; 17 mg cholesterol

Apple Surprise Rolls 

MAKES 16 rolls
PREP 45 minutes **RISE** 30 minutes **BAKE** 12 minutes
OVEN 375°F

- **1 16-ounce package hot roll mix**
- **1 cup finely chopped cooking apple (1 medium)**
- **¼ cup mixed dried fruit bits or raisins**
- **2 tablespoons packed brown sugar**
- **½ teaspoon ground cinnamon**
- **Nonstick cooking spray**
- **½ cup powdered sugar**
- **1½ to 2 teaspoons milk**

1 Preheat oven to 375°F. Prepare hot roll mix according to package directions. Knead the dough; allow to rest as directed. Meanwhile, for filling, in a small bowl stir together apple, dried fruit bits, brown sugar, and cinnamon. Lightly coat 2 baking sheets with cooking spray; set aside.
2 Divide dough into 16 pieces. Flatten each piece into a 3-inch circle. Spoon 1 rounded teaspoon of filling onto each circle. Shape the dough around the filling to enclose, pulling dough until smooth and rounded. Place rolls, rounded sides up, on the prepared baking sheets. Cover and let rise in a warm place until nearly double in size (about 30 minutes).
3 Bake for 12 to 15 minutes or until golden. Transfer rolls to a wire rack and cool slightly. In a small bowl stir together powdered sugar and enough milk to make an icing of drizzling consistency. Drizzle icing over rolls.

PER ROLL 149 calories; 2 g fat (0 g sat.); 4 g protein; 29 g carbohydrate; 0 g fiber; 187 mg sodium; 13 mg cholesterol

bread knife to cut even slices.

Cranberry Twist

page 94

page 75

Fresh Fish &

Shellfish

Menu

Provençal Fish Fillets
[opposite]

Steamed green beans

Salad of hearts of romaine with balsamic vinaigrette

Italian bread slices with olive oil for dipping

Provençal Fish Fillets

Provençal Fish Fillets

MAKES 4 servings
PREP 25 minutes **BROIL** 4 to 6 minutes per ½-inch thickness

- **4 4-ounce fresh or frozen skinless cod, catfish, pollack, or tilapia fillets, ½ to 1 inch thick**
- **1 medium onion, thinly sliced**
- **2 cloves garlic, minced**
- **1 tablespoon olive oil**
- **1 14.5-ounce can whole tomatoes, drained and chopped**
- **2 teaspoons snipped fresh thyme or ½ teaspoon dried thyme, crushed**
- **8 oil-cured Greek olives, pitted and halved, or 8 pitted ripe olives, halved**
- **1 teaspoon capers, drained**
- **Fresh thyme sprigs (optional)**

1 Thaw fish, if frozen. Rinse fish; pat dry with paper towels. Measure thickness of fish. Set aside. For sauce, in a small saucepan cook onion and garlic in hot oil over medium heat about 5 minutes or until tender, stirring occasionally. Add drained tomatoes, thyme, olives, and drained capers. Bring to boiling; reduce heat. Simmer, uncovered, about 10 minutes or until most of the liquid has evaporated.
2 Preheat broiler. Place fish on the greased unheated rack of a broiler pan, tucking under thin edges of fish to make pieces of uniform thickness. Broil 4 inches from the heat until fish flakes easily when tested with a fork. Allow 4 to 6 minutes per ½-inch thickness of fish. (If fillets are 1 inch thick, turn once halfway through broiling.) Serve with sauce. If desired, garnish with fresh thyme sprigs.

PER SERVING 161 calories; 5 g fat (1 g sat.); 21 g protein; 7 g carbohydrate; 2 g fiber; 292 mg sodium; 48 mg cholesterol

Lemon-Parmesan Fish  

MAKES 4 servings
PREP 15 minutes **BAKE** 4 to 6 minutes per ½-inch thickness
OVEN 450°F

- **4 4-ounce fresh or frozen skinless flounder, sole, or orange roughy fillets, ½ to 1 inch thick**
- **Nonstick cooking spray**
- **½ cup crushed cornflakes**
- **1 tablespoon grated Parmesan cheese**
- **1 tablespoon butter, melted**
- **1 teaspoon finely shredded lemon peel**
- **¼ teaspoon black pepper**
- **Lemon wedges**

1 Thaw fish, if frozen. Rinse fish; pat dry with paper towels. Measure thickness of fish. Coat a 15×10×1-inch baking pan with cooking spray. Place fillets in prepared pan, tucking under thin edges of fish to make pieces of uniform thickness.
2 In a small bowl stir together cornflakes, cheese, melted butter, lemon peel, and pepper. Sprinkle crumb mixture on top of fish.
3 Bake in a 450°F oven until fish flakes easily when tested with a fork and crumbs are brown. Allow 4 to 6 minutes per ½-inch thickness of fish. Serve with lemon wedges.

PER SERVING 158 calories; 5 g fat (1 g sat.); 22 g protein; 5 g carbohydrate; 0 g fiber; 221 mg sodium; 62 mg cholesterol

Lemon-Parmesan Fish

Baked Fish with Mushrooms 

MAKES 4 servings
PREP 15 minutes **BAKE** 12 minutes **OVEN** 450°F

- **1 pound fresh or frozen skinless fish fillets, ½ to ¾ inch thick**
- **Salt**
- **2 tablespoons butter**
- **1½ cups sliced fresh mushrooms (4 ounces)**
- **¼ cup sliced green onion (2)**
- **1 teaspoon snipped fresh tarragon or thyme, or ¼ teaspoon dried tarragon or thyme, crushed**

1 Thaw fish, if frozen. Rinse fish; pat dry with paper towels. Cut into four serving-size pieces, if necessary. Arrange fish in a 2-quart rectangular baking dish, tucking under thin edges of fish to make pieces of uniform thickness. Sprinkle with salt. Set aside.
2 In a small saucepan melt butter over medium heat. Add mushrooms, green onion, and dried tarragon (if using); cook and stir until mushrooms and green onion are tender. Spoon mushroom mixture over fish; sprinkle with fresh tarragon (if using).
3 Bake, covered, in a 450°F oven for 12 to 18 minutes or until fish flakes easily when tested with a fork.

PER SERVING 159 calories; 8 g fat (4 g sat.); 22 g protein; 1 g carbohydrate; 0 g fiber; 104 mg sodium; 71 mg cholesterol

Dijon Mustard Fillets 

MAKES 4 servings
START TO FINISH 15 minutes

- **1 pound fresh or frozen skinless fish fillets, ½ to 1 inch thick**
- **½ teaspoon lemon-pepper seasoning**
- **¼ cup dairy sour cream**
- **1 tablespoon milk**
- **1 tablespoon Dijon-style mustard**
- **2 teaspoons snipped fresh chives or chopped green onion tops**
- **2 to 3 teaspoons capers, drained (optional)**

1 Thaw fish, if frozen. Rinse fish; pat dry with paper towels. Cut into four serving-size pieces, if necessary. Measure thickness of fish.
2 Preheat broiler. Place fish on the greased unheated rack of a broiler pan, tucking under thin edges of fish to make pieces of uniform thickness. Sprinkle with lemon-pepper seasoning. Broil 4 inches from the heat until fish flakes easily when tested with a fork. Allow 4 to 6 minutes per ½-inch thickness of fish. (If fillets are 1 inch thick, turn once halfway through broiling.)
3 Meanwhile, in a small saucepan stir together sour cream, milk, mustard, and chives. Heat and stir over low heat until heated through (do not boil). Spoon sauce over fish. If desired, sprinkle with drained capers.

PER SERVING 112 calories; 4 g fat (2 g sat.); 17 g protein; 1 g carbohydrate; 0 g fiber; 237 mg sodium; 28 mg cholesterol

Baked Mediterranean Cod & Asparagus 

MAKES 4 servings
PREP 15 minutes **BAKE** 12 minutes **OVEN** 475°F

- **1½ pounds fresh or frozen skinless cod fillets**
- **2 tablespoons olive oil**
- **Salt and black pepper**
- **1 pound asparagus spears, trimmed**
- **1 recipe Olive Relish**

1 Thaw fish, if frozen. Rinse fish; pat dry with paper towels. Cut fish into four serving-size pieces, if necessary. Lightly coat a 15×10×1-inch baking pan with a little of the olive oil. Arrange fillets on one side of pan, tucking under thin edges of fish to make pieces of uniform thickness. Brush fish with 1 teaspoon of the remaining olive oil. Sprinkle fish with salt and pepper.
2 Bake, uncovered, in a 475°F oven for 5 minutes. Place asparagus in opposite side of pan; brush with remaining olive oil and sprinkle with salt and pepper. Bake for 7 to 10 minutes more or until fish flakes easily when tested with a fork. Serve fish with Olive Relish and the asparagus.
Olive Relish: In a small bowl combine ¾ cup whole pimiento-stuffed green olives, coarsely chopped; ⅓ cup chopped onion; ¼ cup snipped fresh Italian (flat-leaf) parsley; 2 tablespoons capers, drained; 1 small fresh jalapeño chile pepper,* seeded and chopped; and 1 tablespoon white wine vinegar. Season to taste with ground black pepper.
***Note:** Because chile peppers contain volatile oils that can burn your skin and eyes, avoid direct contact with them as much as possible. When working with chile peppers, wear plastic or rubber gloves. If your bare hands do touch the chile peppers, wash your hands and nails well with soap and warm water.

PER SERVING 267 calories; 12 g fat (2 g sat.); 33 g protein; 7 g carbohydrate; 4 g fiber; 594 mg sodium; 73 mg cholesterol

Sesame-Crusted Cod

Sesame-Crusted Cod 

MAKES 4 servings
START TO FINISH 17 minutes

- **1 pound fresh or frozen skinless cod fillets, ¾ inch thick**
- **Salt**
- **Black pepper**
- **2 tablespoons sesame seeds**
- **3 tablespoons butter, melted**
- **1 12-ounce package trimmed fresh tender young green beans**
- **1 medium orange, halved and sliced**
- **3 cloves garlic, thinly sliced**

1 Thaw fish, if frozen. Rinse fish; pat dry with paper towels. Cut fish into four serving-size pieces, if necessary. Preheat broiler. Place fish on the unheated rack of a broiler pan, tucking under thin edges of fish to make pieces of uniform thickness. Sprinkle fish with salt and pepper. In a small bowl stir the sesame seeds into the melted butter. Reserve 1 tablespoon of the butter mixture; set aside. Brush fish with half of the remaining butter mixture. Broil 5 to 6 inches from the heat for 4 minutes; turn fish. Brush with remaining half of the butter mixture. Broil for 5 to 6 minutes more or until fish flakes easily when tested with a fork.

2 Meanwhile, in a large skillet heat the reserved butter mixture over medium-high heat. Add green beans and orange slices. Cover and cook for 2 minutes. Uncover; add garlic. Cook, uncovered, for 5 to 6 minutes more or until beans are crisp-tender, stirring frequently. Serve bean mixture with fish.

PER SERVING 241 calories; 12 g fat (6 g sat.); 23 g protein; 12 g carbohydrate; 4 g fiber; 274 mg sodium; 72 mg cholesterol

Cod Amandine

The best way to thaw fish is to place it in the refrigerator and allow it to defrost overnight. To speed up the thaw, place the wrapped package of fish under cold running water for 1 to 2 minutes. Don't thaw fish or shellfish in warm water or at room temperature and do not refreeze; doing so is unsafe.

Cod Amandine 

MAKES 4 servings
PREP 15 minutes **BAKE** 4 to 6 minutes per ½-inch thickness
OVEN 450°F

- **4 4-ounce fresh or frozen skinless cod, tilapia, trout, or halibut fillets, ½ to 1 inch thick**
- **¼ cup buttermilk**
- **½ cup panko (Japanese-style) bread crumbs or fine dry bread crumbs**
- **2 tablespoons snipped fresh parsley, or 2 teaspoons dried parsley flakes, crushed**
- **½ teaspoon dry mustard**
- **¼ teaspoon salt**
- **⅛ teaspoon black pepper**
- **¼ cup sliced almonds, coarsely chopped**
- **1 tablespoon butter, melted**

1 Thaw fish, if frozen. Rinse fish; pat dry with paper towels. Measure thickness of fish. Set aside. Grease a shallow baking pan; set aside.
2 Pour buttermilk into a shallow dish. In another shallow dish stir together bread crumbs, parsley, mustard, salt, and pepper. Dip fish in buttermilk; coat with crumb mixture. Place coated fish in the prepared baking pan.
3 Sprinkle fish with almonds. Drizzle melted butter over fish. Bake, uncovered, in a 450°F oven until fish flakes easily when tested with a fork. Allow 4 to 6 minutes per ½-inch thickness of fish.

PER SERVING 200 calories; 8 g fat (2 g sat.); 24 g protein; 8 g carbohydrate; 1 g fiber; 266 mg sodium; 56 mg cholesterol

Fish Fillets with Roasted Red Pepper Sauce

MAKES 4 servings
START TO FINISH 25 minutes

- **1 pound fresh or frozen skinless orange roughy or cod fillets**
- **1 12-ounce jar roasted red sweet peppers, drained**
- **2 cloves garlic, minced**
- **1 cup water**
- **2 teaspoons dried basil, crushed**
- **2 tablespoons tomato paste**
- **1 tablespoon red wine vinegar**
- **½ teaspoon sugar**
- **⅛ teaspoon salt**
- **Dash cayenne pepper**
- **1 lemon, sliced**
- **¼ teaspoon salt**
- **¼ teaspoon lemon-pepper seasoning**

1 Thaw fish, if frozen. Rinse fish; pat dry with paper towels. Cut into four serving-size pieces, if necessary. Measure thickness of fish. Set aside.
2 For sauce, in a blender or food processor combine roasted sweet peppers and garlic; cover and blend until nearly smooth. Add ½ cup of the water, the basil, tomato paste, vinegar, sugar, the ⅛ teaspoon salt, and the cayenne pepper. Cover and blend with several on-off turns until sweet pepper mixture is nearly smooth. Transfer sweet pepper mixture to a small saucepan; cook and stir over medium heat until heated through.
3 In a large skillet bring the remaining ½ cup water and half of the lemon slices just to boiling. Carefully add fish. Return just to boiling; reduce heat. Cover and simmer until fish flakes easily when tested with a fork. Allow 4 to 6 minutes per ½-inch thickness of fish.
4 Remove fish from skillet. Gently pat tops of fish dry with paper towels. Sprinkle fish lightly with the ¼ teaspoon salt and the lemon-pepper seasoning. Divide the red pepper sauce among four dinner plates. Place the fillets on top of the sauce. Garnish with remaining lemon slices.

PER SERVING 109 calories; 1 g fat (0 g sat.); 18 g protein; 7 g carbohydrate; 2 g fiber; 358 mg sodium; 23 mg cholesterol

Tilapia with Grape Chutney

Mild-flavored

Tilapia with Herbed Mushroom Sauce 

MAKES 6 servings
PREP 25 minutes **BAKE** 4 to 6 minutes per ½-inch thickness
OVEN 450°F

- **6 6-ounce fresh or frozen skinless tilapia, pollack, or cod fillets (½ to ¾ inch thick)**
- **Nonstick cooking spray**
- **2 teaspoons lemon juice**
- **¼ cup fine dry bread crumbs**
- **¼ to ½ teaspoon black pepper**
- **¼ teaspoon salt**
- **1½ cups shiitake mushrooms, stemmed and thinly sliced**
- **2 tablespoons finely chopped shallot (1 medium) or sweet onion**
- **2 teaspoons olive oil**
- **1 tablespoon all-purpose flour**
- **½ cup dry white wine or reduced-sodium chicken broth**
- **¾ cup reduced-sodium chicken broth**
- **1 tablespoon snipped fresh chives**
- **1 tablespoon snipped fresh parsley**
- **2 teaspoons snipped fresh thyme, or ½ teaspoon dried thyme, crushed**
- **Fresh thyme sprigs (optional)**
- **Lemon slices (optional)**

1 Thaw fish, if frozen. Rinse fish; pat dry with paper towels. Lightly coat a shallow baking pan with cooking spray. Measure thickness of fish. Brush fish lightly with lemon juice. Place fish, skin side down, in the prepared pan. In a small bowl stir together bread crumbs, pepper, and salt. Sprinkle crumb mixture evenly onto fish. Coat fish generously with cooking spray. Measure thickness of fish.
2 Bake, uncovered, in a 450°F oven until fish flakes easily when tested with a fork. Allow 4 to 6 minutes per ½-inch thickness of fish.
3 Meanwhile, for sauce, in a large skillet cook mushrooms and shallot in hot oil over medium-high heat about 3 minutes or until tender, stirring occasionally. Stir flour into skillet. Add white wine; cook and stir until thickened and bubbly. Add chicken broth. Bring to boiling; reduce heat. Simmer, uncovered, for 4 minutes, stirring occasionally. Stir in chives, parsley, and thyme. Serve sauce over fish. If desired, garnish with thyme sprigs and lemon slices.

PER SERVING 220 calories; 4 g fat (1 g sat.); 32 g protein; 11 g carbohydrate; 1 g fiber; 369 mg sodium; 75 mg cholesterol

Tilapia with Grape Chutney 

MAKES 4 servings
START TO FINISH 20 minutes

- **4 4-ounce fresh or frozen skinless tilapia or sole fillets**
- **Salt and black pepper**
- **2 tablespoons cooking oil**
- **1 cup seedless green grapes, halved**
- **½ cup tropical blend mixed dried fruit bits**
- **⅓ cup sliced green onion (3)**
- **⅓ cup apricot spreadable fruit**
- **Cooked brown rice (optional)**

1 Thaw fish, if frozen. Rinse fish; pat dry with paper towels. Cut fish into four serving-size pieces, if necessary. Sprinkle with salt and pepper.
2 In a large skillet cook fish in hot oil over medium-high heat for 3 to 4 minutes or until fish flakes easily when tested with a fork, turning once.
3 Transfer fish to a platter; keep warm. Add grapes, fruit bits, green onion, and spreadable fruit to skillet; cook and stir for 2 minutes. Season to taste with additional salt and pepper. Spoon chutney over fish. If desired, serve with brown rice.

PER SERVING 305 calories; 9 g fat (1 g sat.); 24 g protein; 37 g carbohydrate; 2 g fiber; 208 mg sodium; 57 mg cholesterol

tilapia is a fish kids will love.

Tilapia with Herbed Mushroom Sauce

Salmon with Fruit Salsa

Salmon with Fruit Salsa 

MAKES 4 servings
PREP 20 minutes **BROIL** 8 minutes

- **14 to 16 ounces fresh or frozen skinless salmon or halibut fillets, about 1 inch thick**
- **1 teaspoon olive oil or cooking oil**
- **¼ teaspoon lemon-pepper seasoning**
- **¾ cup chopped fresh strawberries or chopped, peeled peaches or nectarines**
- **⅓ cup chopped, peeled kiwifruit or fresh apricots**
- **1 tablespoon snipped fresh cilantro**
- **1 tablespoon orange juice or apple juice**
- **1 fresh jalapeño chile pepper, seeded and chopped***
- **Fresh cilantro sprigs (optional)**

1 Thaw fish, if frozen. Rinse fish; pat dry with paper towels. Cut into four serving-size pieces, if necessary. Brush both sides of each salmon fillet with oil. Sprinkle with lemon-pepper seasoning. Set aside.
2 For fruit salsa, in a medium bowl stir together strawberries, kiwifruit, snipped cilantro, orange juice, and jalapeño pepper. Set aside.
3 Preheat broiler. Place fish on the greased unheated rack of a broiler pan. Broil 4 inches from the heat for 8 to 12 minutes or until fish flakes easily when tested with a fork, turning once halfway through broiling. Serve fish with the fruit salsa. If desired, garnish with cilantro sprigs.
***Note:** Because chile peppers contain volatile oils that can burn your skin and eyes, avoid direct contact with them as much as possible. When working with chile peppers, wear plastic or rubber gloves. If your bare hands do touch the chile peppers, wash your hands and nails well with soap and warm water.

PER SERVING 123 calories; 5 g fat (1 g sat.); 15 g protein; 5 g carbohydrate; 1 g fiber; 95 mg sodium; 18 mg cholesterol

Citrus-Glazed Salmon 

MAKES 8 servings
PREP 20 minutes **BAKE** 4 to 6 minutes per ½-inch thickness
OVEN 450°F

- **1 2-pound fresh or frozen salmon fillet, skin removed**
- **Salt**
- **Black pepper**
- **¾ cup orange marmalade**
- **¼ cup sliced green onion (2)**
- **1 clove garlic, minced**
- **2 teaspoons dry white wine or water**
- **1 teaspoon grated fresh ginger**
- **1 teaspoon Dijon-style mustard**
- **¼ teaspoon cayenne pepper**
- **⅛ teaspoon five-spice powder**
- **3 tablespoons sliced almonds, toasted**

1 Thaw fish, if frozen. Rinse fish; pat dry with paper towels. Season fillet with salt and black pepper. Place fillet in a shallow baking pan; set aside.
2 In a small bowl stir together orange marmalade, green onion, garlic, wine, ginger, mustard, cayenne pepper, and five-spice powder. Spoon marmalade mixture over salmon.
3 Bake, uncovered, in a 450°F oven until fish flakes easily when tested with a fork. Allow 4 to 6 minutes per ½-inch thickness of fish. Transfer fish and glaze to a serving dish. Sprinkle with toasted almonds.

PER SERVING 227 calories; 6 g fat (1 g sat.); 24 g protein; 21 g carbohydrate; 1 g fiber; 170 mg sodium; 59 mg cholesterol

Salmon & Spinach Salad 

MAKES 4 servings
START TO FINISH 20 minutes

- **12 ounces cooked salmon,* broken into chunks**
- **3 cups fresh baby spinach**
- **1 cup coarsely chopped cucumber (1 small)**
- **½ cup quartered red onion slices**
- **¼ cup Flaxseed Dressing (below)**

1 In a large bowl combine salmon, spinach, cucumber, and onion. Drizzle with Flaxseed Dressing; toss gently to coat.

Flaxseed Dressing: Place 1 tablespoon flaxseeds in a shallow baking pan. Bake in a 350°F oven for 10 minutes, stirring once or twice. Cool. Place toasted flaxseeds in a spice grinder and pulse until ground to a fine powder. In a small bowl whisk together ground flaxseeds, 3 tablespoons champagne vinegar or white wine vinegar, 2 tablespoons olive oil, 1 tablespoon water, 1 tablespoon finely chopped shallot or green onion, 2 teaspoons Dijon-style mustard, and 1 clove garlic, minced.

***Note:** One pound fresh or frozen skinless salmon fillets will yield 12 ounces cooked salmon. Thaw salmon, if frozen. Rinse salmon; pat dry with paper towels. Measure thickness of salmon. Preheat broiler. Place salmon on the unheated rack of a broiler pan. Broil 4 inches from the heat until fish flakes easily when tested with a fork, turning once halfway through broiling. Allow 4 to 6 minutes per ½-inch thickness of fish.

PER SERVING 239 calories; 15 g fat (3 g sat.); 20 g protein; 6 g carbohydrate; 1 g fiber; 102 mg sodium; 54 mg cholesterol

Grilled Salmon Salad

To trim some

4 To serve, divide greens mixture among four serving plates. Arrange grilled salmon on greens mixture. Serve with dressing. If desired, garnish each serving with fresh dill.

Oil-Free Vinaigrette: In a small bowl stir together 1 tablespoon powdered fruit pectin; 1 teaspoon snipped fresh dill or tarragon or 1/4 teaspoon dried dill or tarragon, crushed; and 1/8 teaspoon black pepper. Stir in 1/4 cup water, 2 teaspoons white wine vinegar, and 1 teaspoon honey mustard. Cover and chill for at least 30 minutes or up to 3 days.

PER SERVING 228 calories; 9 g fat (1 g sat.); 30 g protein; 5 g carbohydrate; 2 g fiber; 83 mg sodium; 78 mg cholesterol

Grilled Salmon Salad

MAKES 4 servings
PREP 25 minutes **GRILL** 4 to 6 minutes per ½-inch thickness
CHILL 30 minutes to 3 days

- **1 recipe Oil-Free Vinaigrette**
- **1¼ pounds fresh or frozen salmon fillets**
- **Black pepper**
- **3 cups torn mixed greens**
- **1 cup cucumber slices, quartered**
- **1 cup steamed asparagus or green beans, cut into 2-inch pieces and chilled**
- **½ cup radish slices, quartered**
- **¼ cup sliced green onion (2)**
- **Fresh dill sprigs or tarragon sprigs (optional)**

1 Prepare Oil-Free Vinaigrette; cover and chill. Thaw fish, if frozen. Rinse fish; pat dry with paper towels. Cut salmon into four serving-size portions, if necessary. Measure thickness of salmon. Sprinkle fish with pepper.

2 For a charcoal grill, place fish, skin side up, on a greased grill rack directly over medium coals. Grill, uncovered, until fish flakes easily when tested with a fork, turning once halfway through grilling. Allow 4 to 6 minutes per 1/2-inch thickness of fish. (For a gas grill, preheat grill. Reduce heat to medium. Place fish, skin side up, on greased grill rack over heat. Cover and grill as above.) Using a wide metal spatula, lift fillets away from the skin and transfer to a serving plate. (Scrape skin from grill rack and discard.)

3 In a large bowl toss together greens, cucumber, asparagus, radish, and green onion.

Salmon with Feta & Pasta 

MAKES 5 servings
START TO FINISH 25 minutes

- **12 ounces fresh or frozen skinless salmon fillet**
- **8 ounces dried rotini pasta**
- **2 teaspoons olive oil**
- **Nonstick cooking spray**
- **2 cloves garlic, minced**
- **Salt**
- **2 cups chopped roma tomato (4 large)**
- **1 cup sliced green onion (8)**
- **⅓ cup sliced, pitted ripe olives**
- **3 tablespoons snipped fresh basil**
- **½ teaspoon coarsely ground black pepper**
- **1 4-ounce package feta cheese, crumbled**

1 Thaw fish, if frozen. Rinse fish; pat dry with paper towels. Cut fish into 1-inch pieces. Set aside. Cook pasta according to package directions; drain well. Return pasta to hot pan and toss with oil to coat; cover to keep warm.

2 Meanwhile, lightly coat a large nonstick skillet with cooking spray. Heat skillet over medium-high heat. Add garlic; cook and stir for 15 seconds. Lightly season fish pieces with salt. Add fish to skillet; cook for 4 to 6 minutes or until fish flakes easily when tested with a fork, turning occasionally. Stir in tomato, green onion, olives, basil, and pepper. Heat through.

3 In a large bowl combine hot pasta, salmon mixture, and feta cheese; toss gently.

PER SERVING 373 calories; 13 g fat (5 g sat.); 24 g protein; 41 g carbohydrate; 3 g fiber; 443 mg sodium; 56 mg cholesterol

fat, use reduced-fat feta cheese.

Salmon with Feta & Pasta

Salad Niçoise in Flatbreads 

MAKES 6 servings
START TO FINISH 25 minutes

- **4 ounces fresh green beans, trimmed (if desired) and cut into 1-inch pieces (about 1 cup)**
- **1 12-ounce can chunk white or light tuna (water pack), drained and flaked**
- **1 cup halved cherry tomatoes**
- **⅓ cup chopped, pitted niçoise or kalamata olives**
- **¼ cup finely chopped sweet onion (such as Vidalia, Walla Walla, or Maui)**
- **2 tablespoons snipped fresh mint**
- **1 tablespoon lemon juice**
- **2 teaspoons olive oil**
- **⅛ teaspoon black pepper**
- **3 cups packaged mesclun (mixed salad greens)**
- **3 Greek pita flatbreads**

1 In a medium saucepan cook beans, covered, in boiling water about 4 minutes or until crisp-tender. Drain. Rinse with cold water; drain again.
2 In a large bowl combine beans, drained tuna, tomatoes, olives, onion, and mint. Add lemon juice, oil, and pepper; toss to combine. Stir in mesclun.
3 To serve, cut pita rounds in half crosswise. Cut each half horizontally. Fill pita halves with about ½ cup of the tuna mixture.

PER POCKET 210 calories; 5 g fat (1 g sat.); 17 g protein; 23 g carbohydrate; 3 g fiber; 527 mg sodium; 24 mg cholesterol

Cornmeal-Crusted Tuna Burgers

MAKES 6 burgers
PREP 30 minutes **BAKE** 18 minutes **OVEN** 425°F

- **1½ pounds fresh tuna fillets**
- **½ cup finely shredded carrot (1 medium)**
- **¼ cup chopped green onion (2)**
- **½ cup panko (Japanese-style) bread crumbs**
- **2 tablespoons creamy Dijon-style mustard blend**
- **½ teaspoon salt**
- **¼ teaspoon bottled hot pepper sauce**
- **¼ cup yellow cornmeal**
- **1 recipe Tangy Dill Coleslaw (optional)**

1 Grease a 15×10×1-inch baking pan; set aside. Finely chop tuna. In a large bowl combine tuna, carrot, green onion, ¼ cup of the bread crumbs, the mustard blend, salt, and hot pepper sauce. With wet hands, form mixture into six ½-inch-thick patties.
2 In a shallow dish stir together cornmeal and the remaining bread crumbs; coat tuna patties all over with crumb mixture. Place patties in the prepared baking pan.
3 Bake, uncovered, in a 425°F oven about 18 minutes until done (160°F), turning patties once halfway through baking. If desired, serve burgers with Tangy Dill Coleslaw.

Tangy Dill Coleslaw: In a large bowl combine ¼ cup light mayonnaise dressing, ¼ cup light dairy sour cream, 2 tablespoons creamy Dijon-style mustard blend, 1 tablespoon snipped fresh dill, and 1 tablespoon cider vinegar. Add one 10-ounce package finely shredded green cabbage and ¼ cup finely chopped dill pickle; mix well. Cover and refrigerate until serving time.

PER BURGER (WITH COLESLAW) 277 calories; 10 g fat (2 g sat.); 29 g protein; 17 g carbohydrate; 2 g fiber; 577 mg sodium; 49 mg cholesterol

Seared Tuna with Grapefruit-Orange Relish 

MAKES 4 servings
PREP 20 minutes **COOK** 6 minutes

- **4 4-ounce fresh or frozen tuna steaks, ¾ inch thick**
- **2 teaspoons sherry vinegar or white wine vinegar**
- **2 teaspoons soy sauce**
- **½ teaspoon grated fresh ginger**
- **1 tablespoon olive oil**
- **1 medium grapefruit, peeled and sectioned**
- **1 medium orange, peeled and sliced**
- **2 tablespoons finely chopped red onion**
- **2 tablespoons snipped fresh cilantro**
- **2 teaspoons olive oil**

1 Thaw fish, if frozen. Rinse fish; pat dry with paper towels.
2 For relish, in a small bowl stir together vinegar, soy sauce, and ginger. Whisk in the 1 tablespoon olive oil. Cut grapefruit sections into thirds and coarsely chop orange slices. Stir fruit pieces, red onion, and cilantro into vinegar mixture. Set aside.
3 In a large skillet heat the 2 teaspoons olive oil over medium-high heat. Add fish; cook for 6 to 9 minutes or until fish flakes easily when tested with a fork (tuna can be slightly pink in center), turning once. Serve fish with relish.

PER SERVING 244 calories; 11 g fat (2 g sat.); 27 g protein; 7 g carbohydrate; 1 g fiber; 199 mg sodium; 43 mg cholesterol

Serve these classic salad-filled flatbreads as towering displays. Thread a cherry tomato, kalamata olive, and fresh mint leaf on a short wooden skewer or sandwich pick. Then cut each filled flatbread half in half, forming two sandwich triangles. Stack two triangles and insert a pick to hold the layers together.

Salad Niçoise in Flatbreads

Dilled Tuna Potato Salad

MAKES 6 servings
PREP 25 minutes **CHILL** 4 to 6 hours

- **3 medium red potatoes (about 1 pound)**
- **½ cup light mayonnaise dressing or salad dressing**
- **½ cup plain fat-free yogurt**
- **1 tablespoon snipped fresh dill or 1 teaspoon dried dill**
- **1 tablespoon fat-free milk**
- **½ teaspoon finely shredded lemon peel**
- **¼ teaspoon salt**
- **1 clove garlic, minced**
- **1 cup chopped cucumber (1 small)**
- **¼ cup sliced green onion (2)**
- **¼ cup coarsely chopped radishes**
- **1 9-ounce can chunk white tuna (water pack), drained and broken into chunks**
- **2 hard-cooked eggs, chopped**
- **12 leaves savoy cabbage or napa cabbage**

1 Scrub potatoes; cut into ½-inch cubes. In a covered medium saucepan cook potatoes in a small amount of boiling water for 10 to 12 minutes or just until tender. Drain and cool slightly.
2 Meanwhile, in a large bowl stir together mayonnaise dressing, yogurt, dill, milk, lemon peel, salt, and garlic. Stir in cucumber, green onion, and radishes. Add cooked potatoes, drained tuna, and eggs; toss gently to coat. Cover and chill for 4 to 6 hours.
3 To serve, line six serving bowls with cabbage leaves. Gently stir tuna mixture; spoon on top of cabbage.

PER SERVING 243 calories; 10 g fat (2 g sat.); 18 g protein; 22 g carbohydrate; 5 g fiber; 461 mg sodium; 96 mg cholesterol

Chilly Bow Ties & Tuna

Chilly Bow Ties & Tuna 

MAKES 6 servings
PREP 20 minutes **CHILL** 4 to 24 hours

- **8 ounces dried farfalle pasta (bow ties)**
- **⅓ cup light mayonnaise dressing or salad dressing**
- **⅓ cup bottled reduced-calorie Italian salad dressing**
- **¼ cup thinly sliced green onion (2) (optional)**
- **2 tablespoons orange juice**
- **¼ teaspoon salt**
- **¼ teaspoon black pepper**
- **1 11-ounce can mandarin orange sections, drained**
- **1 12-ounce can chunk white tuna (water pack), drained and broken into chunks**
- **1 cup fresh pea pods, halved**
- **Milk (optional)**

1 Cook pasta according to package directions; drain. Rinse with cold water; drain again.
2 Meanwhile, for dressing, in a large bowl combine mayonnaise dressing, Italian dressing, green onion (if desired), orange juice, salt, and pepper.
3 Add cooked pasta to dressing in bowl. Toss well to coat. Gently stir in drained orange sections, drained tuna, and pea pods. Cover and chill for 4 to 24 hours. Before serving, if necessary, stir in milk, 1 teaspoon at a time, to moisten.

PER SERVING 254 calories; 3 g fat (1 g sat.); 13 g protein; 43 g carbohydrate; 2 g fiber; 433 mg sodium; 13 mg cholesterol

Snapper Veracruz

Snapper Veracruz 

MAKES 6 servings
START TO FINISH 30 minutes

- **1½ pounds fresh or frozen skinless red snapper or other fish fillets, ½ to ¾ inch thick**
- **⅛ teaspoon salt**
- **⅛ teaspoon ground black pepper**
- **1 large onion, sliced and separated into rings**
- **2 cloves garlic, minced**
- **1 tablespoon cooking oil**
- **2 large tomatoes, chopped**
- **¼ cup sliced pimiento-stuffed green olives**
- **¼ cup dry white wine**
- **2 tablespoons capers, drained**
- **1 to 2 fresh jalapeño or serrano chile peppers, seeded and chopped, or 1 to 2 canned jalapeño chile peppers, rinsed, drained, seeded, and chopped***
- **½ teaspoon sugar**
- **1 bay leaf**
- **Snipped fresh parsley (optional)**

1 Thaw fish, if frozen. Rinse fish; pat dry with paper towels. Cut into six serving-size pieces, if necessary. Sprinkle fish with salt and black pepper.
2 For sauce, in a large skillet cook onion and garlic in hot oil until onion is tender. Stir in tomatoes, olives, wine, drained capers, chile peppers, sugar, and bay leaf. Bring to boiling. Add fish to skillet. Return to boiling; reduce heat. Cover and simmer for 6 to 10 minutes or until fish flakes easily when tested with a fork. Use a slotted spatula to carefully transfer fish from skillet to a serving platter. Cover and keep warm.
3 Boil sauce in skillet for 5 to 6 minutes or until reduced to about 2 cups, stirring occasionally. Discard bay leaf. Spoon sauce over fish. If desired, sprinkle with parsley.

***Note:** Because chile peppers contain volatile oils that can burn your skin and eyes, avoid direct contact with them as much as possible. When working with chile peppers, wear plastic or rubber gloves. If your bare hands do touch the chile peppers, wash your hands and nails well with soap and warm water.

PER SERVING 174 calories; 5 g fat (1 g sat.); 24 g protein; 7 g carbohydrate; 6 g fiber; 260 mg sodium; 42 mg cholesterol

Red Snapper with Cilantro-Lime Vinaigrette

MAKES 4 servings
PREP 15 minutes **MARINATE** 30 minutes to 1 hour
BROIL 8 minutes

- **4 6-ounce fresh or frozen skinless red snapper or other firm white-fleshed fish fillets, about 1 inch thick**
- **2 limes**
- **¼ cup olive oil**
- **2 tablespoons sugar**
- **2 tablespoons red wine vinegar**
- **2 tablespoons finely chopped shallot (optional)**
- **1 tablespoon snipped fresh cilantro**
- **1 clove garlic, minced**

1 Thaw fish, if frozen. Rinse fish; pat dry with paper towels. Place fish in a shallow dish.
2 Finely shred enough lime peel to make ½ teaspoon. Squeeze enough juice from a lime to make 2 tablespoons. Cut the remaining lime into wedges; set aside. In a small bowl combine the shredded lime peel, lime juice, oil, sugar, vinegar, shallot (if desired), cilantro, and garlic. Set aside 2 tablespoons of the oil mixture until ready to serve.
3 Pour the remaining oil mixture over fish in dish. Cover and marinate in the refrigerator for at least 30 minutes or up to 1 hour.
4 Preheat broiler. Drain fish, reserving marinade. Place fish on the greased unheated rack of a broiler pan. Broil 4 inches from the heat for 8 to 12 minutes or until fish flakes easily when tested with a fork, turning and brushing once with reserved marinade halfway through broiling. Discard any remaining marinade.
5 Transfer fish to four plates; drizzle with the reserved 2 tablespoons oil mixture. Serve fish with lime wedges.

PER SERVING 249 calories; 9 g fat (1 g sat.); 35 g protein; 6 g carbohydrate; 1 g fiber; 110 mg sodium; 62 mg cholesterol

Broiled Halibut with Dijon Cream 

MAKES 4 servings
PREP 10 minutes **BROIL** 8 minutes

- **4 4- to 5-ounce fresh or frozen halibut steaks, 1 inch thick**
- **1 teaspoon Greek-style or Mediterranean seasoning blend**
- **¼ teaspoon coarsely ground black pepper**
- **¼ cup dairy sour cream**
- **¼ cup creamy Dijon-style mustard blend**
- **1 tablespoon milk**
- **½ teaspoon dried oregano, crushed**

1 Thaw fish, if frozen. Rinse fish; pat dry with paper towels. Preheat broiler. Place fish on a greased unheated rack of a broiler pan. Sprinkle fish with Greek-style seasoning blend and pepper.
2 Broil 4 inches from the heat for 8 to 12 minutes or until fish flakes easily when tested with a fork, turning once halfway through broiling. Invert fish onto a serving platter.
3 Meanwhile, for sauce, in a small bowl combine sour cream, mustard blend, milk, and oregano. Serve sauce over fish.

PER SERVING 168 calories; 5 g fat (2 g sat.); 24 g protein; 4 g carbohydrate; 0 g fiber; 300 mg sodium; 42 mg cholesterol

Basil Halibut Steaks

MAKES 4 servings
PREP 25 minutes **BROIL** 8 minutes

- **4 5- to 6-ounce fresh or frozen halibut steaks, 1 inch thick**
- **½ cup chopped onion (1 medium)**
- **1 clove garlic, minced**
- **1 tablespoon olive oil**
- **2 cups chopped, peeled tomato (4 medium)**
- **¼ teaspoon salt**
- **¼ teaspoon black pepper**
- **4 tablespoons snipped fresh basil**
- **2 tablespoons butter, melted**

1 Thaw fish, if frozen. Rinse fish; pat dry with paper towels. Set aside. In a medium skillet cook onion and garlic in hot oil over medium heat until tender, stirring occasionally. Stir in tomato, salt, and pepper. Bring to boiling; reduce heat. Simmer, uncovered, for 15 minutes. Stir in 2 tablespoons of the basil.
2 Meanwhile, combine melted butter and the remaining 2 tablespoons basil; brush butter mixture over one side of the halibut steaks.
3 Preheat broiler. Place fish, brushed side up, on a greased unheated rack of a broiler pan. Broil 4 inches from heat for 8 to 12 minutes or until fish flakes easily when tested with a fork, turning once halfway through broiling.
4 Season fish to taste with additional salt and pepper. Serve with tomato mixture.

PER SERVING 274 calories; 13 g fat (4 g sat.); 31 g protein; 8 g carbohydrate; 2 g fiber; 273 mg sodium; 61 mg cholesterol

Pollack with Nectarine Salad 

MAKES 4 servings
PREP 20 minutes **GRILL** 8 minutes

- **1 pound fresh or frozen skinless pollack fillets, about 1 inch thick**
- **2 small nectarines, cut into ½-inch pieces (1 cup)**
- **1 small cucumber, seeded and cut into ½-inch pieces (1 cup)**
- **1 kiwifruit, peeled and cut into ½-inch pieces**
- **¼ cup thinly sliced green onion (2)**
- **¼ cup orange juice**
- **2 teaspoons white wine vinegar**
- **1 teaspoon olive oil**
- **½ teaspoon black pepper**
- **6 cups torn mixed salad greens**

1 Thaw fish, if frozen. Rinse fish; pat dry with paper towels. Set aside. For salsa, in a small bowl combine nectarine, cucumber, kiwifruit, green onion, orange juice, and vinegar. Cover and chill until ready to serve.
2 Rub oil over both sides of fish; sprinkle with pepper. Place fish in a greased grill basket. For a charcoal grill, place basket on the grill rack directly over medium coals. Grill, uncovered, for 8 to 12 minutes or until fish flakes easily when tested with a fork, turning once. (For a gas grill, preheat grill. Reduce heat to medium. Place basket on grill rack over heat. Cover and grill as above.)
3 To serve, divide greens among four bowls. Break up fish into pieces; place on top of greens with nectarine mixture.

PER SERVING 181 calories; 3 g fat (0 g sat.); 24 g protein; 15 g carbohydrate; 3 g fiber; 111 mg sodium; 81 mg cholesterol

If nectarines are unavailable, try peaches... they can be used interchangeably.

Pollack with Nectarine Salad

Spicy Fish Kabobs

Halibut in Pepper Water [below]

Salad of fresh spinach, sliced apples, sliced red onion, and honey-mustard dressing

Country-style Italian rolls

Halibut in Pepper Water

MAKES 4 servings

PREP 20 minutes **COOK** 7 minutes plus 4 to 6 minutes per ½-inch thickness

- **4** **5- to 6-ounce fresh or frozen halibut steaks or 4 skinless cod or other whitefish fillets**
- **1½** **cups dry white wine (sauvignon blanc or pinot grigio) or chicken broth**
- **1** **cup water**
- **1½** **cups chopped yellow sweet pepper (2 medium)**
- **3** **tablespoons capers, drained**
- **4** **cloves garlic, minced**
- **¼** **to ½ teaspoon crushed red pepper**
- **Salt and freshly ground black pepper**
- **2** **tablespoons basil oil or olive oil**
- **Coarsely chopped fresh parsley**

1 Thaw fish, if frozen. Rinse fish; pat dry with paper towels. Measure thickness of fish. Set aside.

2 For pepper water, in a large skillet combine wine, water, sweet pepper, drained capers, garlic, and crushed red pepper. Bring to boiling; reduce heat. Simmer, uncovered, for 7 minutes, stirring occasionally.

3 Place fish in a single layer in the pepper water in the skillet. Season fish with salt and black pepper. Spoon liquid over fish. Return to simmer. Cook, covered, until fish flakes easily when tested with a fork. Allow 4 to 6 minutes per ½-inch thickness of fish.

4 Transfer fish to a serving platter. Pour pepper water into a small serving pitcher. Drizzle cooked fish with the oil and a little of the pepper water. Sprinkle with parsley. Serve with remaining pepper water.

PER SERVING 338 calories; 11 g fat (1 g sat.); 37 g protein; 8 g carbohydrate; 1 g fiber; 437 mg sodium; 54 mg cholesterol

Spicy Fish Kabobs 

MAKES 6 servings

PREP 20 minutes **GRILL** 10 minutes

- **1½** **pounds fresh or frozen halibut or swordfish steaks**
- **¾** **cup packaged peeled fresh baby carrots**
- **1½** **cups baby yellow and/or green pattypan squash or 2 small zucchini or yellow summer squash, halved lengthwise and cut crosswise into ½-inch slices**
- **1** **cup fresh sugar snap peas or pea pods, trimmed**
- **1** **teaspoon ground cumin**
- **1** **teaspoon ground coriander**
- **¼** **teaspoon each salt and black pepper**
- **⅛** **teaspoon cayenne pepper**
- **3** **tablespoons olive oil**
- **1** **teaspoon finely shredded orange peel (set aside)**
- **¼** **cup orange juice**
- **1** **cup quick-cooking couscous**
- **1½** **cups reduced-sodium chicken broth**

1 Thaw fish, if frozen. Rinse fish; pat dry with paper towels. Cut fish into 1-inch cubes. Set aside. In a covered medium saucepan cook carrots in a small amount of boiling water for 1 minute; add squash and cook for 1 minute more. Drain. On six 10- to 12-inch-long skewers,* alternately thread fish cubes, squash, carrots, and sugar snap peas, leaving a ¼-inch space between pieces. Set kabobs aside.

2 In a small bowl stir together cumin, coriander, salt, black pepper, and cayenne pepper. In a medium saucepan heat oil over low heat. Add spice mixture; heat and stir for 1 minute. Transfer 2 tablespoons of the oil-spice mixture to a small bowl. Stir orange juice into mixture in the bowl.

3 Stir couscous into remaining oil-spice mixture in saucepan. Cook and stir for 1 minute. Stir in broth and orange peel. Bring to boiling. Cover and remove from heat. Let stand while grilling kabobs.

4 Brush some of the orange juice mixture on the kabobs. For a charcoal grill, place kabobs on the greased grill rack directly over medium coals. Grill, uncovered, about 10 minutes or until fish flakes easily when tested with a fork, turning and brushing with remaining orange juice mixture once halfway through grilling. (For a gas grill, preheat grill. Reduce heat to medium. Place kabobs on grill rack over heat. Cover and grill as above.) Discard any remaining orange juice mixture. Serve kabobs with couscous.

***Note:** If using wooden skewers, soak in enough water to cover for at least 30 minutes before using.

PER SERVING 325 calories; 10 g fat (1 g sat.); 29 g protein; 29 g carbohydrate; 3 g fiber; 317 mg sodium; 36 mg cholesterol

Grilled Shrimp Kabobs

You can use wooden skewers instead of metal. To prevent them from burning, soak skewers in enough water to cover for at least 30 minutes before using.

Grilled Shrimp Kabobs  

MAKES 4 servings
PREP 20 minutes **GRILL** 6 minutes

- **1 pound fresh or frozen large shrimp in shells**
- **1 medium green and/or red sweet pepper, cut into 16 pieces**
- **¼ of a medium fresh pineapple, cut into chunks**
- **4 green onions, cut into 2- to 3-inch pieces**
- **¼ cup bottled low-carb barbecue sauce**

1 Thaw shrimp, if frozen. Peel and devein shrimp, leaving tails intact. Rinse shrimp; pat dry with paper towels. Alternately thread shrimp, sweet pepper, pineapple, and green onion onto eight 10- to 12-inch-long metal skewers.
2 For a charcoal grill, place kabobs on the greased grill rack directly over medium coals. Grill, uncovered, for 6 to 10 minutes or until shrimp are opaque, turning kabobs and brushing with barbecue sauce once halfway through grilling. (For a gas grill, preheat grill. Reduce heat to medium. Place kabobs on greased grill rack over heat. Cover; grill as above.)

PER SERVING 127 calories; 2 g fat (0 g sat.); 18 g protein; 9 g carbohydrate; 1 g fiber; 257 mg sodium; 129 mg cholesterol

Seared Shrimp in Garlic Butter  

MAKES 4 servings
START TO FINISH 20 minutes

- **1½ pounds fresh or frozen medium shrimp in shells**
- **3 cloves garlic, minced**
- **2 tablespoons butter**
- **2 tablespoons dry white wine or chicken broth**
- **1 tablespoon snipped fresh chives (optional)**
- **⅛ teaspoon salt**

1 Thaw shrimp, if frozen. Peel and devein shrimp, removing tails. Rinse shrimp; pat dry with paper towels. Set aside.
2 In a very large skillet cook and stir garlic in 1 tablespoon of the butter over medium-high heat until butter melts. Add shrimp; cook and stir 1 to 3 minutes or until shrimp are opaque. Transfer shrimp to a serving platter. Add wine and remaining butter to the skillet. Cook and stir to loosen any brown bits from pan. Pour wine mixture over shrimp. Sprinkle with chives, if desired, and salt.

PER SERVING 241 calories; 9 g fat (4 g sat.); 35 g protein; 3 g carbohydrate; 0 g fiber; 366 mg sodium; 274 mg cholesterol

Honey-Sauced Shrimp & Veggies 

MAKES 4 servings
START TO FINISH 20 minutes

- **1 pound fresh or frozen medium shrimp in shells**
- **12 ounces fresh baby carrots, peeled and halved lengthwise, or one 12-ounce package peeled fresh baby carrots**
- **3 cups broccoli florets**
- **1 cup cherry tomatoes**
- **1 tablespoon cooking oil**
- **⅓ cup honey**
- **2 tablespoons bottled chili garlic sauce**
- **2 tablespoons orange juice**

1 Thaw shrimp, if frozen. Peel and devein shrimp, leaving tails intact, if desired. Rinse shrimp; pat dry with paper towels. Set aside.
2 In a large saucepan cook carrots, covered, in boiling lightly salted water for 5 minutes. Add broccoli; cook for 3 to 4 minutes more or until vegetables are just tender. Drain.
3 Meanwhile, in a large skillet cook and stir shrimp and tomatoes in hot oil for 3 to 4 minutes or until shrimp are opaque. Transfer shrimp mixture to a serving platter along with carrots and broccoli. In the same skillet stir together honey, chili sauce, and orange juice; heat through. Spoon honey mixture over shrimp and vegetables.

PER SERVING 319 calories; 6 g fat (1 g sat.); 26 g protein; 43 g carbohydrate; 5 g fiber; 361 mg sodium; 172 mg cholesterol

Honey-Sauced Shrimp & Veggies

Seafood Salad with Orange-Cream Dressing

Seafood Salad with Orange-Cream Dressing 

MAKES 6 servings
START TO FINISH 20 minutes

- **1 pound fresh or frozen sea scallops, cooked and chilled***
- **8 ounces fresh or frozen peeled and deveined shrimp, cooked and chilled ****
- **6 cups fresh spinach leaves or torn mixed salad greens**
- **2 large mangoes or small papayas, seeded, peeled, and cut into chunks**
- **1 recipe Orange-Cream Dressing**
- **2 tablespoons cashew halves or sliced almonds, toasted (optional)**

1 Halve any large scallops. In a large salad bowl combine scallops, shrimp, spinach, and mangoes. Drizzle Orange-Cream Dressing over scallop mixture; toss gently to coat.
2 To serve, divide the scallop mixture among six dinner plates. If desired, sprinkle with cashews.

Orange-Cream Dressing: Combine 1/3 cup light dairy sour cream, 2 teaspoons grated fresh ginger, 1 teaspoon white wine vinegar, 1/2 teaspoon finely shredded orange peel, 1 teaspoon orange juice, and dash cayenne pepper.

***Note:** To cook scallops, add 1/2 cup water to a large skillet. Bring to boiling. Add scallops. Return to boiling; reduce heat. Simmer, covered, for 4 to 6 minutes or until scallops are opaque. Drain and chill.

****Note:** If desired, leave the tails on shrimp. To cook shrimp, in a medium saucepan bring 2 cups water to boiling. Add shrimp; return to boiling. Cook, uncovered, for 1 to 3 minutes or until shrimp are opaque. Rinse under cold running water; drain and chill.

PER SERVING 194 calories; 5 g fat (1 g sat.); 23 g protein; 16 g carbohydrate; 2 g fiber; 206 mg sodium; 82 mg cholesterol

Basil-Lemon Shrimp Linguine 

MAKES 4 servings
START TO FINISH 30 minutes

- **1 pound fresh or frozen large shrimp in shells**
- **6 ounces dried linguine or fettuccine pasta**
- **½ teaspoon salt**
- **8 ounces fresh asparagus spears, trimmed and cut diagonally into 1-inch pieces**
- **Nonstick cooking spray**
- **2 cloves garlic, minced**
- **1 cup thin red, yellow, and/or green sweet pepper strips (1 large)**
- **¼ cup snipped fresh basil or 1 tablespoon dried basil, crushed**
- **1 teaspoon finely shredded lemon peel**
- **¼ teaspoon black pepper**
- **¼ cup sliced green onion (2)**
- **2 tablespoons lemon juice**
- **1 tablespoon olive oil**
- **Lemon wedges (optional)**

1 Thaw shrimp, if frozen. Peel and devein shrimp, leaving tails intact, if desired. Rinse shrimp; pat dry with paper towels. Set aside.
2 Cook pasta according to package directions in water with 1/4 teaspoon of the salt and adding asparagus for the last 3 minutes of cooking. Drain and return pasta mixture to pan; cover and keep warm.
3 Meanwhile, lightly coat a large nonstick skillet with cooking spray. Heat skillet over medium heat. Add garlic to skillet; cook and stir for 15 seconds. Add sweet pepper; cook and stir about 2 minutes or until crisp-tender. Add shrimp, dried basil (if using), lemon peel, remaining 1/4 teaspoon salt, and black pepper. Cook and stir about 3 minutes or until shrimp are opaque. Remove from heat.
4 Add shrimp mixture to pasta mixture. Add snipped fresh basil (if using), the green onion, lemon juice, and oil; toss gently to coat. If desired, garnish each serving with lemon wedges.

PER SERVING 336 calories; 6 g fat (1 g sat.); 31 g protein; 39 g carbohydrate; 4 g fiber; 463 mg sodium; 172 mg cholesterol

Make a quick change—try half shrimp and half scallops in this lemony fresh pasta dish.

Basil-Lemon Shrimp Linguine

Shrimp Tacos

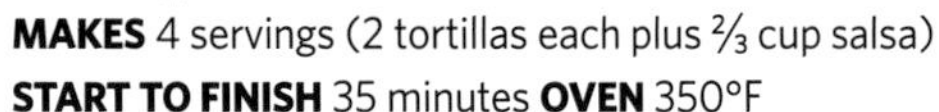

Shrimp Tacos

MAKES 4 servings (2 tortillas each plus ⅔ cup salsa)
START TO FINISH 35 minutes **OVEN** 350°F

- **1 pound fresh or frozen medium shrimp in shells**
- **8 6-inch corn tortillas**
- **1½ cups chopped, seeded tomato (3 medium)**
- **1 cup chopped, seeded cucumber (1 small)**
- **⅓ cup thinly sliced green onion (3)**
- **¼ cup snipped fresh cilantro**
- **3 tablespoons lime juice**
- **¼ teaspoon salt**
- **8 ounces fresh green beans, trimmed**
- **1 teaspoon Jamaican jerk seasoning**
- **1 tablespoon olive oil**
- **Lime wedges**

1 Thaw shrimp, if frozen. Peel and devein shrimp, removing tails. Rinse shrimp; pat dry with paper towels. Set aside.
2 Wrap tortillas in heavy foil. Heat tortillas in a 350°F oven for 10 minutes. Meanwhile, for salsa, in a medium bowl stir together tomato, cucumber, green onion, cilantro, lime juice, and salt; set aside.
3 In a medium bowl toss beans with ½ teaspoon of the jerk seasoning. In a large bowl toss shrimp with remaining ½ teaspoon jerk seasoning. In a large skillet cook and stir beans in hot oil over medium-high heat for 3 minutes. Add shrimp; cook and stir for 2 to 3 minutes more or until shrimp are opaque.
4 To assemble tacos, fill each warm tortilla with about ⅓ cup of the shrimp mixture. Serve with salsa and lime wedges.

PER SERVING 274 calories; 7 g fat (1 g sat.); 22 g protein; 33 g carbohydrate; 7 g fiber; 381 mg sodium; 129 mg cholesterol

Shrimp & Couscous Jambalaya 

MAKES 4 servings
START TO FINISH 25 minutes

- **12 ounces fresh or frozen medium shrimp in shells**
- **1 cup sliced celery (2 stalks)**
- **¾ cup chopped green sweet pepper (1 medium)**
- **½ cup chopped onion (1 medium)**
- **½ teaspoon Cajun seasoning**
- **¼ teaspoon dried oregano, crushed**
- **2 tablespoons cooking oil**
- **1 14.5-ounce can reduced-sodium chicken broth**
- **1 cup couscous**
- **½ cup chopped tomato (1 medium)**
- **Bottled hot pepper sauce (optional)**
- **Lemon wedges (optional)**

1 Thaw shrimp, if frozen. Peel and devein shrimp, leaving tails intact. Rinse shrimp; pat dry with paper towels. Set aside.
2 In a large skillet cook celery, sweet pepper, onion, Cajun seasoning, and oregano in hot oil over medium heat until vegetables are tender, stirring occasionally. Carefully add broth; bring to boiling.
3 Stir in the shrimp; remove from heat. Stir in the couscous and tomato. Cover and let stand for 5 minutes. To serve, fluff mixture with a fork. Transfer mixture to a serving bowl. If desired, serve with hot pepper sauce and lemon wedges.

PER SERVING 317 calories; 8 g fat (1 g sat.); 18 g protein; 42 g carbohydrate; 9 g fiber; 462 mg sodium; 98 mg cholesterol

Shrimp & Couscous Jambalaya

Shrimp Pasta Salad

MAKES 10 to 12 servings
PREP 30 minutes **CHILL** 2 to 24 hours

- **10 ounces dried campanelle or bow tie pasta (about 3 cups)**
- **1½ pounds cooked, peeled and deveined shrimp**
- **1 cup chopped celery (2 stalks)**
- **½ cup chopped red onion (1 small)**
- **½ cup chopped green sweet pepper (1 small)**
- **1 2.25-ounce can sliced, pitted ripe olives, drained**
- **4 roma tomatoes, cut into thin wedges**
- **1 recipe Citrus Vinaigrette or 1¼ cups bottled Italian salad dressing**

1 Cook pasta according to package directions; drain. Rinse with cold water; drain again.
2 In a very large bowl combine pasta, shrimp, celery, onion, sweet pepper, and drained olives. Stir in tomato. Pour Citrus Vinaigrette over pasta mixture. Toss gently to coat. Cover and chill for 2 to 24 hours. Stir before serving.

Citrus Vinaigrette: In a screw-top jar combine ¾ cup grapefruit juice; ½ cup salad oil; 2 tablespoons honey; 1 tablespoon snipped fresh thyme or 1 teaspoon dried thyme, crushed; ¼ teaspoon salt; and ¼ teaspoon black pepper. Cover and shake well.

PER SERVING 308 calories; 13 g fat (2 g sat.); 18 g protein; 29 g carbohydrate; 2 g fiber; 280 mg sodium; 133 mg cholesterol

Shrimp & Watercress Salad 

MAKES 4 servings
START TO FINISH 15 minutes

- **1 pound fresh asparagus spears, trimmed**
- **4 cups watercress, tough stems removed**
- **1 pound cooked, peeled and deveined shrimp (tails on)**
- **2 cups cherry tomatoes, halved**
- **½ cup bottled light raspberry or berry vinaigrette salad dressing**
- **Freshly ground black pepper**

1 In a large skillet cook asparagus, covered, in a small amount of boiling lightly salted water about 3 minutes or until crisp-tender; drain in a colander. Rinse asparagus under cold water until cool; drain well.

2 Divide asparagus among four dinner plates; top with watercress, shrimp, and tomatoes. Drizzle dressing evenly over salads. Sprinkle with pepper.

PER SERVING 257 calories; 8 g fat (1 g sat.); 33 g protein; 14 g carbohydrate; 2 g fiber; 360 mg sodium; 227 mg cholesterol

Shrimp & Watercress Salad

Crab Cakes with Spring Greens Salad

Crab Cakes with Spring Greens Salad

MAKES 6 servings
PREP 30 minutes + chill time **COOK** 8 minutes **OVEN** 300°F

- **1 egg white**
- **3 tablespoons light mayonnaise dressing**
- **1 tablespoon Dijon-style mustard**
- **Few drops bottled hot pepper sauce**
- **3 tablespoons finely chopped red or green sweet pepper**
- **2 tablespoons snipped fresh parsley**
- **1 tablespoon sliced green onion**
- **2 teaspoons snipped fresh dill or cilantro or ½ teaspoon dried dill**
- **1 pound cooked fresh lump crabmeat or three 6- to 6½-ounce cans lump crabmeat, drained, flaked, and cartilage removed**
- **1¼ cups soft whole wheat or white bread crumbs**
- **1 recipe Lime Dressing**
- **8 ounces mixed baby greens (8 cups)**
- **1 head Belgian endive, sliced crosswise**
- **½ cup chopped, seeded tomato (1 medium)**
- **Nonstick cooking spray**
- **Lime wedges (optional)**

1 In a large bowl whisk together egg white, mayonnaise dressing, mustard, and hot pepper sauce. Stir in sweet pepper, parsley, green onion, and dill. Add crab and ½ cup of the bread crumbs; stir until well mixed. Using wet hands, form mixture into six ½-inch-thick patties. Place patties in a 15×10×1-inch baking pan. Cover and chill for 30 minutes.
2 Meanwhile, prepare Lime Dressing; set aside. In a very large bowl combine greens, Belgian endive, and tomato. Cover and chill until ready to serve.
3 Place remaining ¾ cup bread crumbs in a shallow dish. Dip crab cakes in bread crumbs, turning to coat both sides. Coat a large nonstick skillet with cooking spray. Heat skillet over medium heat. Add three of the crab cakes. Cook for 8 to 10 minutes or until golden brown and heated through (160°F), turning once halfway through cooking. Transfer crab cakes to a baking sheet; keep warm in a 300°F oven. Repeat with remaining crab cakes.
4 To serve, toss greens mixture with Lime Dressing to coat; divide among six dinner plates. Top with warm crab cakes. If desired, garnish with lime wedges.
Lime Dressing: In a bowl whisk together 2 tablespoons olive oil; 2 tablespoons lime juice; 1 clove garlic, minced; ⅛ teaspoon salt; and ⅛ teaspoon black pepper.

PER SERVING 181 calories; 9 g fat (1 g sat.); 18 g protein; 8 g carbohydrate; 1 g fiber; 426 mg sodium; 78 mg cholesterol

Pasta with White Clam Sauce 

MAKES 6 servings
PREP 10 minutes **COOK** 8 minutes

- **1 pound dried rigatoni pasta**
- **1 pound fresh asparagus, trimmed and cut into 1-inch pieces**
- **¼ cup olive oil**
- **6 cloves garlic, minced**
- **3 6.5-ounce cans clams, drained and ½ cup clam juice reserved**
- **2 tablespoons lemon juice**
- **4 jarred hot cherry peppers, seeded and thinly sliced**
- **¼ teaspoon salt**
- **2 tablespoons unsalted butter**
- **1 cup fresh Italian parsley, chopped**
- **Olive oil (optional)**

1 Cook pasta according to package directions, adding asparagus for the last 4 minutes of cooking; drain.
2 Meanwhile, in a large skillet heat oil over medium heat. Add garlic; cook and stir for 2 minutes. Add the ½ cup clam juice; cook for 1 minute. Stir in drained clams, lemon juice, cherry peppers, and salt. Cook and stir about 1 minute or until heated through. Stir in butter and parsley.
3 Toss the pasta and asparagus with the clam sauce. If desired, drizzle with additional oil. Serve immediately.

PER SERVING 421 calories; 15 g fat (4 g sat.); 12 g protein; 61 g carbohydrate; 5 g fiber; 403 mg sodium; 13 mg cholesterol

page 114

page 122

Pleasing

Poultry

Sweet-and-Sour Chicken

3 Spoon spinach mixture over chicken; sprinkle with the remaining crumb mixture. Bake in a 350°F oven for 40 to 45 minutes or until the chicken is tender and no longer pink (170°F).

PER SERVING 243 calories; 6 g fat (3 g sat.); 38 g protein; 8 g carbohydrate; 1 g fiber; 474 mg sodium; 95 mg cholesterol

Rosemary Chicken with Vegetables

MAKES 4 servings
START TO FINISH 27 minutes

- **4 skinless, boneless chicken breast halves**
- **½ teaspoon lemon-pepper seasoning**
- **2 tablespoons olive oil**
- **4 ounces refrigerated spinach or plain linguine pasta**
- **2 cloves garlic, minced**
- **2½ cups sliced zucchini and/or yellow summer squash (2 medium)**
- **½ cup apple juice**
- **2 teaspoons snippe**
  dried rosemary, c
- **2 tablespoons dry**
- **2 teaspoons cornst**
- **1 cup halved cherr**

1 Sprinkle chicken with skillet cook chicken in h 12 minutes or until chic turning once. Transfer ch warm. Meanwhile, cook p directions; drain and kee

2 Add garlic to skillet; c zucchini, apple juice, an reduce heat. Cover and s

3 In a small bowl stir to skillet. Cook and stir unt stir for 2 minutes more. chicken on pasta. Spoon desired, garnish with *fre*

PER SERVING 326 calories; 1 25 g carbohydrate; 2 g fiber

Sweet-and-Sour Chicken  

MAKES 4 to 5 servings
START TO FINISH 25 minutes

- **12 ounces skinless, boneless chicken breast halves**
- **1 8-ounce can pineapple chunks (juice pack)**
- **½ cup bottled sweet-and-sour sauce**
- **1 tablespoon reduced-sodium soy sauce**
- **4 teaspoons cooking oil**
- **1 medium red sweet pepper, cut into bite-size strips**
- **½ cup sliced carrot (1 medium)**
- **1 cup fresh pea pods, stems removed**
- **2 cups hot cooked rice**

1 Cut chicken into 1-inch pieces; set aside. Drain pineapple, reserving 2 tablespoons of the juice; set pineapple chunks aside. In a small bowl stir together the reserved pineapple juice and the sweet-and-sour sauce; set aside. In a medium bowl toss chicken with soy sauce; set aside.

2 In a large nonstick skillet heat 3 teaspoons of the oil over medium-high heat. Add sweet pepper and carrot; cook and stir for 3 minutes. Add pea pods; cook and stir about 1 minute more or until vegetables are crisp-tender. Remove from skillet; set aside.

3 Add the remaining 1 teaspoon oil to skillet. Using a slotted spoon, add chicken to skillet. Cook and stir for 3 to 4 minutes or until chicken is no longer pink. Add sweet-and-sour sauce mixture, vegetable mixture, and pineapple chunks; heat through. Serve chicken mixture over hot cooked rice.

PER SERVING 337 calories; 6 g fat (1 g sat.); 23 g protein; 46 g carbohydrate; 3 g fiber; 297 mg sodium; 49 mg cholesterol

Szechwan-Fried Chicken Breasts

Szechwan-Fried Chicken Breasts 

MAKES 4 servings
START TO FINISH 30 minutes

- **1 tablespoon soy sauce**
- **1 teaspoon grated fresh ginger**
- **1 teaspoon chile oil**
- **½ teaspoon sugar**
- **½ cup all-purpose flour**
- **4 skinless, boneless chicken breast halves**
- **1 tablespoon cooking oil**
- **¼ cup apricot preserves**
- **¼ cup chicken broth**
- **Shredded orange peel (optional)**
- **Snipped fresh chives (optional)**
- **Hot cooked rice (optional)**

1 In a small bowl stir together soy sauce, ginger, ½ teaspoon of the chile oil, and the sugar; set aside.

2 Place flour in a shallow dish. Brush both sides of chicken with soy sauce mixture. Dip chicken in flour to coat. In a large nonstick skillet cook chicken in hot oil over medium-high heat for 8 to 12 minutes or until chicken is no longer pink (170°F), turning once. Remove chicken from skillet; cover and keep warm.

3 For sauce, add apricot preserves, broth, and the remaining ½ teaspoon chile oil to the skillet. Cook and stir over medium heat until preserves melt and mixture is heated through. Spoon sauce over chicken. If desired, sprinkle with orange peel. If desired, stir chives into hot cooked rice; serve with chicken.

PER SERVING 315 calories; 7 g fat (1 g sat.); 35 g protein; 25 g carbohydrate; 1 g fiber; 374 mg sodium; 82 mg cholesterol

Triple-Mango Chicken 30

MAKES 4 servings
START TO FINISH 20 minutes

- 4 skinless, boneless chicken breast halves
- 1 tablespoon olive oil
- 1 cup cubed, peeled seeded mango (1 medium)
- ½ cup mango-blend fruit drink*
- ¼ cup mango chutney
- 2 medium zucchini, thinly sliced lengthwise
- ¼ cup water
- Salt and crushed red pepper

1 In a very large skillet cook chicken in hot oil over medium heat for 6 minutes; turn chicken. Add mango cubes, mango drink, and chutney. Cook for 4 to 6 minutes more or until chicken is no longer pink (170°F), stirring mango mixture occasionally.
2 Meanwhile, place zucchini and the water in a microwave-safe 2-quart dish. Cover with vented plastic wrap. Microwave on 100-percent power (high) for 2 to 3 minutes or until crisp-tender, stirring once. Drain. Serve chicken and mango mixture on top of zucchini. Season to taste with salt and crushed red pepper.
***Note:** Mango nectar, carrot juice, or orange juice may be substituted for the mango-blend drink.

PER SERVING 274 calories; 9 g fat (1 g sat.); 28 g protein; 22 g carbohydrate; 2 g fiber; 277 mg sodium; 66 mg cholesterol

Triple-Mango Chicken

Tangy Len

MAKES 4 serv
PREP 10 minut

- 4 skinle
- ½ cup bo
- 1 tables
- ¼ cup le

1 Place the c shallow dish. salad dressing *pepper.* Pour chicken. Mari up to 4 hours
2 Drain chick place chicken uncovered, fo pink (170°F), halfway throu (For a gas gril chicken on gr

PER SERVING 17 2 g carbohydra

Spinach-C

MAKES 12 ser
PREP 25 minu

- ¾ cup s
- ¼ cup g
- 12 skinle
- ½ cup sl
- 2 table
- 2 table
- 1 cup m
- 1 10-ou and w
- 1 4-our

1 In a shallo Lightly coat Arrange chicl aside. Reserv
2 In a large medium heat Cook and stir 1 minute mo

Chicken with Marsala Sauce

MAKES 4 servings
START TO FINISH 45 minutes

- 2 tablespoons all-purpose flour
- 4 skinless, boneless chicken breast halves
- 2 medium carrots, cut into thin bite-size strips
- 2 tablespoons olive oil
- 1 small yellow sweet pepper, cut into thin bite-size strips
- 1 small red sweet pepper, cut into thin bite-size strips
- ¼ teaspoon salt
- ¼ teaspoon black pepper
- 3 cloves garlic, minced
- ⅔ cup dry Marsala wine
- ½ cup chicken broth
- 2 teaspoons cornstarch
- 1 tablespoon snipped fresh thyme or ½ teaspoon dried thyme, crushed
- Fresh thyme sprigs (optional)

1 Place flour in a shallow dish. Coat chicken lightly with flour. Set aside.
2 In a large skillet cook and stir carrot in 1 tablespoon hot oil over medium heat for 3 minutes. Add sweet peppers, salt, black pepper, and garlic; cook and stir for 2 to 3 minutes more or until vegetables are crisp-tender. Remove vegetables from skillet; cover and keep warm.
3 In the same skillet cook chicken in the remaining 1 tablespoon hot oil over medium heat for 8 to 12 minutes or until chicken is no longer pink (170°F), turning once. Remove chicken from skillet; cover and keep warm.
4 In a small bowl stir together Marsala, broth, and cornstarch; add to skillet along with thyme. Cook and stir until thickened and bubbly, scraping up any brown bits from skillet. Cook and stir for 2 minutes more.
5 To serve, spoon vegetables onto dinner plates. Top with chicken. Pour Marsala mixture over chicken. If desired, garnish with thyme sprigs.

PER SERVING 357 calories; 9 g fat (1 g sat.); 35 g protein; 12 g carbohydrate; 2 g fiber; 357 mg sodium; 82 mg cholesterol

Chicken with Marsala Sauce

Chicken with Cherry-Ginger Chutney 

MAKES 4 servings
START TO FINISH 20 minutes

- 4 skinless, boneless chicken breast halves
- Salt
- Black pepper
- ½ teaspoon ground ginger
- 1 tablespoon olive oil or cooking oil
- ½ cup dried tart red cherries
- 1 large apple, thinly sliced horizontally*
- ⅓ cup coarsely chopped walnuts
- ¼ cup water
- 3 tablespoons cider vinegar
- 4 teaspoons packed brown sugar

1 Cut chicken breast halves into quarters. Sprinkle chicken lightly with salt, pepper, and ¼ teaspoon ginger.
2 In a large skillet cook chicken in hot oil over medium heat for 8 to 12 minutes or until chicken is no longer pink (170°F). Transfer chicken to a serving platter; cover and keep warm. Add cherries, apple, and walnuts to skillet; cook and stir for 2 minutes. In a small bowl stir together water, vinegar, brown sugar, and remaining ¼ teaspoon ginger; add to skillet. Cook and stir for 1 minute. Serve cherry mixture with chicken.
***Note:** If you wish, use an apple corer to remove the core and seeds before slicing the apple.

PER SERVING 364 calories; 12 g fat (2 g sat.); 35 g protein; 30 g carbohydrate; 3 g fiber; 249 mg sodium; 82 mg cholesterol

Chicken with
Cherry-Ginger Chutney

Apricots, Chicken, & Orzo

Apricots, Chicken, & Orzo 

MAKES 4 servings
START TO FINISH 20 minutes

- **1¼ cups dried orzo (about 8 ounces)**
- **1 15-ounce can unpeeled apricot halves in light syrup**
- **4 skinless, boneless chicken breast halves**
- **Salt and black pepper**
- **1½ teaspoons curry powder**
- **2 tablespoons olive oil or cooking oil**
- **6 green onions**

1 Cook orzo according to package directions; drain. Drain apricot halves, reserving ½ cup syrup.
2 Meanwhile, sprinkle chicken with salt, pepper, and ½ teaspoon of the curry powder. In a large skillet cook chicken in hot oil over medium heat for 8 to 10 minutes or until chicken is no longer pink (170°F), turning once, and adding apricots, cut sides down, to the skillet for the last 2 minutes of cooking. Transfer to serving plates.
3 While chicken cooks, cut green tops of 2 of the green onions into thick diagonal slices; set aside. Chop remaining green onions. Add chopped green onion and the remaining 1 teaspoon curry powder to skillet; cook and stir for 1 minute. Stir in reserved apricot syrup and orzo. Spoon orzo mixture onto plates. Sprinkle with green onion tops.

PER SERVING 458 calories; 9 g fat (1 g sat.); 34 g protein; 59 g carbohydrate; 4 g fiber; 230 mg sodium; 66 mg cholesterol

Middle Eastern Chicken Kabobs

MAKES 6 servings
PREP 25 minutes **MARINATE** 1 hour **BROIL** 8 minutes

- **1 pound skinless, boneless chicken breast halves**
- **¼ cup plain low-fat yogurt**
- **1 tablespoon lemon juice**
- **1 teaspoon dry mustard**
- **1 teaspoon ground cinnamon**
- **1 teaspoon curry powder**
- **½ teaspoon salt**
- **¼ to ½ teaspoon crushed red pepper**
- **1 large red sweet pepper, cut into 1-inch pieces**
- **1 medium yellow summer squash, halved lengthwise and cut into ½-inch slices**
- **1 recipe Tomato Relish (optional)**

1 Cut chicken into 1-inch pieces. Place chicken pieces in a resealable plastic bag set in a shallow dish. For marinade, in a small bowl stir together yogurt, lemon juice, mustard, cinnamon, curry powder, salt, and crushed red pepper. Pour marinade over chicken; seal bag. Turn to coat chicken. Marinate in refrigerator for 1 to 4 hours, turning bag once.
2 Preheat broiler. On six 10- to 12-inch metal skewers alternately thread chicken, sweet pepper, and squash, leaving a ¼-inch space between pieces. Place skewers on the unheated rack of a broiler pan. Broil 4 to 5 inches from the heat for 8 to 10 minutes or until chicken is no longer pink, turning once. If desired, serve with Tomato Relish.
Tomato Relish: Combine ⅔ cup coarsely chopped roma tomato; ½ cup grape tomatoes, halved; 1 teaspoon snipped fresh oregano or ¼ teaspoon dried oregano, crushed; 1 teaspoon snipped fresh thyme or ¼ teaspoon dried thyme, crushed; 1 clove garlic, minced; 1 tablespoon white balsamic or balsamic vinegar; and 1 teaspoon honey. Season to taste with salt and black pepper. Cover and chill for up to 4 hours.

PER SERVING 107 calories; 2 g fat (0 g sat.); 19 g protein; 4 g carbohydrate; 1 g fiber; 254 mg sodium; 44 mg cholesterol

Chicken with Balsamic Succotash

MAKES 4 servings
PREP 10 minutes **COOK** 30 minutes

- **4 teaspoons chili powder**
- **½ teaspoon salt**
- **¼ teaspoon black pepper**
- **4 skinless, boneless chicken breast halves**
- **2 tablespoons olive oil**

- 2 **cloves garlic, minced**
- 1 **cup chopped sweet onion (1 large)**
- ¾ **cup coarsely chopped red sweet pepper (1 medium)**
- 2 **cups frozen corn, thawed**
- 2 **cups frozen lima beans, thawed**
- 3 **tablespoons balsamic vinegar**
- ¼ **cup chicken broth or water**

1 In a small bowl combine 3 teaspoons of the chili powder, the salt, and black pepper. Sprinkle chicken with chili powder mixture; rub in with your fingers.
2 In a large nonstick skillet cook chicken in 1 tablespoon hot oil over medium heat for 8 to 12 minutes or until chicken is no longer pink (170°F). Remove chicken from skillet; cover and keep warm.
3 In the same skillet cook garlic in remaining 1 tablespoon oil over low heat for 3 to 4 minutes or until garlic is soft. Increase heat to medium. Add onion and sweet pepper; cook for 5 minutes. Add corn, lima beans, remaining 1 teaspoon chili powder, and the vinegar; cook for 5 minutes. Add broth and heat through. Serve succotash with chicken.

PER SERVING 446 calories; 10 g fat (2 g sat.); 47 g protein; 42 g carbohydrate; 8 g fiber; 627 mg sodium; 99 mg cholesterol

Chicken with Balsamic Succotash

Asian Chicken Strips

MAKES 4 servings
PREP 15 minutes **MARINATE** 15 minutes to 2 hours
GRILL 10 minutes

- 1 pound skinless, boneless chicken breast halves
- ⅓ cup vinegar
- ¼ cup bottled hoisin sauce
- ½ teaspoon crushed red pepper
- 1 clove garlic, minced
- 12 cherry tomatoes
- 2 cups packaged shredded broccoli (broccoli slaw mix)
- 1 tablespoon chopped peanuts (optional)

1 Cut chicken into bite-size strips. Place chicken in a resealable plastic bag set in a shallow dish. In a small bowl stir together vinegar, hoisin sauce, crushed red pepper, and garlic. Set aside half of the vinegar mixture. Pour remaining vinegar mixture over chicken; seal bag. Turn to coat chicken. Marinate in the refrigerator for at least 15 minutes or up to 2 hours, turning bag once.
2 Drain chicken, reserving marinade. On four 12-inch metal skewers thread chicken, accordion-style. For a charcoal grill, place skewers on the grill rack directly over medium coals. Grill, uncovered, for 10 to 12 minutes or until chicken is no longer pink (170°F), turning once halfway through grilling and brushing twice with reserved marinade during the first 5 minutes of grilling. Discard any remaining marinade. Add tomatoes to ends of skewers for the last 2 minutes of grilling. (For a gas grill, preheat grill. Reduce heat to medium. Place kabobs on grill rack over heat. Cover and grill as above.)
3 Serve kabobs on a bed of shredded broccoli. Drizzle with the reserved vinegar mixture. If desired, sprinkle peanuts over kabobs.
Broiler Directions: Preheat broiler. Prepare as directed, except place skewers on the unheated rack of a broiler pan. Broil 4 to 5 inches from the heat for 10 to 12 minutes or until chicken is no longer pink (170°F), turning once halfway through broiling and brushing twice with reserved marinade during the first 5 minutes of broiling. Discard any remaining marinade. Add tomatoes to ends of skewers for the last 2 minutes of broiling. Serve as directed.

PER SERVING 202 calories; 4 g fat (1 g sat.); 23 g protein; 15 g carbohydrate; 2 g fiber; 400 mg sodium; 59 mg cholesterol

Turn the extra shredded broccoli into a tasty salad to serve alongside your favorite sandwich. Toss some of the shredded broccoli with a spoonful of mayonnaise and a little milk. Then add a handful of dried cranberries and some toasted sliced almonds.

Garlic Chicken 

MAKES 4 servings
PREP 20 minutes **MARINATE** 30 minutes **COOK** 6 minutes

- 1 pound skinless, boneless chicken breast halves
- 1 cup water
- 3 tablespoons reduced-sodium soy sauce
- 2 tablespoons chicken broth
- 1 tablespoon cornstarch
- 2 tablespoons cooking oil
- 10 green onions, bias-sliced into 1-inch pieces
- 1 cup thinly sliced assorted fresh mushrooms
- 12 cloves garlic, peeled and thinly sliced, or 2 tablespoons bottled minced garlic
- ½ cup sliced water chestnuts
- Hot cooked rice (optional)

1 Cut chicken into bite-size pieces. Place chicken in a resealable plastic bag set in a shallow bowl. In a measuring cup stir together the water, the soy sauce, and broth. Pour over chicken in bag; seal bag. Marinate in the refrigerator for 30 minutes.
2 Drain chicken, reserving marinade. Stir cornstarch into the reserved marinade; set aside.
3 In a wok or large skillet heat oil over medium-high heat. Add green onions, mushrooms, and garlic; cook and stir for 1 to 2 minutes or until tender. Remove vegetables from wok. Add chicken to wok; cook and stir for 2 to 3 minutes or until no longer pink, adding more oil if necessary. Push chicken from center of wok. Stir marinade mixture; add to center of wok. Cook and stir until thickened and bubbly.
4 Return cooked vegetables to wok. Add water chestnuts. Cook and stir about 1 minute more or until combined and heated through. If desired, serve with hot cooked rice.

PER SERVING 352 calories; 9 g fat (1 g sat.); 32 g protein; 34 g carbohydrate; 3 g fiber; 555 mg sodium; 66 mg cholesterol

Garlic Chicken

Chicken & Wild Rice Casserole 

MAKES 6 servings
PREP 50 minutes **BAKE** 50 minutes **OVEN** 350°F

- **1 10.75-ounce can reduced-fat and reduced-sodium condensed cream of mushroom soup**
- **1 6.5-ounce container light semisoft cheese with garlic and herbs, softened**
- **½ cup evaporated fat-free milk**
- **1 14- to 15-ounce can bean sprouts, rinsed and drained**
- **2¼ cups cubed cooked chicken breast**
- **1 cup cooked wild rice**
- **⅔ cup thinly sliced celery**
- **½ cup coarsely shredded carrot (1 medium)**
- **1 4-ounce can (drained weight) sliced mushrooms, drained**
- **1 tablespoon chopped shallot or green onion**
- **½ cup soft whole wheat bread crumbs**
- **2 teaspoons dried parsley flakes**
- **Butter-flavored nonstick cooking spray**

1 In a large bowl whisk together soup, cheese, and evaporated milk until smooth. Stir in bean sprouts, chicken, wild rice, celery, carrot, drained mushrooms, and shallot. Spoon chicken mixture into a 2-quart casserole. Bake, covered, in a 350°F oven for 30 minutes.

2 Meanwhile, in a medium bowl stir together bread crumbs and parsley flakes; coat lightly with cooking spray. Toss gently; coat again with cooking spray. Sprinkle crumb mixture over the partially baked casserole. Bake, uncovered, for 20 to 25 minutes more or until filling is bubbly and topping is golden brown.

PER SERVING 258 calories; 8 g fat (4 g sat.); 26 g protein; 20 g carbohydrate; 2 g fiber; 576 mg sodium; 71 mg cholesterol

Chicken Caesar Lasagna 

MAKES 9 servings
PREP 35 minutes **BAKE** 50 minutes **STAND** 15 minutes
OVEN 325°F

- **9 dried whole wheat or regular lasagna noodles**
- **2 10-ounce containers refrigerated light Alfredo sauce**
- **3 tablespoons lemon juice**
- **½ teaspoon coarsely ground black pepper**
- **3 cups chopped cooked chicken breast***
- **1 10-ounce package frozen chopped spinach, thawed and well drained**
- **1 cup bottled roasted red sweet peppers, drained and chopped**
- **Nonstick cooking spray**
- **¾ cup shredded Italian blend cheese (3 ounces)**

1 Cook noodles according to package directions; drain. Rinse with cold water; drain again. Meanwhile, in a large bowl stir together Alfredo sauce, lemon juice, and black pepper. Stir in chicken, spinach, and sweet peppers.
2 Lightly coat a 3-quart rectangular baking dish with cooking spray. Lay 3 noodles in bottom of prepared dish. Top with one-third of chicken mixture. Repeat layers twice.
3 Cover and bake in a 325°F oven for 45 to 55 minutes or until heated through. Uncover; sprinkle with cheese. Bake, uncovered, about 5 minutes more or until cheese melts. Let stand for 15 minutes before serving.
***Note:** For 3 cups chopped cooked chicken, sprinkle 2 pounds raw skinless, boneless chicken breast halves with ¼ teaspoon salt and ⅛ teaspoon black pepper. In a large skillet cook chicken in 1 tablespoon hot oil over medium heat for 8 to 12 minutes or until no longer pink (170°F), turning once. Cool chicken slightly before chopping.

PER SERVING 268 calories; 10 g fat (6 g sat.); 24 g protein; 20 g carbohydrate; 2 g fiber; 557 mg sodium; 68 mg cholesterol

Buffalo Chicken Pizzas

Buffalo Chicken Pizzas  

MAKES 4 servings
START TO FINISH 20 minutes **OVEN** 450°F

- **4 pita bread rounds**
- **¼ cup bottled blue cheese salad dressing**
- **1 9-ounce package refrigerated Southwest-flavored cooked chicken breast strips**
- **¾ cup thinly sliced celery (1½ stalks)**
- **Blue cheese crumbles (optional)**
- **Bottled hot pepper sauce or buffalo wing sauce (optional)**

1 Place pita rounds on a large baking sheet. Brush with blue cheese dressing. Scatter chicken strips and celery over blue cheese dressing. Bake in a 450°F oven about 10 minutes or until heated through and pita rounds are crisp.
2 Transfer pizzas to plates. If desired, sprinkle with blue cheese and pass hot pepper sauce.

PER SERVING 353 calories; 14 g fat (3 g sat.); 21 g protein; 36 g carbohydrate; 2 g fiber; 1,084 mg sodium; 45 mg cholesterol

Parmesan Chicken Salad

Chicken Enchilada Sandwiches 

MAKES 6 sandwiches
PREP 25 minutes **CHILL** up to 24 hours

- **2 skinless, boneless chicken breast halves**
- **1 tablespoon butter**
- **1 teaspoon chili powder**
- **½ teaspoon ground cumin**
- **1 clove garlic, minced**
- **Dash cayenne pepper**
- **1 3-ounce package cream cheese, softened**
- **½ cup shredded sharp cheddar cheese (2 ounces)**
- **¼ cup dairy sour cream**
- **1 10-ounce can diced tomatoes and green chile peppers, drained**
- **¼ cup thinly sliced green onion (2)**
- **2 tablespoons snipped fresh cilantro**
- **12 slices white sandwich bread, crusts removed, or six 8-inch flour tortillas**
- **Cucumber slices, avocado slices, or tomato slices (optional)**
- **12 leaves Boston, Bibb, or green leaf lettuce**

1 Finely chop chicken. In a large skillet cook chicken in hot butter over medium heat until chicken is no longer pink. Stir in chili powder, cumin, garlic, and cayenne pepper; cook and stir for 1 minute more. Cool slightly.
2 In a medium bowl combine cream cheese, cheddar cheese, and sour cream; beat on low to medium speed of an electric mixer until creamy. Fold in chicken mixture, tomatoes, green onion, and cilantro. Cover and chill for up to 24 hours.
3 Spread chicken mixture on six slices of the bread. If desired, top with cucumber, avocado, or tomato slices. Add lettuce and the remaining six slices bread. (Or spread chicken mixture evenly over one edge of tortillas; top with lettuce, and, if desired, cucumber, avocado, or tomato slices. Roll up tortillas.)

PER SANDWICH 324 calories; 15 g fat (8 g sat.); 20 g protein; 28 g carbohydrate; 2 g fiber; 543 mg sodium; 62 mg cholesterol

Parmesan Chicken Salad  

MAKES 6 servings
START TO FINISH 10 minutes

- **½ cup low-fat mayonnaise dressing**
- **1 tablespoon lemon juice**
- **2 teaspoons snipped fresh basil**
- **2½ cups chopped cooked chicken or turkey**
- **¼ cup grated Parmesan cheese**
- **¼ cup thinly sliced green onion (2)**
- **3 tablespoons finely chopped celery**
- **Salt**
- **Black pepper**
- **Toasted wheat bread (optional)**

1 In a small bowl stir together mayonnaise dressing, lemon juice, and basil. Set aside.
2 In a medium bowl stir together chicken, cheese, green onion, and celery. Pour mayonnaise mixture over chicken mixture; toss to coat. Season to taste with salt and pepper. Serve immediately or cover and chill for 1 to 4 hours. If desired, serve on toasted wheat bread.

PER SERVING 194 calories; 12 g fat (3 g sat.); 18 g protein; 2 g carbohydrate; 0 g fiber; 366 mg sodium; 61 mg cholesterol

Champion Chicken Pockets  

MAKES 4 pockets
START TO FINISH 15 minutes

- **¼ cup plain low-fat yogurt**
- **¼ cup bottled reduced-fat ranch salad dressing**
- **1½ cups chopped cooked chicken or turkey**
- **½ cup chopped broccoli**

- ¼ cup shredded carrot
- ¼ cup chopped pecans or walnuts (optional)
- 2 6- to 7-inch whole wheat pita bread rounds, halved crosswise

1 In a small bowl stir together yogurt and salad dressing. In a medium bowl combine chicken, broccoli, carrot, and, if desired, pecans. Pour yogurt mixture over chicken; toss to coat. Spoon chicken mixture into pita halves.
Make-Ahead Directions: Sandwiches can be tightly wrapped in plastic wrap and chilled for up to 24 hours.

PER FILLED PITA HALF 231 calories; 8 g fat (1 g sat.); 20 g protein; 21 g carbohydrate; 3 g fiber; 392 mg sodium; 53 mg cholesterol

Chicken-Vegetable Ratatouille 

MAKES 4 to 5 servings
START TO FINISH 30 minutes

- 1 cup chopped onion (1 large)
- 2 cloves garlic, minced
- 1 tablespoon olive oil or cooking oil
- 1 medium eggplant, cut into 1-inch pieces
- 2 cups frozen zucchini, carrots, cauliflower, lima beans, and Italian beans
- 1 14.5-ounce can diced tomatoes, undrained
- 1 teaspoon dried Italian seasoning, crushed
- ¾ teaspoon seasoned salt
- ¼ teaspoon black pepper
- 2⅔ cups dried penne, ziti, or wagon wheel pasta (8 ounces)
- 1½ cups chopped cooked chicken

1 In a 4-quart Dutch oven cook onion and garlic in hot oil over medium heat for 2 minutes. Stir in eggplant, frozen vegetables, undrained tomatoes, Italian seasoning, seasoned salt, and pepper. Bring to boiling; reduce heat. Simmer, uncovered, for 10 to 12 minutes or until eggplant is tender.
2 Meanwhile, in a large saucepan cook pasta according to package directions; drain. Cover and keep warm.
3 Add chicken to vegetable mixture; heat through. Serve chicken mixture over pasta.

PER SERVING 442 calories; 9 g fat (2 g sat.); 28 g protein; 64 g carbohydrate; 11 g fiber; 578 mg sodium; 50 mg cholesterol

Chicken-Vegetable Ratatouille

Chicken Salad-Stuffed Shells 

MAKES 2 servings
START TO FINISH 25 minutes

- **½ of a medium cantaloupe, halved and seeded**
- **4 dried jumbo macaroni shells**
- **⅔ cup chopped cooked chicken breast**
- **¼ cup finely chopped honeydew melon**
- **2 tablespoons plain fat-free yogurt**
- **1 tablespoon lemon juice**
- **1½ teaspoons chopped fresh chives**
- **½ teaspoon Dijon-style mustard**
- **Fresh thyme sprigs (optional)**

1 Cut the cantaloupe half into three wedges; cover and chill two of the wedges. Peel and finely chop the remaining wedge; set aside.
2 Cook pasta shells according to package directions; drain. Rinse with cold water; drain again. Set aside.
3 In a small bowl stir together chopped cantaloupe, chicken, honeydew, yogurt, lemon juice, chives, and mustard. Spoon about ¼ cup of the mixture into each pasta shell. Arrange two filled shells and a chilled cantaloupe wedge on each of two shallow bowls. If desired, garnish with thyme sprigs.

PER SERVING 176 calories; 2 g fat (0 g sat.); 14 g protein; 28 g carbohydrate; 2 g fiber; 55 mg sodium; 26 mg cholesterol

Chicken & Spinach Salad with Avocado Dressing

MAKES 8 servings
START TO FINISH 40 minutes

- **6 cups fresh baby spinach**
- **4 cups chopped or shredded cooked chicken**
- **1 medium cucumber, halved lengthwise, seeded, and sliced**
- **1 cup cherry tomatoes, halved**
- **2 medium red, yellow, and/or green sweet peppers, cut into thin strips**
- **1 small red onion, thinly sliced**
- **¼ cup snipped fresh cilantro**
- **1 large ripe avocado, halved, pitted, peeled, and cut up**
- **2 cloves garlic, minced**
- **2 teaspoons finely shredded lime peel**
- **2 tablespoons lime juice**
- **⅔ cup dairy sour cream**
- **2 tablespoons snipped fresh cilantro**
- **½ teaspoon salt**
- **⅛ teaspoon black pepper**
- **Bottled hot pepper sauce**

1 In a large serving bowl toss together spinach, chicken, cucumber, cherry tomatoes, sweet peppers, half of the onion, and the ¼ cup cilantro. Set aside.
2 For dressing, in a food processor* combine avocado, remaining onion, the garlic, and lime juice. Cover and process until smooth. Stir in lime peel, sour cream, the 2 tablespoons cilantro, the salt, and black pepper. Season to taste with bottled hot pepper sauce. If desired, stir in 1 to 2 tablespoons water to make dressing of desired consistency.
3 Spoon dressing over spinach mixture. Toss gently to coat.
***Note:** If you don't have a food processor, mash avocado with a fork or a potato masher. Finely chop the onion. Stir dressing ingredients together.

PER SERVING 232 calories; 12 g fat (4 g sat.); 23 g protein; 9 g carbohydrate; 3 g fiber; 238 mg sodium; 69 mg cholesterol

Honey Chicken Sandwiches

Honey Chicken Sandwiches  

MAKES 4 servings
START TO FINISH 20 minutes

- **3 tablespoons honey**
- **2 teaspoons snipped fresh thyme or ½ teaspoon dried thyme, crushed**
- **1 small red onion, halved and thinly sliced**
- **12 ounces cooked chicken, cut up**
- **4 baked biscuits, split**

1 In a medium skillet combine honey and thyme; stir in onion. Cook and stir over medium-low heat until just hot. (Do not boil.) Stir in chicken; heat through. Arrange chicken mixture on biscuit bottoms. Add tops.

PER SANDWICH 342 calories; 12 g fat (3 g sat.); 27 g protein; 31 g carbohydrate; 1 g fiber; 443 mg sodium; 76 mg cholesterol

Springtime Pasta

Springtime Pasta 

MAKES 8 servings

PREP 15 minutes **COOK** about 15 minutes

- **1½ pounds skinless, boneless chicken breast halves**
- **1 pound dried cavatappi or other corkscrew-shape pasta**
- **1 pound fresh asparagus, trimmed and cut into 2-inch pieces**
- **1 tablespoon olive oil**
- **1 sweet yellow pepper, seeded and cut into thin strips**
- **1 pint cherry tomatoes, halved**
- **1 5.2-ounce package spreadable herb cheese (such as Boursin)**
- **¼ teaspoon salt**
- **¼ teaspoon black pepper**

1 Cut chicken into 1-inch pieces; set aside. Cook pasta according to package directions for 8 minutes, adding asparagus for the last 2 minutes of cooking. Drain, reserving ¼ cup pasta water.

2 Meanwhile, in a large nonstick skillet cook chicken in hot oil over medium-high heat for 5 minutes, stirring occasionally. Add sweet pepper; cook and stir for 1 minute more. Remove from heat.

3 In a large bowl combine hot pasta mixture, chicken mixture, tomatoes, cheese, reserved pasta water, salt, and black pepper; toss until well blended and cheese melts.

PER SERVING 395 calories; 10 g fat (5 g sat.); 30 g protein; 47 g carbohydrate; 3 g fiber; 248 mg sodium; 74 mg cholesterol

Southwest Chicken Salad with Mango Salsa

MAKES 6 servings

PREP 30 minutes **MARINATE** 30 minutes **GRILL** 12 minutes

- **2 tablespoons chili powder**
- **1 teaspoon salt**
- **1 teaspoon garlic powder**
- **1 teaspoon ground cumin**
- **½ teaspoon black pepper**
- **¼ teaspoon cayenne pepper**
- **3 tablespoons olive oil or cooking oil**
- **6 skinless, boneless chicken breast halves**
- **3 cups cubed, peeled, seeded mango (3 medium)**
- **1 cup blueberries**
- **⅓ cup finely chopped red onion**
- **3 tablespoons lime juice**
- **2 tablespoons snipped fresh mint**
- **2 tablespoons honey**
- **¼ teaspoon crushed red pepper**
- **8 cups torn mixed greens**

1 In a small bowl stir together chili powder, salt, garlic powder, cumin, black pepper, and cayenne pepper. Stir in oil. Brush mixture on both sides of chicken. Place chicken in a shallow dish; cover and chill for 30 minutes.

2 Meanwhile, for mango salsa, in a medium bowl combine mango, blueberries, onion, lime juice, mint, honey, and crushed red pepper.

3 For a charcoal grill, place chicken on the grill rack directly over medium coals. Grill, uncovered, for 12 to 15 minutes or until chicken is no longer pink (170°F), turning once halfway through grilling. (For a gas grill, preheat grill. Reduce heat to medium. Place chicken on grill rack over heat. Cover and grill as above.)

4 Slice chicken into bite-size strips; toss with greens and mango salsa.

PER SERVING 335 calories; 10 g fat (2 g sat.); 33 g protein; 31 g carbohydrate; 5 g fiber; 497 mg sodium; 77 mg cholesterol

Pasta Salad with Orange Dressing

MAKES 4 servings
PREP 30 minutes **CHILL** 2 to 24 hours

- **6** **ounces dried whole grain or plain pasta, such as penne or bow tie (1½ cups)**
- **1** **15-ounce can black beans, rinsed and drained**
- **1** **cup chopped cooked chicken**
- **½** **of a large green sweet pepper, seeded and cut into thin bite-size strips**
- **½** **cup thin wedges of red onion**
- **1** **orange**
- **1** **8-ounce carton light dairy sour cream**
- **¼** **teaspoon salt**
- **¼** **teaspoon black pepper**
- **Milk**
- **1½** **cups lightly packed arugula leaves, coarsely shredded**
- **3** **tablespoons snipped fresh cilantro**

1 Cook pasta according to package directions; drain. Rinse with cold water; drain again. Transfer pasta to salad bowl. Add beans, chicken, sweet pepper, and onion; set aside.
2 Finely shred enough orange peel to get 1½ teaspoons. Place shredded orange peel in a small bowl; stir in sour cream, salt, and black pepper. Juice the orange. Add 3 tablespoons orange juice to sour cream mixture; mix well.
3 Add sour cream mixture to pasta mixture; toss to coat. Cover and chill for 2 to 24 hours. Before serving, stir in enough milk, 1 tablespoon at a time, until salad is desired consistency. Stir in arugula and cilantro.

PER SERVING 390 calories; 10 g fat (5 g sat.); 23 g protein; 57 g carbohydrate; 9 g fiber; 624 mg sodium; 51 mg cholesterol

Pasta Salad with Orange Dressing

Peruvian-Style Chicken Tacos 

MAKES 12 tacos
START TO FINISH 30 minutes **OVEN** 350°F

- **1 pound uncooked ground chicken**
- **½ cup chopped onion (1 medium)**
- **2 teaspoons ground coriander**
- **2 teaspoons ground cumin**
- **1 teaspoon salt**
- **1 14.5-ounce can diced tomatoes, undrained**
- **1 cup finely chopped, peeled potato (1 medium)**
- **¼ cup snipped pitted dried plums**
- **¼ cup chopped pimiento-stuffed green olives**
- **12 6- to 7-inch corn or flour tortillas**
- **1 to 1½ cups shredded Cotija or Monterey Jack cheese (4 to 6 ounces)**
- **Chopped onion**
- **Snipped fresh cilantro**

1 In a large skillet cook chicken and the ½ cup onion over medium heat until chicken is no longer pink and onion is tender, stirring to break apart. If necessary, drain off fat. Add coriander, cumin, and salt; cook and stir for 1 to 2 minutes. Add undrained tomatoes, the potato, dried plums, and olives. Bring to boiling; reduce heat. Simmer, covered, for 12 to 15 minutes or until potato is tender. Uncover; cook 5 minutes more or until most of the liquid has evaporated.
2 Meanwhile, wrap tortillas in foil; place in a 350°F oven about 15 minutes or until heated. To assemble, place ⅓ cup chicken mixture in center of each tortilla. Top with cheese. Sprinkle with additional chopped onion and cilantro. Roll up tortillas.

PER TACO 194 calories; 10 g fat (0 g sat.); 11 g protein; 18 g carbohydrate; 3 g fiber; 328 mg sodium; 9 mg cholesterol

Peruvian-Style Chicken Tacos

Tamale Pie

MAKES 6 servings
PREP 35 minutes **BAKE** 25 minutes **OVEN** 350°F

- **Nonstick cooking spray**
- **1⅓ cups water**
- **½ cup yellow cornmeal**
- **½ cup cold water**
- **¼ teaspoon salt**
- **8 ounces ground uncooked turkey breast**
- **½ cup chopped onion (1 medium)**
- **½ cup chopped green and/or red sweet pepper (1 small)**
- **1 clove garlic, minced**
- **1 tablespoon chili powder**
- **¼ teaspoon salt**
- **1 14.5-ounce can no-salt-added diced tomatoes, drained**
- **1 11-ounce can whole kernel corn, drained**
- **2 tablespoons tomato paste**
- **2 tablespoons snipped fresh cilantro or parsley**
- **½ cup shredded reduced-fat cheddar or Monterey Jack cheese (2 ounces)**
- **Snipped fresh cilantro or parsley (optional)**

1 Lightly coat a 2-quart square baking dish with cooking spray; set aside. In a small saucepan bring the 1⅓ cups water to boiling. In a small bowl stir together the cornmeal, the ½ cup cold water, and ¼ teaspoon salt. Slowly add the cornmeal mixture to the boiling water, stirring constantly. Cook and stir until mixture returns to boiling; reduce heat. Cook over low heat about 10 minutes or until very thick, stirring occasionally. Pour the hot cornmeal mixture into the prepared dish. Cover and chill while preparing filling.
2 For filling, in a large skillet cook turkey, onion, sweet pepper, and garlic over medium heat until turkey is no longer pink, stirring to break apart. If necessary, drain off fat. Stir in chili powder and the remaining ¼ teaspoon salt; cook and stir for 1 minute. Stir in drained tomatoes, drained corn, tomato paste, and the 2 tablespoons cilantro. Spoon turkey mixture over chilled cornmeal mixture in baking dish.
3 Bake, uncovered, in a 350°F oven for 25 minutes or until heated through. Sprinkle with cheese. If desired, garnish with additional cilantro.

PER SERVING 182 calories; 3 g fat (1 g sat.); 14 g protein; 25 g carbohydrate; 4 g fiber; 546 mg sodium; 22 mg cholesterol

Tamale Pie

When making the polentalike mixture that serves as the base for this Southwestern-style casserole, use a sturdy wire whisk for stirring. A whisk will help keep the mixture free from lumps as it begins to thicken and bubble.

Turkey Enchiladas 

MAKES 12 enchiladas
PREP 35 minutes **BAKE** 44 minutes **OVEN** 350°F

- ½ cup chopped onion (1 medium)
- ½ of an 8-ounce package reduced-fat cream cheese (Neufchâtel), softened
- 1 tablespoon water
- 1 teaspoon ground cumin
- ¼ teaspoon black pepper
- ⅛ teaspoon salt
- 4 cups chopped cooked turkey or chicken breast
- ¼ cup chopped pecans, toasted
- 12 7- to 8-inch whole wheat flour tortillas
- Nonstick cooking spray
- 1 10.75-ounce can reduced-fat and reduced-sodium condensed cream of chicken soup
- 1 8-ounce carton light dairy sour cream
- 1 cup milk
- 2 to 4 tablespoons finely chopped, pickled jalapeño chile peppers*
- ½ cup shredded reduced-fat sharp cheddar cheese (2 ounces)
- Chopped tomatoes (optional)
- Chopped sweet pepper (optional)
- Snipped fresh cilantro or parsley (optional)

1 For filling, in a small covered saucepan cook onion in a small amount of water until tender; drain. In a large bowl stir together cream cheese, the 1 tablespoon water, the cumin, black pepper, and salt. Stir in cooked onion, turkey, and pecans; set aside. Wrap tortillas in foil; place in a 350°F oven about 15 minutes or until heated.

2 Coat a 3-quart rectangular baking dish with cooking spray. For each enchilada, spoon about ¼ cup of the filling onto a tortilla; roll up. Place filled tortillas, seam sides down, in the prepared baking dish.

3 For sauce, in a medium bowl stir together soup, sour cream, milk, and jalapeño peppers. Pour sauce over enchiladas. Bake, covered, in the 350°F oven about 40 minutes or until heated through. Sprinkle with cheddar cheese. Bake, uncovered, for 4 to 5 minutes more or until cheese melts. If desired, top with tomatoes, sweet pepper, and cilantro.

***Note:** Because chile peppers contain volatile oils that can burn your skin and eyes, avoid direct contact with them as much as possible. When working with chile peppers, wear plastic or rubber gloves. If your bare hands do touch the chile peppers, wash your hands and nails well with soap and warm water.

PER ENCHILADA 246 calories; 9 g fat (4 g sat.); 21 g protein; 18 g carbohydrate; 9 g fiber; 475 mg sodium; 55 mg cholesterol

Turkey Saltimbocca

Turkey Saltimbocca 

MAKES 4 servings
START TO FINISH 20 minutes

- **2 turkey breast tenderloins**
- **¼ teaspoon coarsely ground black pepper**
- **2 tablespoons butter**
- **2 ounces thinly sliced deli ham**
- **½ cup orange juice**
- **2 9- to 10-ounce packages fresh spinach**
- **Salt and black pepper**
- **Orange wedges (optional)**

1 Cut each tenderloin in half horizontally. Season turkey with the ¼ teaspoon pepper. In a very large skillet cook turkey in hot butter over medium-high heat about 12 minutes or until turkey is no longer pink (170°F), turning once. Meanwhile, cut ham into bite-size strips.

2 Remove turkey from skillet; cover and keep warm. Add ham to skillet; cook and stir for 1 to 2 minutes or until ham is heated through and starts to crisp. Using a slotted spoon, remove ham from skillet. Add orange juice to skillet; bring to boiling. Add spinach, half at a time, to skillet; cook and stir about 1 minute or just until it starts to wilt.

3 Using tongs, transfer spinach to dinner plates. Sprinkle with salt and pepper. Top spinach with sliced turkey and ham. Drizzle any remaining pan drippings over turkey. If desired, serve with orange wedges.

PER SERVING 244 calories; 8 g fat (4 g sat.); 34 g protein; 9 g carbohydrate; 3 g fiber; 528 mg sodium; 94 mg cholesterol

Cobb Salad 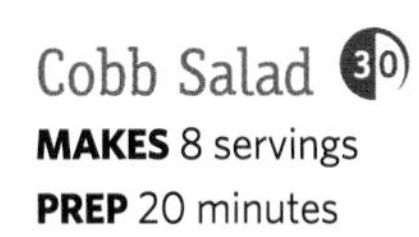

MAKES 8 servings
PREP 20 minutes

- 1 large head romaine lettuce
- 1 large head chicory
- 1 small avocado, halved, pitted, peeled, and cut lengthwise into thin wedges
- 2 ounces blue cheese, crumbled (about ½ cup)
- 1 cup cherry tomatoes, halved
- 2 hard-cooked eggs, shelled and quartered
- 6 strips turkey bacon, cooked and crumbled
- 4 ounces cooked turkey breast, cut into matchstick-size pieces (¾ cup)
- 1 recipe Cran-Raspberry Vinaigrette

1 Tear lettuce and chicory into bite-size pieces. Place in large shallow bowl. Arrange avocado, blue cheese, tomatoes, eggs, turkey bacon, and turkey breast in rows over the lettuce mixture. Serve with Cran-Raspberry Vinaigrette.

Cran-Raspberry Vinaigrette: Place ¾ cup raspberries in a sieve over a bowl. Press to remove seeds; discard seeds. In a food processor or blender combine raspberry puree, ½ cup cranberry juice, ½ cup red wine vinegar, ¼ cup hot water, 1 tablespoon olive oil, ¾ teaspoon salt, and ¼ teaspoon sugar. Process until smooth.

PER SERVING 176 calories; 8 g fat (3 g sat.); 14 g protein; 14 g carbohydrate; 8 g fiber; 699 mg sodium; 71 mg cholesterol

Cobb Salad

Herbed Lemon Turkey with Wild Mushroom Gravy

MAKES 6 to 8 servings
PREP 20 minutes **ROAST** 1½ hours **STAND** 15 minutes
OVEN 325°F

- ½ cup dried cherries
- 2 tablespoons olive oil
- 1½ teaspoons snipped fresh sage
- 1 4½- to 5-pound whole turkey breast (with bone)
- 1 lemon, quartered
- 1 medium onion, quartered
- ½ cup dried porcini, oyster, and shiitake mushrooms
- 1 cup boiling water
- ¼ cup all-purpose flour
- Chicken broth
- 2 tablespoons dry sherry or chicken broth

1 In a food processor or blender combine dried cherries, 1 tablespoon of the olive oil, and the sage. Cover and process just until cherries are finely chopped.

2 Slip your fingers between the skin and meat of the turkey breast to loosen the skin. Lift the skin and, using a spatula, carefully spread the cherry mixture over turkey under skin. Place the turkey on a rack in a shallow roasting pan. Place the lemon and onion underneath the turkey. Insert an oven-going meat thermometer into the thickest part of the turkey breast. (The thermometer should not touch bone.) Brush turkey with remaining 1 tablespoon oil.

3 Roast, uncovered, in a 325°F oven for 1½ to 2¼ hours or until turkey is no longer pink (170°F), covering with foil for the last 45 minutes of roasting to prevent overbrowning. Let stand, covered, for 15 minutes before carving.

4 Meanwhile, place mushrooms in a small bowl. Pour the boiling water over mushrooms to cover. Let stand for 10 minutes. Drain mushrooms, reserving liquid. Strain mushroom-soaking liquid through a fine-mesh sieve lined with 100-percent-cotton cheesecloth; reserve strained liquid. Rinse and drain mushrooms a second time.

5 Pour pan drippings from turkey into a large measuring cup. Skim and reserve fat from drippings. Pour ¼ cup of the fat (if necessary, add butter) into a medium saucepan. Stir in the flour. Add enough of the strained mushroom liquid and chicken broth to the remaining drippings in the measuring cup to equal 2 cups. Add broth mixture all at once to flour mixture; cook and stir over medium heat until thickened and bubbly. Stir in mushrooms and sherry; cook and stir for 1 minute more. Season to taste with *salt* and *black pepper.*

PER SERVING 293 calories; 13 g fat (3 g sat.); 35 g protein; 7 g carbohydrate; 0 g fiber; 198 mg sodium; 99 mg cholesterol

Turkey Tenderloin with Bean-and-Corn Salsa

Turkey Tenderloin with Bean-and-Corn Salsa (30)

MAKES 4 servings
START TO FINISH 20 minutes

- **2 turkey breast tenderloins**
- **Salt and black pepper**
- **¼ cup red jalapeño chile pepper jelly**
- **1¼ cups purchased black bean and corn salsa**
- **2 tablespoons fresh cilantro leaves**

1 Preheat broiler. Cut each turkey tenderloin in half horizontally. Place turkey on the unheated rack of a broiler pan. Sprinkle with salt and black pepper. Broil 4 to 5 inches from heat for 5 minutes.
2 Meanwhile, in a small saucepan melt jelly over low heat. Remove 2 tablespoons of the jelly from pan. Turn turkey over; spoon the 2 tablespoons jelly evenly over turkey. Broil for 4 to 6 minutes more or until turkey is tender and no longer pink (170°F).
3 Transfer turkey to a serving plate. Spoon remaining jelly over turkey; cover and keep warm. In a small saucepan heat salsa. Spoon salsa over turkey. Sprinkle with cilantro.

PER SERVING 196 calories; 2 g fat (1 g sat.); 27 g protein; 16 g carbohydrate; 1 g fiber; 377 mg sodium; 66 mg cholesterol

Turkey Breast with Raspberry Salsa

MAKES 8 servings
PREP 10 minutes **GRILL** 1¼ hours **STAND** 15 minutes

- **⅓ cup seedless raspberry jam**
- **1 tablespoon Dijon-style mustard**
- **1 teaspoon finely shredded orange peel**
- **½ cup bottled mild salsa**
- **1 2- to 2½-pound turkey breast portion (with bone)**

1 In a small bowl stir together jam, mustard, and orange peel. Stir 3 tablespoons of the jam mixture into the salsa. Cover both mixtures and chill.

Try whole wheat

2 Skin turkey breast, if desired. Insert an oven-going meat thermometer into thickest part of the breast. (The thermometer should not touch bone.)
3 For a charcoal grill, arrange medium-hot coals around a drip pan. Test for medium heat above pan. Place turkey, bone side down, on grill rack over drip pan. Cover and grill for 1¼ to 2 hours or until juices run clear and turkey is no longer pink (170°F), brushing occasionally with reserved jam mixture during the last 15 minutes of grilling. (For a gas grill, preheat grill. Reduce heat to medium. Adjust for indirect cooking. Grill as above.)
4 Transfer turkey to a cutting board. Cover with foil; let stand 15 minutes before carving. Serve with salsa mixture.

PER SERVING 149 calories; 3 g fat (1 g sat.); 20 g protein; 11 g carbohydrate; 0 g fiber; 147 mg sodium; 46 mg cholesterol

Sesame-Ginger Turkey Wraps

MAKES 12 wraps
PREP 20 minutes **COOK** 6 to 7 hours (low) or 3 to 3½ hours (high) **STAND** 5 minutes **OVEN** 350°F

- **3 turkey thighs**
- **Nonstick cooking spray**
- **1 cup bottled sesame-ginger stir-fry sauce**
- **¼ cup water**
- **1 16-ounce package shredded broccoli (broccoli slaw mix)**
- **12 8-inch flour tortillas**
- **¾ cup sliced green onion (6)**

1 Skin turkey; set aside. Lightly coat a 3½- or 4-quart slow cooker with cooking spray. Place turkey in prepared cooker. In a small bowl stir together stir-fry sauce and the water. Pour over turkey in cooker.
2 Cover and cook on low-heat setting for 6 to 7 hours or on high-heat setting for 3 to 3½ hours.
3 Remove turkey from cooker; cool slightly. Remove turkey from bones; discard bones. Using two forks, shred turkey into bite-size pieces. Return turkey to cooker. Add broccoli to cooker; stir to coat. Cover and let stand for 5 minutes. Using a slotted spoon, remove turkey mixture from cooker.
4 Meanwhile, wrap tortillas in foil; place in a 350°F oven about 15 minutes or until heated. To assemble, place some of the turkey mixture on each tortilla. Top turkey mixture with green onion. If desired, spoon some of the sauce from cooker on top. Roll up tortillas.

PER WRAP 207 calories; 5 g fat (1 g sat.); 20 g protein; 20 g carbohydrate; 2 g fiber; 422 mg sodium; 67 mg cholesterol

tortillas as a more healthful option.

Sesame-Ginger Turkey Wraps

page 154
page 159

Mouth-Watering Meats

Spicy Beef Sloppy Joes 

MAKES 6 servings + reserved meat mixture
PREP 20 minutes **COOK** 8 to 10 hours (low) or 4 to 5 hours (high)

- **2 pounds lean ground beef**
- **2 16-ounce jars salsa**
- **3 cups sliced fresh mushrooms (8 ounces)**
- **1½ cups shredded carrot (3 medium)**
- **1½ cups finely chopped red and/or green sweet pepper (2 medium)**
- **⅓ cup tomato paste**
- **2 teaspoons dried basil, crushed**
- **1 teaspoon dried oregano, crushed**
- **½ teaspoon salt**
- **¼ teaspoon cayenne pepper**
- **4 cloves garlic, minced**
- **6 kaiser rolls, split and toasted**

1 In a large skillet cook ground beef over medium heat until brown. Drain off fat. In a 5- or 6-quart slow cooker stir together cooked beef, salsa, mushrooms, carrot, sweet pepper, tomato paste, basil, oregano, salt, cayenne pepper, and garlic.
2 Cover and cook on low-heat setting for 8 to 10 hours or high-heat setting for 4 to 5 hours.
3 Reserve 5 cups of the meat mixture for another time; place in an airtight container and refrigerate for up to 3 days or freeze for up to 3 months. Serve remaining meat mixture on kaiser rolls.

PER SERVING 294 calories; 8 g fat (3 g sat.); 18 g protein; 37 g carbohydrate; 3 g fiber; 756 mg sodium; 36 mg cholesterol

Veggie-Filled Hamburgers

Veggie-Filled Hamburgers

MAKES 4 servings
PREP 25 minutes **GRILL** 11 minutes

- **2 tablespoons fat-free milk**
- **½ cup finely shredded carrot**
- **¼ cup thinly sliced green onion (2)**
- **¼ cup soft whole wheat bread crumbs**
- **¼ teaspoon dried Italian seasoning, crushed**
- **¼ teaspoon garlic salt**
- **Dash black pepper**
- **12 ounces extra-lean ground beef or uncooked ground turkey breast or chicken breast**
- **4 whole wheat hamburger buns, split and toasted**
- **4 lettuce leaves**
- **½ cup sliced or shredded zucchini**
- **4 slices tomato**
- **Curry Mustard (optional)**

1 In a medium bowl stir together milk, carrot, green onion, bread crumbs, Italian seasoning, garlic salt, and pepper. Add the ground beef; mix well. Divide the beef mixture into four portions. Shape each portion into a ½-inch-thick patty.
2 For a charcoal grill, place patties on the grill rack directly over medium coals. Grill, uncovered, for 11 to 14 minutes or until an instant-read thermometer inserted into the side of the patties registers 160°F for beef and 165°F for chicken or turkey, turning once halfway through grilling. (For a gas grill, preheat grill. Reduce heat to medium. Place patties on grill rack over heat. Cover and grill as directed above.)
3 To serve, place patties on bottom halves of buns. Layer with lettuce leaves, zucchini, tomato, and, if desired, Curry Mustard. Add bun top.

Curry Mustard: In a small bowl stir together ¼ cup Dijon-style mustard and ½ teaspoon curry powder.

Make-Ahead Directions: Prepare patties as directed in Step 1. Place patties in a single layer in a freezer container. Seal, label, and freeze for up to 3 months. Thaw in the refrigerator overnight. To serve, continue with Step 2.

PER SERVING 254 calories; 6 g fat (2 g sat.); 24 g protein; 27 g carbohydrate; 3 g fiber; 359 mg sodium; 53 mg cholesterol

Greek Burgers with Feta Sauce

Greek Burgers with Feta Sauce

MAKES 4 servings
PREP 30 minutes **GRILL** 12 minutes

- **12 ounces lean ground beef**
- **½ cup quick-cooking rolled oats**
- **⅓ cup finely chopped red onion (1 small)**
- **1 egg white**
- **3 tablespoons snipped fresh mint or basil**
- **½ teaspoon garlic salt**
- **1 small red sweet pepper, quartered**
- **1 6-ounce carton plain low-fat or fat-free yogurt**
- **⅓ cup crumbled feta cheese with garlic and herb (1½ ounces)**
- **2 large whole wheat pita bread rounds, halved, or 4 whole wheat hamburger buns, split and toasted**
- **1 cup fresh baby spinach leaves**

1 In a medium bowl combine ground beef, oats, red onion, egg white, 2 tablespoons of the mint, and the garlic salt; mix well. Form beef mixture into four ¾-inch-thick patties.

2 For a charcoal grill, place patties on the grill rack directly over medium coals. Grill, uncovered, for 12 to 14 minutes or until an instant-read thermometer inserted into the side of the patties registers 160°F, turning once halfway through grilling. Add sweet pepper quarters to grill for the last 8 to 10 minutes of grilling or until skins are charred and sweet pepper quarters are tender, turning once. (For a gas grill, preheat grill. Reduce heat to medium. Place patties on the grill rack over heat. Cover and grill as directed above.)

3 Meanwhile, for sauce, in a small bowl stir together yogurt and feta cheese.

4 Cut sweet pepper quarters into strips, peeling off any loose skin, if desired. Serve burgers with pita halves, pepper strips, sauce, and spinach. Sprinkle with the remaining 1 tablespoon mint. (If using hamburger buns, spread sauce mixture on bottoms of buns. Top with spinach, burgers, pepper strips, and remaining 1 tablespoon mint. Replace bun tops.)

PER SERVING 348 calories; 13 g fat (5 g sat.); 27 g protein; 31 g carbohydrate; 4 g fiber; 585 mg sodium; 64 mg cholesterol

Mexican Beef & Veggies

Mexican Beef & Veggies [below]

Salad of romaine lettuce, avocado slices, red onion slices, and cilantro-lime vinaigrette

Frozen vanilla yogurt with diced fresh mango

Mexican Beef & Veggies 

MAKES 4 to 6 servings
START TO FINISH 30 minutes

- **12 ounces lean ground beef**
- **1 medium (1¼ pounds) butternut squash, peeled, seeded, and cubed (about 3 cups)**
- **2 cloves garlic, minced**
- **1 teaspoon ground cumin**
- **½ teaspoon salt**
- **⅛ teaspoon ground cinnamon**
- **1 14.5-ounce can diced tomatoes, undrained**
- **1 medium zucchini, halved lengthwise and sliced ¼ inch thick**
- **¼ cup water**
- **¼ cup snipped fresh cilantro**
- **2 to 3 cups hot cooked white or brown rice**
- **Bottled hot pepper sauce (optional)**

1 In a large skillet cook ground beef, squash, garlic, cumin, salt, and cinnamon over medium heat until beef is brown. Drain off fat.
2 Stir in undrained tomatoes. Bring to boiling; reduce heat. Simmer, covered, about 8 minutes or until squash is just tender. Stir in zucchini and the water. Cover and simmer about 4 minutes more or until zucchini is tender. Stir in cilantro. Serve over hot cooked rice. If desired, season to taste with hot pepper sauce.

PER SERVING 313 calories; 9 g fat (3 g sat.); 20 g protein; 39 g carbohydrate; 3 g fiber; 504 mg sodium; 54 mg cholesterol

Beef Ragu with Beans 

MAKES 8 servings + reserved meat sauce
PREP 15 minutes **COOK** 8½ hours (low) or 5½ hours (high) + 30 minutes

- **1½ cups coarsely chopped carrot (2 large)**
- **1 cup coarsely chopped celery (2 stalks)**
- **1 cup coarsely chopped onion (1 large)**
- **4 cloves garlic, peeled**
- **2 pounds ground beef**
- **2 14.5-ounce cans diced tomatoes, undrained**
- **2 cups beef broth**
- **1 15-ounce can cannellini (white kidney) beans, rinsed and drained**
- **3 tablespoons tomato paste**
- **2 teaspoons sugar**
- **1½ teaspoons dried Italian seasoning**
- **1½ teaspoons salt**
- **1 teaspoon red pepper flakes**
- **1 pound dried rigatoni pasta**
- **Grated Parmesan cheese (optional)**

1 Place carrot, celery, onion, and garlic in a food processor; pulse until finely chopped. In a large bowl stir together chopped vegetables, ground beef, undrained tomatoes, broth, beans, tomato paste, and sugar. Stir in ¾ teaspoon of the Italian seasoning, ¾ teaspoon of the salt, and ½ teaspoon of the red pepper flakes. Transfer meat mixture to a 6-quart slow cooker.
2 Cover and cook on low-heat setting for 8½ hours or on high-heat setting for 5½ hours. Stir in remaining Italian seasoning, salt, and red pepper flakes. Cover and cook for 30 minutes more.
3 Meanwhile, cook pasta according to package directions; drain. Toss half of the meat mixture with rigatoni; if desired, serve with grated cheese. Store remaining sauce in an airtight container for future use. Refrigerate reserved meat mixture for up to 3 days or freeze for up to 3 months.

PER SERVING 359 calories; 8 g fat (3 g sat.); 22 g protein; 52 g carbohydrate; 4 g fiber; 505 mg sodium; 41 mg cholesterol

Easy Shepherd's Pie (30)

MAKES 6 servings
START TO FINISH 30 minutes

- 1 pound lean ground beef or uncooked ground turkey or chicken
- 1 medium onion, chopped
- 1 10-ounce package frozen mixed vegetables, thawed
- ¼ cup water
- 1 10.75-ounce can condensed tomato soup
- 1 teaspoon Worcestershire sauce
- ¼ teaspoon dried thyme, crushed
- 1 20-ounce package refrigerated mashed potatoes or 3 cups leftover mashed potatoes
- ½ cup shredded cheddar cheese (2 ounces)

1 In a large skillet cook ground beef and onion over medium heat until beef is brown and onion is tender. Drain off fat. Stir mixed vegetables and the water into beef mixture in skillet. Bring to boiling; reduce heat. Simmer, covered, about 5 minutes or until vegetables are tender.
2 Stir in soup, Worcestershire sauce, and thyme. Return to boiling; reduce heat. Drop mashed potatoes in 6 mounds on top of hot mixture. Sprinkle potatoes with cheese. Cover and simmer for 10 to 15 minutes or until potatoes are heated through.

PER SERVING 301 calories; 12 g fat (5 g sat.); 20 g protein; 27 g carbohydrate; 3 g fiber; 570 mg sodium; 58 mg cholesterol

Greek-Style Beef & Vegetables

MAKES 6 servings
PREP 15 minutes **COOK** 6 to 8 hours (low) or 3 to 4 hours (high) + 30 minutes

- 1 pound ground beef
- 1 cup chopped onion (1 large)
- 3 cloves garlic, minced
- 1 14-ounce can beef broth
- 3 cups frozen mixed vegetables
- 1 14.5-ounce can diced tomatoes, undrained
- 3 tablespoons tomato paste
- 1 teaspoon dried oregano, crushed
- ⅛ teaspoon ground cinnamon
- ⅛ teaspoon ground nutmeg
- 2 cups dried medium shell macaroni
- 1 cup shredded Monterey Jack or crumbled feta cheese (4 ounces)

1 In a large skillet cook ground beef, onion, and garlic over medium heat until beef is brown and onion is tender. Drain off fat. Place meat mixture in a 3½- to 4-quart slow cooker. Stir in broth, frozen vegetables, undrained tomatoes, tomato paste, oregano, cinnamon, and nutmeg.
2 Cover and cook on low-heat setting for 6 to 8 hours or on high-heat setting for 3 to 4 hours. If using low-heat setting, turn to high-heat setting. Add pasta. Cover and cook about 30 minutes more or until pasta is tender. Top each serving with cheese.

PER SERVING 446 calories; 16 g fat (7 g sat.); 28 g protein; 46 g carbohydrate; 5 g fiber; 539 mg sodium; 64 mg cholesterol

Traditional beef goulash gets a makeover with the addition of vitamin-loaded veggies and Greek-style seasonings.

Greek-Style Beef & Vegetables

Spaghetti or any long noodle makes a tasty bed to cradle this saucy steak.

Beefy Italian Skillet

Beefy Italian Skillet 

MAKES 4 servings
PREP 35 minutes **COOK** 1¼ hours

- 1 pound boneless beef round steak
- Nonstick cooking spray
- 2 cups sliced fresh mushrooms
- 1 cup chopped onion (1 large)
- 1 cup coarsely chopped green sweet pepper (1 large)
- ½ cup chopped celery (1 stalk)
- 2 cloves garlic, minced
- 1 14.5-ounce can diced tomatoes, undrained
- ½ teaspoon dried basil, crushed
- ¼ teaspoon dried oregano, crushed
- ¼ teaspoon crushed red pepper (optional)
- 8 ounces dried spaghetti
- 2 tablespoons grated Parmesan cheese (optional)

1 Trim fat from steak. Cut steak into four serving-size pieces. Lightly coat an unheated large skillet with cooking spray. Heat skillet over medium heat. Brown steak on both sides; remove from skillet.
2 Add mushrooms, onion, sweet pepper, celery, and garlic to skillet. Cook until vegetables are nearly tender, stirring occasionally. Stir in undrained tomatoes, basil, oregano, and, if desired, crushed red pepper. Add steak to skillet, spooning vegetable mixture over the steak. Reduce heat to medium-low. Simmer, covered, about 1¼ hours or until steak is tender, stirring occasionally.
3 Meanwhile, cook spaghetti according to package directions. Transfer steak to a serving platter. Spoon vegetable mixture over steak. Serve with spaghetti. If desired, sprinkle with cheese.

PER SERVING 438 calories; 8 g fat (3 g sat.); 37 g protein; 55 g carbohydrate; 4 g fiber; 273 mg sodium; 56 mg cholesterol

Beef & Cabbage Wraps 

MAKES 4 servings
START TO FINISH 20 minutes **OVEN** 350°F

- 8 8-inch flour tortillas
- 12 ounces lean ground beef
- ½ cup chopped onion (1 medium)
- 1 cup frozen whole kernel corn
- ½ to ⅔ cup bottled barbecue sauce
- 2 cups packaged shredded cabbage with carrot (coleslaw mix)

1 Wrap tortillas tightly in foil; place on baking sheet. Heat in a 350°F oven about 10 minutes or until heated through.
2 Meanwhile, in a large skillet cook ground beef and onion over medium heat until beef is brown and onion is tender. Drain off fat. Stir in corn and ⅓ cup barbecue sauce. Cook and stir until heated through.
3 To serve, spread one side of tortillas with some of the remaining barbecue sauce. Spoon about ½ cup meat mixture on each tortilla. Top evenly with shredded cabbage mix. Roll up tortillas to enclose filling to make wraps.

PER SERVING 391 calories; 14 g fat (4 g sat.); 21 g protein; 46 g carbohydrate; 3 g fiber; 535 mg sodium; 54 mg cholesterol

Beef & Cabbage Wraps

Sirloin with Mustard & Chives

Check the beef ads for your local supermarket weekly. When there's a sale on a specific cut of beef you like, stock up on it. Order steaks bundled in the number you want per package and ask that they be wrapped in freezer paper. You can safely store beef in the freezer for up to one year.

Sirloin with Mustard & Chives 

MAKES 4 servings
START TO FINISH 20 minutes

- 4 **boneless beef sirloin or ribeye steaks, cut ¾ inch thick**
- 1½ **teaspoons garlic-pepper seasoning**
- ½ **cup light dairy sour cream**
- 2 **tablespoons Dijon-style mustard**
- 1 **tablespoon snipped fresh chives**
- ½ **teaspoon garlic-pepper seasoning**

1 Sprinkle both sides of steaks evenly with the 1½ teaspoons garlic-pepper seasoning. For a charcoal grill, place steaks on the grill rack directly over medium coals. Grill, uncovered, to desired doneness, turning once halfway through grilling. Allow 9 to 11 minutes for medium rare (145°F) and 11 to 13 minutes for medium (160°F). (For a gas grill, preheat grill. Reduce heat to medium. Place steaks on grill rack over heat. Cover and grill as above.)
2 Meanwhile, in a small bowl stir together sour cream, mustard, chives, and the ½ teaspoon garlic-pepper seasoning. Spoon sour cream mixture onto steaks.

PER SERVING 256 calories; 9 g fat (4 g sat.); 37 g protein; 2 g carbohydrate; 0 g fiber; 421 mg sodium; 112 mg cholesterol

Steak with Sweet Potato-Mango Chutney 

MAKES 4 servings
START TO FINISH 20 minutes

- 1 **large sweet potato (12 ounces), peeled and diced**
- 4 **boneless beef eye of round steaks, about ¾ inch thick**
- **Salt**
- **Steak seasoning**
- ⅓ **cup mango chutney**
- ¼ **cup dried cranberries**
- **Rosemary sprigs (optional)**

1 In a medium saucepan bring lightly salted water to boiling. Add sweet potato; simmer, covered, for 8 to 10 minutes or until tender. Drain and keep warm.
2 Sprinkle steaks lightly with salt and steak seasoning. In a large nonstick skillet cook steaks over medium heat to desired doneness, turning once. Allow 8 to 10 minutes for medium rare (145°F) to medium (160°F). Transfer to serving plates; cover to keep warm.
3 Add sweet potatoes to skillet; cook and stir for 2 minutes. Add chutney and cranberries to skillet; stir gently to heat through. Season to taste with additional salt and steak seasoning. Serve sweet potato with steaks. If desired, garnish with rosemary.

PER SERVING 344 calories; 5 g fat (2 g sat.); 40 g protein; 32 g carbohydrate; 4 g fiber; 418 mg sodium; 70 mg cholesterol

Steak with Sweet Potato-Mango Chutney

Menu

Beef with Cucumber Raita [below right]

Greek pita flatbread

Salad of romaine lettuce, cucumber slices, red onion slices, tomato wedges, and Greek-style vinaigrette

Lemon Sorbet

Beef with Cucumber Raita

Honey-and-Onion-Smothered Steak

MAKES 4 servings
START TO FINISH 35 minutes

- **¼ cup red wine vinegar**
- **3 tablespoons honey**
- **2 tablespoons water**
- **½ teaspoon dried thyme, crushed**
- **1 large onion, thinly sliced**
- **1 pound boneless beef sirloin steak, cut 1 inch thick**
- **½ to 1 teaspoon seasoned pepper**
- **1 tablespoon cooking oil**

1 In a medium bowl stir together vinegar, honey, the water, and the thyme; mix well. Stir in onion; set aside.
2 Trim fat from steak. Season both sides of steak with seasoned pepper. In a large nonstick skillet cook steak in hot oil over medium heat for 8 minutes, turning once. Remove steak from skillet; cover and keep warm. Add onion mixture to skillet. Cook for 3 to 4 minutes or until onion is crisp-tender, stirring occasionally. Return steak to skillet. Reduce heat. Simmer, uncovered, for 8 to 15 minutes or until steak is desired doneness (145°F for medium rare to 160°F for medium).
3 To serve, transfer steak to a serving platter. Spoon onion mixture over steak.

PER SERVING 205 calories; 4 g fat (1 g sat.); 25 g protein; 17 g carbohydrate; 1 g fiber; 62 mg sodium; 53 mg cholesterol

Beef with Cucumber Raita 

MAKES 4 servings
START TO FINISH 30 minutes

- **1 8-ounce carton plain fat-free or low-fat yogurt**
- **¼ cup coarsely shredded unpeeled cucumber**
- **1 tablespoon finely chopped red onion or sweet onion**
- **1 tablespoon snipped fresh mint**
- **¼ teaspoon sugar**
- **Salt and black pepper**
- **1 pound boneless beef top sirloin steak, cut 1 inch thick**
- **½ teaspoon lemon-pepper seasoning**
- **Fresh mint leaves (optional)**

1 Preheat broiler. For raita, in a small bowl stir together yogurt, cucumber, onion, snipped mint, and sugar. Season to taste with salt and pepper; set aside.
2 Trim fat from steak. Sprinkle steak with lemon-pepper seasoning. Place steak on the unheated rack of a broiler pan. Broil 4 inches from heat for 15 to 17 minutes for medium rare (145°F) or 20 to 22 minutes for medium (160°F), turning once halfway through broiling. Thinly slice steak across the grain. Serve with raita. If desired, garnish with fresh mint leaves.

PER SERVING 176 calories; 4 g fat (1 g sat.); 28 g protein; 5 g carbohydrate; 0 g fiber; 312 mg sodium; 55 mg cholesterol

Beef Fajitas

MAKES 8 servings
PREP 25 minutes **COOK** 7 to 8 hours (low) or 3½ to 4 hours (high)

- **1 large onion, cut into thin wedges**
- **2 pounds boneless beef sirloin steak**
- **1 teaspoon ground cumin**
- **1 teaspoon ground coriander**
- **½ teaspoon salt**
- **½ teaspoon black pepper**
- **2 medium red or green sweet peppers, cut into thin bite-size strips**
- **¼ cup beef broth**
- **8 7- to 8-inch whole wheat or plain flour tortillas, warmed**
- **1 cup shredded carrot (2 medium)**
- **1 cup coarsely shredded lettuce**
- **Salsa, guacamole, and/or dairy sour cream**

1 Place onion in a 3½- to 4-quart slow cooker. Trim fat from steak. Sprinkle one side of the steak with cumin, coriander, salt, and black pepper; rub in with your fingers. Thinly slice steak across grain into bite-size strips. Add steak strips to cooker. Top with sweet peppers. Pour broth over all.

2 Cover and cook on low-heat setting for 7 to 8 hours or on high-heat setting for 3½ to 4 hours.

3 To serve, use a slotted spoon to fill tortillas with meat mixture. Top meat mixture with carrot and lettuce. Roll up tortillas. Serve with salsa, guacamole, and/or sour cream.

PER SERVING 327 calories; 10 g fat (3 g sat.); 33 g protein; 22 g carbohydrate; 12 g fiber; 642 mg sodium; 70 mg cholesterol

Steak with Pear Brandy-Pepper Sauce

Steak with Pear Brandy-Pepper Sauce 

MAKES 4 servings
START TO FINISH 30 minutes

- **½ cup snipped dried pears**
- **⅓ cup pear brandy or pear nectar**
- **4 teaspoons all-purpose flour**
- **1 teaspoon cracked black pepper**
- **½ teaspoon salt**
- **4 beef tenderloin steaks or beef top loin steaks, cut 1 inch thick**
- **3 tablespoons butter**
- **¼ cup finely chopped shallot (2 medium) or green onion (2)**
- **¼ cup reduced-sodium beef broth**

1 In a small bowl stir together dried pears and pear brandy; cover and let stand for 15 minutes.

2 Meanwhile, in a shallow dish stir together flour, pepper, and salt. Coat steaks in flour mixture. In a large skillet cook steaks in 2 tablespoons of the hot butter over medium heat to desired doneness, turning once. For tenderloin steaks, allow 10 to 13 minutes for medium rare (145°F) to medium (160°F). For top loin steaks, allow 12 to 15 minutes for medium rare to medium. Transfer steaks to a serving platter, reserving drippings in skillet; keep warm.

3 For sauce, in the same skillet cook shallot in the reserved drippings over medium heat for 1 minute. Remove from heat. Let skillet stand for 1 minute. Carefully stir in dried pear mixture and beef broth. Bring to boiling. Boil gently, uncovered, over medium heat about 3 minutes or until sauce has thickened slightly, stirring occasionally. Whisk in the remaining 1 tablespoon butter. Spoon sauce over steaks.

PER SERVING 322 calories; 17 g fat (8 g sat.); 24 g protein; 6 g carbohydrate; 0 g fiber; 465 mg sodium; 81 mg cholesterol

Bail-Out Beef Stroganoff 

MAKES 4 servings
START TO FINISH 30 minutes

- 3 cups dried wide noodles
- 3 cups broccoli florets (12 ounces)
- ½ cup light dairy sour cream
- 1½ teaspoons prepared horseradish
- ½ teaspoon fresh dill
- 1 pound beef ribeye steak
- 1 small onion, cut into ½-inch slices
- 1 clove garlic, minced
- 1 tablespoon cooking oil
- 4 teaspoons all-purpose flour
- ½ teaspoon black pepper
- 1 14-ounce can beef broth
- 3 tablespoons tomato paste
- 1 teaspoon Worcestershire sauce

1 Cook noodles according to package directions, adding broccoli for the last 5 minutes of cooking. Drain. Return pasta mixture to hot pan; cover to keep warm.
2 Meanwhile, in a small serving bowl stir together the sour cream, horseradish, and dill; cover and chill until serving time.
3 Trim fat from steak. Cut steak into bite-size strips. In a large skillet cook and stir half of the steak strips, the onion, and garlic in hot oil over medium heat until onion is tender and steak strips are desired doneness. Remove meat mixture from skillet. Add remaining steak strips to skillet; cook and stir until steak strips are desired doneness. Return meat mixture to the skillet; sprinkle flour and pepper over all. Stir to coat.
4 Stir in broth, tomato paste, and Worcestershire sauce. Cook and stir until thickened and bubbly. Cook and stir for 1 minute more. Divide noodle mixture among four bowls. Spoon meat mixture evenly over noodle mixture. Top with the sour cream mixture.

PER SERVING 413 calories; 16 g fat (6 g sat.); 33 g protein; 33 g carbohydrate; 3 g fiber; 504 mg sodium; 103 mg cholesterol

This updated stroganoff puts a twist on a classic. Instead of sour cream swirled throughout the red sauce, it's spooned over the top. And, for extra zip, it's laced with prepared horseradish.

Bail-Out
Beef Stroganoff

Flank Steak & Caramelized Onion Sandwiches

MAKES 6 sandwiches
PREP 35 minutes **COOK** 30 minutes **STAND** 10 minutes

- **1½ teaspoons dried oregano, crushed**
- **1½ teaspoons coriander seeds, crushed**
- **1 teaspoon salt**
- **1 teaspoon freshly ground black pepper**
- **2 tablespoons butter**
- **2 large sweet onions, cut into ¼-inch slices (about 4 cups)**
- **2 cloves garlic, minced**
- **1½ pounds beef flank steak**
- **6 small romaine lettuce leaves**
- **6 bakery sourdough rolls or buns or 12 slices sourdough bread, toasted**
- **1 recipe Horseradish Sauce**

1 In a small bowl stir together oregano, coriander, salt, and pepper; set aside. In a large nonstick or cast-iron skillet melt butter over medium-low heat. Add onions, garlic, and half of the spice mixture. Cook, covered, for 13 to 15 minutes or until onions are tender, stirring occasionally. Uncover; cook and stir over medium-high heat for 5 to 8 minutes more or until onions are golden. Remove from skillet; set aside. Wipe skillet clean.

2 Score both sides of steak in a diamond pattern by making shallow diagonal cuts at 1-inch intervals. Rub steak on both sides with the remaining spice mixture. Heat the same skillet over medium-high heat until very hot. Add steak. Cook, uncovered, for 12 to 16 minutes or until steak is medium rare (145°F), turning once. Transfer steak to a cutting board; cover with foil and let stand for 10 minutes. Slice steak thinly across the grain.

3 To serve, arrange lettuce leaves and steak evenly on bottoms of buns. Top with onions and Horseradish Sauce. Add bun tops.

Horseradish Sauce: In a small bowl combine ¾ cup mayonnaise, 1 to 2 tablespoons prepared horseradish, 1 tablespoon lime juice, and ½ teaspoon dried oregano, crushed.

PER SANDWICH 399 calories; 14 g fat (6 g sat.); 31 g protein; 37 g carbohydrate; 4 g fiber; 799 mg sodium; 56 mg cholesterol

Five-Spice Steak Wraps 

MAKES 4 wraps
START TO FINISH 25 minutes

- **12 ounces boneless beef top round steak or sirloin steak**
- **½ teaspoon five-spice powder**
- **¼ teaspoon salt**
- **2 cups packaged shredded cabbage with carrot (coleslaw mix)**
- **¼ cup thin strips red and/or green sweet pepper**
- **¼ cup thin strips carrot**
- **¼ cup snipped fresh chives**
- **2 tablespoons rice vinegar**
- **½ teaspoon toasted sesame oil**
- **Nonstick cooking spray**
- **¼ cup plain low-fat yogurt or light dairy sour cream**
- **4 8-inch flour tortillas**

1 Trim fat from steak. Thinly slice steak across the grain into bite-size strips. Sprinkle steak strips with five-spice powder and salt; set aside. In a medium bowl combine shredded cabbage, sweet pepper, carrot, and chives. In a small bowl combine rice vinegar and sesame oil. Pour vinegar mixture over coleslaw mixture; toss to coat; set aside.

2 Coat a large nonstick skillet with cooking spray. Heat skillet over medium-high heat. Add beef strips; cook and stir for 3 to 4 minutes or until brown.

3 To assemble, spread yogurt down the center of each tortilla. Top with beef strips. Stir coleslaw mixture; spoon over beef strips. Fold in sides of tortillas and roll up.

PER WRAP 237 calories; 7 g fat (2 g sat.); 22 g protein; 20 g carbohydrate; 2 g fiber; 329 mg sodium; 51 mg cholesterol

Flank Steak &
Caramelized Onion
Sandwiches

Lemony Flank Steak ✪

MAKES 4 servings

PREP 15 minutes **MARINATE** 2 to 24 hours **BROIL** 15 minutes

- **1 1½-pound beef flank steak**
- **1 teaspoon finely shredded lemon peel**
- **½ cup lemon juice**
- **2 tablespoons sugar**
- **2 tablespoons reduced-sodium soy sauce**
- **2 teaspoons snipped fresh oregano or ½ teaspoon dried oregano, crushed**
- **⅛ teaspoon black pepper**
- **Lemon slices (optional)**
- **Fresh oregano sprigs (optional)**

1 Score both sides of steak in a diamond pattern by making shallow diagonal cuts at 1-inch intervals. Place steak in a resealable plastic bag set in a shallow dish. Set aside. For marinade, in a small bowl stir together lemon peel, lemon juice, sugar, soy sauce, oregano, and pepper. Pour marinade over steak; seal bag. Turn to coat steak. Marinate in the refrigerator for 2 to 24 hours.

2 Drain steak, reserving marinade. Pat steak dry with paper towels. Preheat broiler. Place steak on the unheated rack of a broiler pan. Broil 3 to 4 inches from the heat for 15 to 18 minutes or until medium doneness (160°F), turning and brushing once with reserved marinade halfway through broiling. Discard any remaining marinade.
3 To serve, thinly slice steak diagonally across the grain. If desired, garnish with lemon slices and fresh oregano sprigs.

PER SERVING 301 calories; 12 g fat (5 g sat.); 38 g protein; 9 g carbohydrate; 0 g fiber; 378 mg sodium; 68 mg cholesterol

Lemony Flank Steak

Flank Steak with Sweet Pepper Relish

MAKES 4 servings
PREP 30 minutes **MARINATE** 30 minutes **GRILL** 17 to 21 minutes

- **1 1½-pound beef flank steak**
- **⅓ cup red wine vinegar**
- **2 large cloves garlic, minced**
- **2 tablespoons Dijon-style mustard**
- **2 tablespoons snipped fresh cilantro**
- **¼ teaspoon crushed red pepper**
- **4 10-inch flour tortillas**
- **Shredded lettuce**
- **1 recipe Sweet-Pepper Salsa**

1 Score both sides of steak in a diamond pattern by making shallow diagonal cuts at 1-inch intervals. Place steak in a large resealable plastic bag set in a shallow dish. Set aside. For marinade, in a small bowl stir together the vinegar, garlic, mustard, cilantro, and red pepper. Pour vinegar mixture over steak; seal bag. Turn to coat steak. Marinate in the refrigerator for 30 minutes. Drain steak, discarding the marinade.
2 For a charcoal grill, place steak on the grill rack directly over medium coals. Grill, uncovered, for 17 to 21 minutes for medium (160°F). (For a gas grill, preheat grill. Reduce heat to medium. Place steak on grill rack over heat. Cover and grill as above.)
3 To serve, thinly slice steak diagonally across the grain. Wrap and chill half of the steak for up to 3 days for another use. Serve remaining steak in flour tortillas with the shredded lettuce. Top with Sweet-Pepper Salsa.
Sweet-Pepper Salsa: In a medium bowl toss together 1½ cups finely chopped green and/or yellow sweet peppers (2 medium); 1 fresh serrano pepper, seeded and chopped;* ½ cup finely chopped, peeled jicama; ¼ cup finely chopped red onion; 2 tablespoons snipped fresh cilantro; 1 tablespoon red wine vinegar, and ¼ teaspoon salt. Cover and chill.
***Note:** Because chile peppers contain volatile oils that can burn your skin and eyes, avoid direct contact with them as much as possible. When working with chile peppers, wear plastic or rubber gloves. If your bare hands do touch the chile peppers, wash your hands and nails well with soap and warm water.

PER SERVING 271 calories; 9 g fat (3 g sat.); 22 g protein; 23 g carbohydrate; 1 g fiber; 270 mg sodium; 34 mg cholesterol

Italian Beef Sandwiches

Beef Brisket with Potatoes

Italian Beef Sandwiches

MAKES 2 sandwiches
PREP 15 minutes **COOK** 7 to 8 hours (low) or 3½ to 4 hours (high)

- **6 ounces beef flank steak**
- **½ teaspoon dried oregano, crushed**
- **Dash crushed red pepper**
- **1 clove garlic, minced**
- **½ cup low-sodium tomato juice**
- **¼ cup bottled roasted red sweet pepper strips (optional)**
- **2 4-inch-long pieces French bread, split and toasted**
- **¼ cup shredded provolone cheese (1 ounce)**

1 If necessary, cut steak to fit in a 1½-quart slow cooker. Place steak in cooker. Sprinkle steak with oregano, red pepper, and garlic. Pour tomato juice over all.
2 Cover and cook on low-heat setting for 7 to 8 hours or on high-heat setting for 3½ to 4 hours. (If no heat setting is available, cook for 6 to 7 hours.)
3 Remove steak from cooker, reserving cooking juices. Using two forks, shred the steak. If desired, stir roasted sweet pepper strips into shredded steak. Place shredded steak on the bottoms of bread pieces. Drizzle enough of the cooking juices over shredded steak to moisten. Sprinkle shredded steak with cheese. Cover with tops of bread pieces.

PER SANDWICH 302 calories; 11 g fat (5 g sat.); 26 g protein; 23 g carbohydrate; 2 g fiber; 442 mg sodium; 44 mg cholesterol

Beef Brisket with Potatoes

MAKES 8 servings
PREP 20 minutes **COOK** 10 hours (low) or 5 to 5½ hours (high)

- **1 pound baking potatoes, peeled and cut into 1-inch cubes**
- **1 pound sweet potatoes, peeled and cut into 1-inch cubes**
- **1 3- to 3½-pound fresh beef brisket**
- **½ cup bottled hoisin sauce**
- **½ cup purchased salsa**
- **2 tablespoons quick-cooking tapioca**
- **2 cloves garlic, minced**

1 In a 5- to 6-quart slow cooker, combine baking potatoes and sweet potatoes. Trim fat from beef. Top potatoes in cooker with beef. In a small bowl stir together hoisin sauce, salsa, tapioca, and garlic. Pour salsa mixture over beef in cooker; spread evenly.
2 Cover and cook on low-heat setting for 10 hours or on high-heat setting for 5 to 5½ hours. Transfer beef to a cutting board. Thinly slice beef across the grain. Serve with cooking liquid and potatoes.

PER SERVING 344 calories; 11 g fat (3 g sat.); 38 g protein; 22 g carbohydrate; 2 g fiber; 382 mg sodium; 103 mg cholesterol

Best-Ever Roast Beef ✪

MAKES 12 servings
PREP 15 minutes **ROAST** 1¼ hours **STAND** 15 minutes
OVEN 400°F

- **Nonstick cooking spray**
- **2 large onions, cut into ¼-inch rings**
- **1 cup dry red wine**
- **1 3-pound beef eye of round roast**
- **¼ cup ketchup**
- **2 tablespoons bottled teriyaki sauce**
- **2 tablespoons Dijon-style mustard**
- **1 tablespoon balsamic vinegar***
- **½ cup water**
- **3 tablespoons all-purpose flour**
- **2 cups beef broth**

1 Coat a roasting pan with cooking spray. Scatter onion rings over bottom of pan. Pour red wine into the pan. Place roast on top of onion rings. Set aside.
2 In a small bowl stir together ketchup, teriyaki sauce, mustard, and vinegar. Reserve 2 tablespoons of the ketchup mixture for gravy; brush the remaining ketchup mixture over the top and sides of the roast.
3 Roast, uncovered, in a 400°F oven about 1¼ hours or until meat thermometer registers 135°F. Transfer the roast to a cutting board. Cover and let stand for 15 minutes before slicing. The temperature of the roast after standing should be 145°F. Transfer onions to a bowl; cover and keep warm.
4 Add the water to reserved 2 tablespoons ketchup mixture; whisk in flour until smooth. Place roasting pan on stovetop over medium-high heat. Add broth; cook for 2 minutes, stirring and scraping up any brown bits from bottom of pan. Slowly whisk in flour mixture; cook and stir about 3 minutes or until thickened and bubbly. Pour gravy into serving bowl. Thinly slice roast. Serve with onions and gravy.
***Note:** While there's no true substitute for the rich, complex flavor of balsamic vinegar, in a pinch, you can use 1 tablespoon cider vinegar or red-wine vinegar plus ½ teaspoon sugar for each tablespoon of balsamic vinegar called for in a recipe.

PER SERVING 251 calories; 12 g fat (5 g sat.); 24 g protein; 7 g carbohydrate; 1 g fiber; 457 mg sodium; 60 mg cholesterol

Best-Ever Roast Beef

Beef & Sweet Potato Pan Roast

MAKES 6 servings
PREP 25 minutes **ROAST** 30 minutes **STAND** 10 minutes
OVEN 425°F

- **1 tablespoon dried Italian seasoning**
- **6 cloves garlic, minced**
- **1 teaspoon salt**
- **½ teaspoon crushed red pepper**
- **3 tablespoons olive oil**
- **2 pounds medium orange and/or white sweet potatoes, peeled and cut into 1-inch wedges**
- **4 6- to 8-ounce beef shoulder petite tenders or 1½- to 2-pound beef tenderloin***
- **1 cup cherry tomatoes**
- **1 recipe Chopped Parsley Topping**

1 In a small bowl stir together Italian seasoning, garlic, salt, and crushed red pepper. Stir in oil. Divide seasoning mixture between two large resealable plastic bags. Place sweet potatoes in one bag. Seal bag and shake to coat potatoes. Spread potatoes in a single layer in a greased shallow roasting pan. Roast, uncovered, in a 425°F oven for 15 minutes.

2 Meanwhile, place beef in the second bag. Seal bag and shake to coat beef. Remove beef from bag. In a large skillet brown meat over medium-high heat.

3 Stir sweet potatoes in roasting pan and push to edges of pan. Place beef in center of pan. Roast, uncovered, for 5 minutes. Add tomatoes; roast for 10 to 15 minutes more or until beef is desired doneness (145°F for medium rare to 160°F for medium). Cover and let stand for 10 minutes before slicing. Serve with Chopped Parsley Topping.

Chopped Parsley Topping: In a small bowl stir together ¼ cup snipped fresh parsley; 2 teaspoons finely shredded orange peel; 2 cloves garlic, minced; and ⅛ teaspoon salt.

***Note:** To substitute beef tenderloin for shoulder petite tenders, prepare potatoes and beef as directed, except do not roast potatoes before adding beef. Place brown tenderloin in center of greased roasting pan. Place potato wedges around pan edges. Roast, uncovered, 30 to 45 minutes or until desired doneness (145°F for medium rare to 160°F for medium). Let stand for 5 minutes before slicing.

PER SERVING 362 calories; 14 g fat (3 g sat.); 26 g protein; 32 g carbohydrate; 5 g fiber; 587 mg sodium; 65 mg cholesterol

Beef & Sweet Potato Pan Roast

The versatile beef shoulder petite tender is relatively new to the market. This juicy, lean cut from the top of the shoulder requires little or no marinating. Serve it roasted or grilled.

Mexican Beef & Tortillas

Mexican Beef & Tortillas  

MAKES 4 servings
START TO FINISH 20 minutes

- **8 6-inch corn tortillas**
- **1 17-ounce package refrigerated beef pot roast with juices**
- **1 14.5-ounce can diced tomatoes with green chilies, undrained**
- **1 green sweet pepper, cut into strips**
- **1 lime, cut into wedges**
- **Dairy sour cream (optional)**
- **Fresh cilantro sprigs (optional)**

1 Wrap tortillas in paper towels. Microwave on 100-percent power (high) 45 to 60 seconds or until warm. Cover and keep warm; set aside.

2 Microwave beef according to package directions. Meanwhile, place undrained tomatoes in a small saucepan; heat through.

3 Transfer beef to a cutting board, reserving juices. Slice beef across grain. Serve beef on tortillas with tomatoes, sweet pepper strips, and a drizzle of reserved juices. Pass lime wedges and, if desired, sour cream and cilantro.

PER SERVING 319 calories; 10 g fat (5 g sat.); 27 g protein; 34 g carbohydrate; 5 g fiber; 857 mg sodium; 64 mg cholesterol

Braised Short Ribs with Beets

MAKES 8 servings
PREP 20 minutes **COOK** 1½ hours

- 2 pounds boneless beef short ribs, cut into serving-size pieces
- 1 tablespoon cooking oil
- ¾ cup reduced-sodium chicken broth
- ½ teaspoon black pepper
- ½ teaspoon dried rosemary, crushed
- ½ teaspoon dried thyme, crushed
- ¼ teaspoon salt
- 16 baby red, pink, or golden beets, or 4 medium carrots, cut into 1-inch pieces
- 4 medium leeks
- 2 teaspoons finely shredded lemon peel
- 8 ounces fresh mushrooms, halved
- Reduced-sodium chicken broth (optional)
- ⅓ cup light dairy sour cream
- 1 tablespoon all-purpose flour

1 Trim fat from ribs. In a 4-quart Dutch oven brown ribs in hot oil over medium-high heat. Drain off fat. Add the ¾ cup chicken broth, the pepper, rosemary, thyme, and salt to the Dutch oven. Bring to boiling; reduce heat. Simmer, covered for 1 hour.

2 Meanwhile, remove beet roots and all but 1 inch of stems; wash beets well. Do not peel. Cut in half lengthwise. Remove any tough outer leaves from leeks. Trim roots from base. Cut away tops, leaving white portion. Slit lengthwise and wash well. Cut leeks crosswise into 2-inch slices; set aside.

3 Add beets and lemon peel to Dutch oven after 1 hour. Return to boiling; reduce heat. Cover and simmer for 20 minutes. Add mushrooms and leeks. Cover and simmer about 10 minutes more or until vegetables and ribs are tender. Using a slotted spoon, transfer ribs and vegetables to a platter, reserving juices in Dutch oven; keep warm.

4 Skim fat from juices. Measure 1 cup of the juices. If necessary, add enough chicken broth to equal 1 cup. Return to Dutch oven. In a small bowl stir together sour cream and flour. Stir into juices. Cook and stir over medium heat until thickened and bubbly. Cook and stir for 1 minute more. Spoon ribs and vegetables into serving bowls. Spoon sauce over ribs and vegetables.

PER SERVING 263 calories; 13 g fat (5 g sat.); 26 g protein; 12 g carbohydrate; 2 g fiber; 290 mg sodium; 55 mg cholesterol

Country Italian Beef

MAKES 6 to 8 servings
PREP 25 minutes **COOK** 8 to 10 hours (low) or 4 to 5 hours (high)

- 2 pounds boneless beef chuck pot roast
- 8 ounces tiny new potatoes, halved or quartered
- 2 medium carrots or parsnips, peeled and cut into 1- to 2-inch pieces
- 1 cup chopped onion (1 large)
- 1 medium fennel bulb, trimmed and cut into ½-inch wedges
- 1 teaspoon dried rosemary, crushed
- 1 14-ounce can beef broth
- 1 cup dry red wine or beef broth
- 1 6-ounce can tomato paste
- 2 tablespoons quick-cooking tapioca
- ½ teaspoon black pepper
- 4 cloves garlic, minced
- 1 to 2 cups fresh basil leaves, spinach leaves, or torn escarole

1 Trim fat from roast. Cut roast into 2-inch pieces. Set aside. In a 4- to 5-quart slow cooker combine potatoes, carrots, onion, and fennel. Add roast to cooker; sprinkle with rosemary.

2 In a medium bowl whisk together broth, wine, tomato paste, tapioca, pepper, and garlic. Pour over meat mixture in cooker.

3 Cover and cook on low-heat setting for 8 to 10 hours or on high-heat setting for 4 to 5 hours. Just before serving, stir in basil.

PER SERVING 327 calories; 6 g fat (2 g sat.); 37 g protein; 25 g carbohydrate; 4 g fiber; 609 mg sodium; 89 mg cholesterol

Country Italian Beef

Menu

Veal Chops with Mushroom Sauce
[below]

Garlic or regular mashed potatoes

Steamed broccolini or green beans

Mixed salad greens with berries and balsamic vinaigrette

Veal Chops with Mushroom Sauce

MAKES 4 servings
START TO FINISH 25 minutes

- **4** veal loin chops or pork loin chops, cut ¾ inch thick (about 1¾ pounds)
- Salt and black pepper
- **¾** cup sliced fresh mushrooms
- **2** tablespoons sliced green onion (1)
- **1** tablespoon butter
- **1** tablespoon all-purpose flour
- **2** teaspoons snipped fresh thyme or ¼ teaspoon dried thyme, crushed
- **1** cup half-and-half, light cream, or milk
- **2** tablespoons dry white wine or 1 tablespoon water plus 2 teaspoons Worcestershire sauce for chicken
- Salt and black pepper (optional)

1 Preheat broiler. Place chops on the unheated rack of a broiler pan. Sprinkle lightly with salt and pepper. Broil 3 to 4 inches from the heat until meat is 160°F, turning once halfway through broiling. For veal, allow 14 to 16 minutes for medium; for pork, allow 9 to 12 minutes.
2 Meanwhile, for sauce, in a medium saucepan cook mushrooms and green onion in hot butter until tender. Stir in flour and dried thyme (if using). Add half-and-half all at once. Cook and stir until thickened and bubbly. Cook and stir for 1 minute more. Stir in wine and fresh thyme (if using). If desired, season sauce with salt and pepper. To serve, spoon some of the sauce over the chops. Pass any remaining sauce.

PER SERVING 219 calories; 13 g fat (7 g sat.); 19 g protein; 5 g carbohydrate; 0 g fiber; 267 mg sodium; 97 mg cholesterol

Veal with Orange Sauce

MAKES 4 servings
START TO FINISH 25 minutes

- **2** medium oranges
- **12** ounces veal leg cutlets or boneless veal leg round steak or sirloin steak, cut ¼ inch thick
- **¼** teaspoon salt
- **¼** teaspoon black pepper
- **2** teaspoons olive oil
- **⅓** cup sliced green onion (3)
- **2** cloves garlic, minced
- **1** teaspoon grated fresh ginger
- **1** cup orange juice
- **1** tablespoon white wine vinegar
- **2** teaspoons cornstarch
- **¼** cup golden raisins
- **⅛** teaspoon salt

1 Finely shred ½ teaspoon peel from one of the oranges; set peel aside. Peel and section oranges, discarding seeds. Set orange sections aside.
2 Sprinkle veal with the ¼ teaspoon salt and the pepper. In a large nonstick skillet cook veal in hot oil over medium-high heat for 4 to 6 minutes or until brown, turning once. Remove from skillet; set aside. Add green onion, garlic, and ginger to drippings in skillet. Cook and stir over medium heat for 1 minute.
3 In a small bowl, stir together orange juice, vinegar, and cornstarch; add to skillet. Cook and stir until slightly thickened and bubbly. Add the orange peel, orange sections, raisins, and the ⅛ teaspoon salt to skillet. Toss gently to coat. Return veal to skillet; spoon sauce over veal. Heat through.

PER SERVING 196 calories; 4 g fat (1 g sat.); 19 g protein; 21 g carbohydrate; 2 g fiber; 265 mg sodium; 66 mg cholesterol

Lamb & Peppers 30

MAKES 4 servings
START TO FINISH 25 minutes

- 8 lamb rib or loin chops, cut 1 inch thick
- 3 small green, red, and/or yellow sweet peppers, cut into 1-inch pieces
- 2 cloves garlic, minced
- 1 tablespoon snipped fresh oregano
- 1 tablespoon olive oil or cooking oil
- ¼ cup sliced pitted green or ripe olives
- Fresh oregano sprigs (optional)

1 Preheat broiler. Place chops on the unheated rack of a broiler pan. Broil 3 to 4 inches from the heat for 10 to 15 minutes for medium (160°F), turning once halfway through broiling. Transfer chops to a serving platter.
2 Meanwhile, in a large skillet cook sweet peppers, garlic, and snipped oregano in hot oil over medium heat for 8 to 10 minutes or until sweet peppers are crisp-tender. Stir in olives. Cook and stir until heated through. Spoon pepper mixture over chops. If desired, garnish with oregano sprigs.

PER SERVING 186 calories; 10 g fat (2 g sat.); 20 g protein; 4 g carbohydrate; 1 g fiber; 257 mg sodium; 60 mg cholesterol

Lamb Chops with Tomatoes 30

MAKES 4 servings
START TO FINISH 20 minutes

- 8 lamb loin chops, cut 1 inch thick
- Salt and black pepper
- 1 8.8-ounce pouch cooked long grain rice
- 4 medium roma tomatoes, cut up
- 4 green onions, cut into 1-inch pieces
- 1 tablespoon snipped fresh oregano
- 1 tablespoon balsamic vinegar

1 Sprinkle chops with salt and pepper. For a charcoal grill, place chops on the grill rack directly over medium coals. Grill, uncovered, to desired doneness, turning once halfway through grilling. Allow 12 to 14 minutes for medium rare (145°F) and 15 to 17 minutes for medium doneness (160°F). (For a gas grill, preheat grill. Reduce heat to medium. Place chops on grill rack over heat. Cover and grill as above.)

2 Meanwhile, cook rice in the microwave according to package directions. In a food processor combine tomatoes, green onions, and oregano; pulse with on/off turns until coarsely chopped. Transfer tomato mixture to bowl; stir in vinegar. Season to taste with salt and pepper. Arrange chops on rice; top with tomato mixture.

PER SERVING 273 calories; 7 g fat (2 g sat.); 25 g protein; 26 g carbohydrate; 3 g fiber; 153 mg sodium; 70 mg cholesterol

Minted Lamb Chops

MAKES 4 servings
PREP 20 minutes **MARINATE** 4 to 24 hours **GRILL** 12 minutes

- **8 lamb rib chops, cut 1 inch thick**
- **¼ cup snipped fresh mint**
- **¼ cup lemon juice**
- **2 tablespoons cooking oil**
- **2 tablespoons water**
- **1 tablespoon grated fresh ginger**
- **1½ teaspoons paprika**
- **1 teaspoon ground cumin**
- **½ teaspoon salt**
- **⅛ teaspoon cayenne pepper**
- **1 large clove garlic, minced**
- **1 to 2 tablespoons finely shredded fresh mint**

1 Trim fat from chops. Place chops in a resealable plastic bag set in a shallow dish. For marinade, in a small bowl stir together the snipped mint, lemon juice, oil, the water, the ginger, paprika, cumin, salt, cayenne pepper, and garlic. Pour marinade over chops; seal bag. Turn to coat chops. Marinate in the refrigerator for 4 to 24 hours, turning bag occasionally.

2 Drain chops, discarding marinade. For a charcoal grill, place chops on the grill rack directly over medium coals. Grill, uncovered, to desired doneness, turning once halfway through grilling. Allow 12 to 14 minutes for medium rare (145°F) and 15 to 17 minutes for medium (160°F). (For a gas grill, preheat grill. Reduce heat to medium. Place chops on grill rack over heat. Cover and grill as above.)

3 Transfer chops to a serving platter. Sprinkle with the shredded mint.

Broiler Directions: Preheat broiler. Place chops on the unheated rack of a broiler pan. Broil 3 to 4 inches from the heat until desired doneness, turning once halfway through broiling. Allow 7 to 9 minutes for medium rare (145°F) or 10 to 15 minutes for medium (160°F).

PER SERVING 236 calories; 14 g fat (4 g sat.); 25 g protein; 1 g carbohydrate; 0 g fiber; 234 mg sodium; 80 mg cholesterol

Menu

Apple-Pecan Pork Chops [below]

Mashed new potatoes with skins

Buttered peas

Salad of Bibb lettuce, tomato wedges, and light blue cheese dressing

Apple-Pecan Pork Chops

Jamaican Pork Chops with Melon Salsa

MAKES 4 servings

PREP 15 minutes **CHILL** up to 8 hours **GRILL** 11 minutes

- **1 cup chopped honeydew melon**
- **1 cup chopped cantaloupe**
- **1 tablespoon snipped fresh mint**
- **1 tablespoon honey**
- **4 boneless pork top loin chops, cut ¾ to 1 inch thick**
- **4 teaspoons Jamaican jerk seasoning**
- **Fresh mint sprigs (optional)**

1 For melon salsa, in a medium bowl combine honeydew, cantaloupe, snipped mint, and honey. Cover and chill for up to 8 hours.

2 Trim fat from chops. Sprinkle Jamaican jerk seasoning evenly over both sides of each chop; rub in with your fingers. For a charcoal grill, place chops on the grill rack directly over medium coals. Grill, uncovered, for 11 to 14 minutes or until chops are slightly pink in center (160°F), turning once halfway through grilling. (For a gas grill, preheat grill. Reduce heat to medium. Place chops on grill rack over heat. Cover and grill as above.)

3 Serve melon salsa with grilled chops. If desired, garnish with mint sprigs.

PER SERVING 201 calories; 5 g fat (2 g sat.); 25 g protein; 12 g carbohydrate; 1 g fiber; 354 mg sodium; 62 mg cholesterol

Apple-Pecan Pork Chops  

MAKES 4 servings

START TO FINISH 20 minutes

- **4 boneless pork loin chops, cut ¾ to 1 inch thick**
- **Salt**
- **Black pepper**
- **2 tablespoons butter**
- **1 medium red apple, cored and thinly sliced**
- **¼ cup coarsely chopped pecans**
- **2 tablespoons packed brown sugar**

1 Trim fat from chops. Sprinkle with salt and pepper. Set aside.

2 In a large skillet melt butter over medium heat until it sizzles. Add apple; cook and stir for 2 minutes. Push apple to side of skillet. Add chops; cook for 4 minutes. Turn chops, moving apple aside as needed. Spoon apple over chops. Sprinkle with pecans and brown sugar.

3 Cook, covered, for 4 to 8 minutes more or until chops are slightly pink in center (160°F). Serve apples and cooking juices over chops.

PER SERVING 250 calories; 13 g fat (5 g sat.); 22 g protein; 12 g carbohydrate; 1 g fiber; 360 mg sodium; 66 mg cholesterol

Pork Chops with Red Cabbage & Pears 30

MAKES 6 servings
START TO FINISH 30 minutes

- ¼ cup cider vinegar
- 2 tablespoons packed brown sugar
- ¼ teaspoon dried sage, crushed
- 6 pork loin chops, cut ½ inch thick
- ½ teaspoon dried thyme, crushed
- ¼ teaspoon salt
- ¼ teaspoon dried sage, crushed
- ⅛ teaspoon black pepper
- 2 teaspoons canola oil
- 6 cups coarsely shredded red cabbage
- 1 cup sliced onion (1 medium)
- 2 medium pears, cored and sliced
- Snipped fresh sage and/or thyme (optional)

1 In a small bowl stir together cider vinegar, brown sugar, and the ¼ teaspoon sage. Reserve 1 tablespoon of the vinegar mixture. Set all aside.

2 Trim fat from chops. Sprinkle chops with thyme, salt, the ¼ teaspoon sage, and the pepper. In a very large skillet cook chops in hot oil over medium-high heat for 6 to 8 minutes or until chops are slightly pink in the center (160°F), turning chops once halfway through cooking and brushing with the 1 tablespoon vinegar mixture for the last 1 minute of cooking. Transfer chops to a platter; cover and keep warm.

3 Add cabbage and onion to skillet. Cook and stir over medium-high heat for 6 minutes. Add the remaining vinegar mixture and the pears to skillet. Bring to boiling; reduce heat. Simmer, covered, for 5 minutes. Top with chops; heat through. If desired, sprinkle chops with fresh sage.

PER SERVING 239 calories; 4 g fat (1 g sat.); 30 g protein; 20 g carbohydrate; 4 g fiber; 323 mg sodium; 70 mg cholesterol

Cranberry Pork Loin Chops 

MAKES 4 servings
START TO FINISH 20 minutes

- **4 boneless pork loin chops, cut ½ inch thick**
- **⅛ teaspoon salt**
- **⅛ teaspoon black pepper**
- **Nonstick cooking spray**
- **½ cup canned whole cranberry sauce**
- **2 tablespoons frozen orange juice concentrate, thawed**
- **1 tablespoon honey**
- **¼ teaspoon ground ginger**
- **⅛ teaspoon ground nutmeg**

1 Trim fat from chops. Sprinkle chops with salt and pepper. Lightly coat a large nonstick skillet with cooking spray. Cook chops in hot skillet over medium heat for 8 to 10 minutes or until chops are slightly pink in center (160°F), turning once. Remove chops from skillet; keep warm.
2 Meanwhile, in a small bowl stir together cranberry sauce, orange juice concentrate, honey, ginger, and nutmeg. Add cranberry mixture to skillet. Cook, uncovered, for 1 to 2 minutes or until slightly thickened. Spoon over chops.

PER SERVING 285 calories; 7 g fat (2 g sat.); 31 g protein; 21 g carbohydrate; 1 g fiber; 172 mg sodium; 89 mg cholesterol

Peppered Pork Chops with Mediterranean Relish

Peppered Pork Chops with Mediterranean Relish

MAKES 6 servings
PREP 10 minutes **MARINATE** 15 minutes **GRILL** 13 minutes

- **6 boneless pork top loin chops, cut ¾ inch thick**
- **1 6.5-ounce jar marinated artichoke hearts**
- **1 teaspoon bottled hot pepper sauce**
- **1½ cups chopped tomato (3 medium)**
- **½ cup bottled roasted red sweet peppers, drained and chopped**
- **¼ cup pitted ripe olives, sliced**
- **1 small fresh jalapeño chile pepper, seeded and finely chopped* (optional)**
- **Fresh oregano (optional)**

1 Trim fat from chops. Place chops in a large resealable plastic bag set in a shallow dish. Drain artichoke hearts, reserving marinade. Add hot pepper sauce to reserved marinade; pour over chops. Seal bag; turn to coat chops. Marinate in the refrigerator for 15 to 30 minutes.
2 For relish, coarsely chop artichoke hearts. In a medium bowl stir together the artichoke hearts, tomato, roasted sweet peppers, olives, and chile pepper (if using).
3 Drain chops, discarding marinade. For a charcoal grill, place chops on the grill rack directly over medium coals. Grill, uncovered, for 11 to 14 minutes or until chops are slightly pink in center (160°F), turning once halfway through grilling. (For a gas grill, preheat grill. Reduce heat to medium. Place chops on grill rack over heat. Cover and grill as above.)
4 Serve chops with relish. If desired, garnish with oregano.
***Note:** Because chile peppers contain volatile oils that can burn your skin and eyes, avoid direct contact with them as much as possible. When working with chile peppers, wear plastic or rubber gloves. If your bare hands do touch the chile peppers, wash your hands and nails well with soap and warm water.

PER SERVING 215 calories; 6 g fat (1 g sat.); 35 g protein; 6 g carbohydrate; 1 g fiber; 390 mg sodium; 83 mg cholesterol

Grilled Pork & Pineapple 

MAKES 4 servings
START TO FINISH 18 minutes

- **4 boneless pork top loin chops, cut ¾ inch thick**
- **Salt (optional)**
- **Black pepper**
- **1 peeled and cored fresh pineapple**
- **3 tablespoons orange marmalade**
- **½ cup plain yogurt**
- **¼ cup roasted, lightly salted cashew halves and/or pieces or toasted pecans, coarsely chopped**
- **Fresh thyme (optional)**

1 Sprinkle both sides of chops lightly with salt (if desired) and pepper. Cut pineapple crosswise into ½-inch slices; set aside.

2 For a charcoal grill, place chops on the grill rack directly over medium coals. Grill, uncovered, for 4 minutes. Turn; add pineapple to grill rack. Brush chops and pineapple with 2 tablespoons of the marmalade. Grill for 3 to 5 minutes more or until chops are slightly pink in center (160°F), turning pineapple once halfway through grilling. (For a gas grill, preheat grill. Reduce heat to medium. Place chops on grill rack over heat. Cover and grill as above).

3 Meanwhile, stir together yogurt and the remaining 1 tablespoon marmalade; season to taste with additional black pepper.

4 Arrange chops and pineapple on serving plates. Spoon yogurt mixture over chops and pineapple; sprinkle with nuts and, if desired, garnish with thyme.

PER SERVING 317 calories; 7 g fat (2 g sat.); 35 g protein; 29 g carbohydrate; 2 g fiber; 313 mg sodium; 80 mg cholesterol

Thai Pork Stir-Fry

You choose... brown or white rice.

Thai Pork Stir-Fry

MAKES 6 servings
START TO FINISH 30 minutes

- **2 tablespoons olive oil**
- **1 tablespoon reduced-sodium soy sauce**
- **½ teaspoon garlic powder**
- **½ teaspoon finely chopped fresh ginger or ¼ teaspoon ground ginger**
- **½ teaspoon black pepper**
- **½ teaspoon ground cardamom**
- **½ teaspoon chili powder**
- **1½ pounds lean boneless pork, cut into bite-size strips**
- **2 cups broccoli florets**
- **1 cup thinly sliced carrot (2 medium)**
- **1 cup cauliflower florets**
- **2 tablespoons white vinegar**
- **1 tablespoon curry powder**
- **2 cups hot cooked brown rice or white rice**

1 In a very large skillet stir together oil, soy sauce, garlic powder, ginger, pepper, cardamom, and chili powder. Add half of the pork; cook and stir pork over medium-high heat for 3 minutes. Remove pork from skillet. Repeat with remaining half of the pork. Return all pork to the skillet.
2 Add broccoli, carrot, cauliflower, vinegar, and curry powder to meat mixture. Bring to boiling; reduce heat. Simmer, covered, for 3 to 5 minutes or until vegetables are crisp-tender, stirring occasionally. Serve pork mixture over rice.

PER SERVING 301 calories; 11 g fat (3 g sat.); 28 g protein; 21 g carbohydrate; 3 g fiber; 206 mg sodium; 71 mg cholesterol

Mu Shu-Style Pork Roll-Ups 

MAKES 4 servings
START TO FINISH 20 minutes **OVEN** 350°F

- **4 10-inch flour tortillas**
- **1 teaspoon toasted sesame oil**
- **12 ounces lean boneless pork, cut into strips**
- **2 cups frozen stir-fry vegetables (any combination)**
- **¼ cup bottled plum or hoisin sauce**

1 Wrap tortillas tightly in foil. Heat in a 350°F oven for 10 minutes to soften. (Or wrap tortillas in paper towels and microwave on 100-percent power [high] for 45 to 60 seconds or until tortillas are warm.) Cover and keep warm; set aside.
2 Meanwhile, in a large skillet heat sesame oil over medium-high heat. Add pork strips; cook and stir for 2 to 3 minutes or until no longer pink. Add stir-fry vegetables; cook and stir for 3 to 4 minutes or until vegetables are crisp-tender.
3 Spread 1 tablespoon of the plum sauce on each tortilla. Spoon pork mixture evenly down centers of tortillas. Fold in the sides of the tortillas and roll up.

PER SERVING 296 calories; 8 g fat (2 g sat.); 22 g protein; 32 g carbohydrate; 1 g fiber; 325 mg sodium; 53 mg cholesterol

Mu Shu-Style Pork Roll-Ups

Pork Wraps with Corn-Tomato Relish
[right]

Fresh pear slices

Baked potato chips

Snickerdoodles
[page 286]

Pork Wraps with Corn-Tomato Relish

MAKES 10 wraps
PREP 50 minutes **GRILL** 30 minutes **STAND** 15 minutes

- **2 1-pound pork tenderloins**
- **Salt**
- **Black pepper**
- **2 tablespoons honey**
- **2 tablespoons Dijon-style mustard**
- **⅛ teaspoon ground cumin**
- **Shredded napa cabbage (optional)**
- **1 recipe Corn-Tomato Relish**
- **10 8- to 10-inch plain or flavored flour tortillas**

1 Trim fat from tenderloins. Sprinkle tenderloins with salt and pepper. In a small bowl stir together honey, mustard, and cumin; set aside.

2 For a charcoal grill, arrange hot coals around a drip pan. Test for medium-high heat above the pan. Place tenderloins on the grill rack over pan. Cover; grill for 30 to 35 minutes or until a meat thermometer registers 155°F, brushing with honey-mustard mixture the last 5 to 10 minutes of grilling. (For gas grill, preheat grill. Reduce heat to medium-high. Adjust for indirect cooking. Grill as above.)

3 Cover tenderloin with foil and let stand for 15 minutes. (The meat's temperature will rise to 160°F.) Slice tenderloin into thin bite-size strips. To serve, divide tenderloin strips, cabbage (if desired), and Corn-Tomato Relish among tortillas. Fold in the sides of tortillas and roll up.

Corn-Tomato Relish: Thaw one 16-ounce package frozen whole kernel corn; drain well and pat dry with paper towels, or use 3 cups fresh whole kernel corn. In a large skillet cook corn, ½ cup finely chopped red onion (1 small) and/or green onion (8), ¼ cup finely chopped celery or green sweet pepper, 1 teaspoon minced garlic, ¾ teaspoon salt, ½ teaspoon ground cumin or chili powder, and ⅛ teaspoon cayenne or black pepper in 2 tablespoons hot oil over medium heat about 10 minutes or until vegetables are tender, stirring occasionally. Remove from heat. Stir in ¾ cup finely chopped and seeded tomato (1 large), ¼ cup snipped fresh parsley, ¼ cup mayonnaise, and 1 tablespoon lime juice. Cover and chill for at least 1 hour or up to 24 hours.

PER WRAP 323 calories; 12 g fat (3 g sat.); 23 g protein; 30 g carbohydrate; 2 g fiber; 501 mg sodium; 62 mg cholesterol

Pork Wraps with Corn-Tomato Relish

Jamaican Pork Stir-Fry

Jamaican Pork Stir-Fry 

MAKES 4 servings
START TO FINISH 20 minutes

- **1 tablespoon cooking oil**
- **1 16-ounce package frozen yellow, green, and red peppers and onion stir-fry vegetables**
- **12 ounces pork strips for stir-frying***
- **2 to 3 teaspoons Jamaican jerk seasoning**
- **½ cup bottled plum sauce**
- **Soy sauce (optional)**
- **Peanuts (optional)**
- **2 cups hot cooked rice or pasta**

1 In a wok or large skillet heat oil over medium-high heat. Add frozen vegetables; cook and stir for 5 to 7 minutes or until vegetables are crisp-tender. Remove from wok.
2 Toss pork with jerk seasoning; add to hot wok. Add more oil if necessary. Cook and stir for 2 to 5 minutes or until pork is no longer pink.
3 Add plum sauce and return vegetables to wok; toss gently to coat and heat through. If desired, season with soy sauce and sprinkle with peanuts. Serve over rice.
***Note:** If you can't find pork strips, cut your own from boneless pork loin.

PER SERVING 357 calories; 9 g fat (2 g sat.); 22 g protein; 45 g carbohydrate; 2 g fiber; 405 mg sodium; 54 mg cholesterol

Sweet Pepper & Olive Pork

Pork tenderloin is often found vacuum-packed with two per package. If the recipe you are making calls for only one pork tenderloin, place the other in a freezer bag and store it in the freezer for up to six months.

Sweet Pepper & Olive Pork 

MAKES 4 servings
START TO FINISH 30 minutes

- 1 **12-ounce pork tenderloin**
- **Nonstick cooking spray**
- 1½ **cups coarsely chopped green sweet pepper (2 medium)**
- 1 **cup coarsely chopped onion (2 medium)**
- ½ **cup sliced fresh mushrooms**
- ½ **teaspoon ground cumin**
- 2 **cloves garlic, minced**
- ⅓ **cup chopped pimiento-stuffed green olives**
- ⅛ **teaspoon salt**
- ⅛ **teaspoon black pepper**
- 2 **teaspoons olive oil**

1 Trim fat from pork. Cut pork crosswise into 8 pieces. Press each piece in the palm of your hand to make it 1 inch thick. Set aside.
2 Lightly coat a large nonstick skillet with cooking spray. Cook sweet pepper, onion, mushrooms, cumin, and garlic in hot skillet over medium heat about 4 minutes or until crisp-tender. Stir in olives; heat through. Transfer vegetable mixture to a serving platter; keep warm.
3 Sprinkle pork slices with salt and black pepper. Cook pork slices, half at a time, in the same skillet in hot oil over medium-high heat for 2 to 3 minutes or until pork slices are slightly pink in center, turning once. Arrange the pork slices on top of vegetable mixture.

PER SERVING 171 calories; 9 g fat (2 g sat.); 14 g protein; 9 g carbohydrate; 2 g fiber; 342 mg sodium; 38 mg cholesterol

Pork Tenderloin with Nutty Pear Stuffing

MAKES 4 servings
PREP 20 minutes **ROAST** 35 minutes **OVEN** 425°F

- ½ **cup chopped pear**
- ¼ **cup chopped hazelnuts (filberts) or almonds, toasted**
- ¼ **cup finely shredded carrot**
- ¼ **cup soft bread crumbs**
- 2 **tablespoons chopped onion**
- 1 **teaspoon grated fresh ginger**
- ¼ **teaspoon salt**
- ¼ **teaspoon black pepper**
- 1 **12-ounce pork tenderloin**
- 1 **teaspoon cooking oil**
- 2 **tablespoons orange marmalade**

1 For stuffing, in a small bowl stir together pear, nuts, carrot, bread crumbs, onion, ginger, salt, and pepper; set aside.
2 Trim fat from pork. Make a lengthwise slit down the center of the tenderloin to within ½ inch of the underside. Open flat; pound with the flat side of a meat mallet to about ¼-inch thickness.
3 Spread stuffing evenly over pork. Fold in ends. Starting from a long side, roll up pork. Tie with 100-percent-cotton string to secure. Place meat roll on a rack in a shallow roasting pan. Brush lightly with oil. Insert an oven-going meat thermometer into center of meat roll.
4 Roast in a 425°F oven for 30 to 40 minutes or until meat thermometer registers 155°F. Brush orange marmalade over top of meat. Roast about 5 minutes more or until meat thermometer registers 160°F.

PER SERVING 198 calories; 9 g fat (1 g sat.); 20 g protein; 10 g carbohydrate; 2 g fiber; 193 mg sodium; 55 mg cholesterol

Pork Medallions with Lemon-Pecan Spinach 30

MAKES 4 servings
START TO FINISH 20 minutes

- 1 pound pork tenderloin
- ¼ teaspoon salt
- ¼ teaspoon coarsely ground black pepper
- 1 tablespoon canola oil
- 2 tablespoons lemon juice
- ⅛ teaspoon bottled hot pepper sauce
- 1 10-ounce package frozen chopped spinach, thawed and well drained
- ¼ cup sliced green onion (2)
- 2 tablespoons chopped pecans
- 1 tablespoon snipped fresh parsley
- ⅛ teaspoon salt
- Lemon slices, halved (optional)

1 Trim fat from pork. Cut pork crosswise into 8 pieces. Press each piece in the palm of your hand to make it 1 inch thick. Sprinkle pork lightly with the ¼ teaspoon salt and the pepper. In a large skillet cook the pork in hot oil over medium-high heat for 6 to 8 minutes or until pork is slightly pink in center, turning once halfway through cooking. Remove pork from skillet, reserving drippings in the skillet. Cover pork and keep warm.

2 Stir lemon juice and hot pepper sauce into reserved drippings in skillet. Stir in spinach, green onion, pecans, parsley, and the ⅛ teaspoon salt. Cook over low heat until spinach mixture is heated through. Place spinach mixture on serving plate; arrange pork on top. If desired, garnish with lemon slices.

PER SERVING 213 calories; 10 g fat (2 g sat.); 27 g protein; 5 g carbohydrate; 3 g fiber; 318 mg sodium; 73 mg cholesterol

Pork Medallions with Lemon-Pecan Spinach

Cornmeal-Crusted Pork  

MAKES 4 servings
START TO FINISH 20 minutes

- **1 pound pork tenderloin**
- **½ cup yellow cornmeal**
- **½ teaspoon salt**
- **½ teaspoon black pepper**
- **1 egg, lightly beaten**
- **1 tablespoon water**
- **2 tablespoons olive oil or cooking oil**
- **12 ounces fresh green beans, trimmed**
- **2½ cups thinly bias-sliced zucchini and/or yellow summer squash (2 medium)**
- **2 tablespoons fresh oregano leaves**

1 Trim fat from pork. Cut pork crosswise into ½-inch slices. Set aside. In a shallow dish stir together cornmeal, salt, and pepper. In another shallow dish combine egg and water. Dip pork in egg mixture, then coat with cornmeal mixture.

2 In a very large skillet cook pork slices in hot oil over medium-high heat for 4 to 5 minutes or until pork slices are slightly pink in center, turning once. Transfer pork to a serving platter; keep warm.

3 Add beans and zucchini to skillet; cook and stir for 6 to 8 minutes or until crisp-tender. Season to taste with additional salt and pepper. Serve vegetables with pork slices. Sprinkle with oregano.

PER SERVING 310 calories; 13 g fat (3 g sat.); 29 g protein; 21 g carbohydrate; 5 g fiber; 385 mg sodium; 127 mg cholesterol

Cornmeal-Crusted Pork

Pork with Parsnips & Pears

Pork with Parsnips & Pears

MAKES 8 to 10 servings
PREP 30 minutes **COOK** 11 to 12 hours (low) or 5½ to 6 hours (high)

- **1½ pounds parsnips and/or carrots, peeled and cut into 1½- to 2-inch pieces***
- **2 medium pears, peeled, quartered, and cored (stems intact, if desired)**
- **2 tablespoons quick-cooking tapioca**
- **1 2½- to 3-pound boneless pork top loin roast (single loin)**
- **1 tablespoon cooking oil**
- **6 cloves garlic, minced**
- **1 teaspoon dried rosemary, crushed**
- **1 teaspoon dried thyme, crushed**
- **½ teaspoon salt**
- **¼ teaspoon black pepper**
- **½ cup port wine or apple juice**
- **Salt and black pepper**

1 Place parsnips and pears in a 5- to 6-quart slow cooker; sprinkle with tapioca. In a large skillet brown pork on all sides in hot oil over medium-high heat. Place pork on top of parsnips and pears in cooker. Sprinkle pork with garlic, rosemary, thyme, the ½ teaspoon salt, and the ¼ teaspoon pepper. Pour wine over all in cooker.
2 Cover and cook on low-heat setting for 11 to 12 hours or on high-heat setting for 5½ to 6 hours.
3 Transfer pork to a serving platter, reserving cooking liquid. Use a slotted spoon to transfer parsnips and pears to serving platter. Slice pork. Season sauce to taste with additional salt and pepper. Serve reserved cooking liquid with pork and vegetables.
***Note:** Cut any thick parsnip or carrot pieces in half lengthwise.

PER SERVING 340 calories; 9 g fat (3 g sat.); 32 g protein; 27 g carbohydrate; 6 g fiber; 292 mg sodium; 78 mg cholesterol

Pork with Hot Pear Relish

MAKES 8 servings
PREP 30 minutes **COOK** 12 minutes **ROAST** 1¼ hours
STAND 15 minutes **OVEN** 350°F

- **1 cup finely chopped sweet onion (1 large)**
- **¾ cup finely chopped red sweet pepper (1 medium)**
- **1 fresh jalapeño chile pepper, seeded and finely chopped***
- **1 tablespoon olive oil**
- **2 cups chopped peeled firm ripe pears (2 medium)**
- **½ cup sugar**
- **½ cup white balsamic vinegar**
- **1 teaspoon dry mustard**
- **¼ teaspoon salt**
- **1 2- to 2½-pound boneless pork top loin roast (single loin)**
- **Salt and black pepper**

1 For relish, in a large skillet cook onion, sweet pepper, and jalapeño pepper in hot oil over medium heat for 2 minutes. Stir in pears, sugar, vinegar, mustard, and salt. Bring to boiling over medium-high heat, stirring occasionally; reduce heat. Simmer, uncovered, 10 minutes or until pears are soft.
2 Place pork on a rack in a shallow roasting pan. Insert an oven-going meat thermometer into center of roast. Sprinkle with salt and pepper. Roast, uncovered, in a 350°F oven for 1 hour. Top with ½ cup of the relish. Roast for 15 to 30 minutes more or until meat thermometer registers 150°F.
3 Cover pork with foil and let stand for 15 minutes. The temperature of the pork after standing should be 160°F. Slice pork and serve with remaining pear relish.
***Note:** Because hot chile peppers contain volatile oils that can burn your skin and eyes, avoid direct contact with them as much as possible. When working with chile peppers, wear plastic or rubber gloves. If your bare hands do touch the chile peppers, wash your hands well with soap and water.

PER SERVING 309 calories; 11 g fat (3 g sat.); 25 g protein; 26 g carbohydrate; 2 g fiber; 174 mg sodium; 74 mg cholesterol

Menu

Roasted Pork with Peach Sauce [below]

Steamed broccoli or asparagus

Salad of romaine with cucumber slices, feta cheese crumbles, and vinaigrette

Apple-Cranberry Crisp [page 296]

Roasted Pork with Peach Sauce

MAKES 8 servings
PREP 10 minutes **COOK** 6 hours (low) or 3 hours (high)
STAND 10 minutes

- **Nonstick cooking spray**
- **1 3-pound boneless pork top loin roast (double loin, tied)**
- **¼ teaspoon onion salt**
- **¼ teaspoon black pepper**
- **1 15.25-ounce can sliced peaches in heavy syrup**
- **½ cup bottled chili sauce**
- **⅓ cup packed light brown sugar**
- **3 tablespoons apple cider vinegar**
- **1 teaspoon pumpkin pie spice**
- **1 tablespoon cornstarch mixed with 2 tablespoons water**
- **Hot cooked egg noodles (optional)**

1 Coat a 6-quart slow cooker with cooking spray. Place pork in cooker; sprinkle with onion salt and pepper.
2 Drain peaches, reserving the syrup. Combine the reserved syrup, the chili sauce, brown sugar, vinegar, and pumpkin pie spice. Pour over pork; scatter peaches over pork.
3 Cover and cook on low-heat setting for 6 hours or on high-heat setting for 3 hours.
4 Transfer pork to a cutting board. Cover with foil and let stand for 10 minutes. Using a slotted spoon, remove peach slices from cooker; set aside and keep warm. Place cooking liquid in a small saucepan; bring to a boil. Stir in cornstarch mixture; heat and stir about 30 seconds until sauce is thickened and bubbly.
5 To serve, slice pork and spoon reserved peach slices over slices. Serve with sauce and, if desired, egg noodles.

PER SERVING 363 calories; 12 g fat (5 g sat.); 37 g protein; 25 g carbohydrate; 1 g fiber; 368 mg sodium; 103 mg cholesterol

Boneless Pork Loin Roast with Herbed Pepper Rub

MAKES 12 servings
PREP 15 minutes **ROAST** 1¼ hours **STAND** 15 minutes
OVEN 350°F

- **2 tablespoons grated Parmesan cheese**
- **1 to 2 tablespoons coarsely ground black pepper**
- **2 teaspoons dried basil, crushed**
- **2 teaspoons dried rosemary, crushed**
- **2 teaspoons dried thyme, crushed**
- **¼ teaspoon garlic powder**
- **¼ teaspoon salt**
- **1 3-pound boneless pork top loin roast (single loin)**
- **1 recipe Black-Eyed Pea Salsa**
- **Lemon wedges (optional)**
- **Fresh thyme sprigs (optional)**

1 Preheat oven to 350°F. For rub, in a small bowl stir together Parmesan cheese, pepper, basil, rosemary, dried thyme, garlic powder, and salt.
2 On a sheet of waxed paper, sprinkle rub in an even layer. Roll roast in rub to coat on all sides. Place roast on a rack in a shallow roasting pan. Insert an oven-going meat thermometer into center of roast. Roast in a 350°F oven for 1¼ to 1½ hours or until meat thermometer registers 150°F. Cover roast with foil and let stand for 15 minutes. The temperature of the roast after standing should be 160°F.
3 Slice roast and serve with cold or hot Black-Eyed Pea Salsa. If desired, garnish with lemon wedges and fresh thyme.

Black-Eyed Pea Salsa: In a medium bowl stir together two 15-ounce cans black-eyed peas, rinsed and drained; one 16-ounce jar salsa; ½ cup sliced green onion (4); and ½ teaspoon coarsely ground black pepper. Cover and chill until serving time. (Or, if desired, place salsa in a medium saucepan; bring just to boiling over medium heat. Remove from heat; cover to keep warm.)

PER SERVING 242 calories; 6 g fat (2 g sat.); 30 g protein; 15 g carbohydrate; 4 g fiber; 528 mg sodium; 63 mg cholesterol

The herb crust locks in juices so you can serve pork that's deliciously moist.

Boneless Pork Loin Roast with Herbed Pepper Rub

Saucy Apple Pork Roast 

MAKES 10 to 12 servings

PREP 15 minutes **ROAST** 2 hours **STAND** 15 minutes **OVEN** 325°F

- **1 3½- to 4-pound boneless pork top loin roast (double loin, tied)**
- **3 cloves garlic, cut into thin slices**
- **1 teaspoon coarse salt or salt**
- **1 teaspoon dried rosemary, crushed**
- **½ teaspoon coarsely ground black pepper**
- **3 medium apples, cored and cut into wedges**
- **¼ cup apple juice or apple cider**
- **2 tablespoons packed brown sugar**
- **2 tablespoons lemon juice**
- **2 teaspoons dry mustard**

1 Trim fat from roast. Cut small slits (about ½ inch wide and 1 inch deep) in roast; insert a piece of garlic in each slit. In a small bowl stir together salt, rosemary, and pepper. Sprinkle rosemary mixture evenly over roast; rub in with your fingers. Place roast on a rack in a shallow roasting pan. Insert an oven-going meat thermometer into center of roast. Roast in a 325°F oven about 2 hours or until meat thermometer registers 150°F.

2 Meanwhile, in a large bowl combine apples, apple juice, brown sugar, lemon juice, and mustard. Add apple mixture to roasting pan for the last 30 minutes of roasting.

3 Transfer roast to a serving platter. Cover roast with foil and let stand for 15 minutes. The temperature of the roast after standing should be 160°F.

4 While roast stands, remove rack from roasting pan. Stir apple wedges into pan juices. Serve roast with apple mixture.

PER SERVING 262 calories; 8 g fat (3 g sat.); 35 g protein; 10 g carbohydrate; 1 g fiber; 252 mg sodium; 87 mg cholesterol

Saucy Apple Pork Roast

Spicy Maple-Glazed Pork Loin

MAKES 8 servings

PREP 35 minutes **GRILL** 2 hours **STAND** 15 minutes

- **¾ cup beer (½ of a 12-ounce can)**
- **¼ cup maple-flavored syrup or mild-flavored molasses**
- **1 to 2 canned chipotle chile peppers in adobo sauce, finely chopped***
- **2 tablespoons creamy peanut butter**
- **1 tablespoon Worcestershire sauce**
- **2 teaspoons Dijon-style mustard**
- **½ teaspoon ground cinnamon**
- **2 cloves garlic, minced**
- **1 4- to 5-pound pork loin center rib roast (backbone loosened**)**
- **¼ teaspoon salt**
- **¼ teaspoon black pepper**

1 For glaze, in a small saucepan stir together beer, syrup, chipotle peppers, peanut butter, Worcestershire sauce, mustard, cinnamon, and garlic. Bring to boiling; reduce heat. Simmer, uncovered, for 20 to 30 minutes or until desired consistency, stirring occasionally. Set aside.

2 Meanwhile, trim fat from roast. Sprinkle roast with salt and pepper.

3 For a charcoal grill, arrange medium-hot coals around a drip pan. Test for medium heat above pan. Place roast, bone side down, on grill rack over pan. Cover and grill for 2 to 2¾ hours or until a meat thermometer registers 150°F, brushing with glaze during the last 20 minutes of grilling. (For a gas grill, preheat grill. Reduce heat to medium. Adjust for indirect cooking. Grill as above.)

4 Remove roast from grill. Cover roast with foil and let stand for 15 minutes. The temperature of the roast after standing should be 160°F.

***Note:** Because chile peppers contain volatile oils that can burn your skin and eyes, avoid direct contact with them as much as possible. When working with chile peppers, wear plastic or rubber gloves. If your bare hands do touch the chile peppers, wash your hands and nails well with soap and warm water.

****Note:** Ask your butcher to loosen the backbone for you.

PER SERVING 378 calories; 13 g fat (4 g sat.); 51 g protein; 10 g carbohydrate; 0 g fiber; 264 mg sodium; 142 mg cholesterol

Cajun Pork

Cajun Pork

MAKES 6 to 8 servings
PREP 20 minutes **COOK** 7 to 8 hours (low) or 3½ to 4 hours (high) + 30 minutes

- **2½ to 3 pounds boneless pork shoulder**
- **Nonstick cooking spray**
- **2 medium yellow sweet peppers, cut into 1-inch pieces**
- **1 tablespoon Cajun seasoning**
- **1 14.5-ounce can diced tomatoes with green pepper and onion, undrained**
- **1 16-ounce package frozen cut okra**
- **1 6-ounce package quick-cooking brown rice**
- **Bottled hot pepper sauce (optional)**

1 Trim fat from pork. Cut pork into 1-inch pieces. Lightly coat a large skillet with cooking spray. In hot skillet brown pork, half at a time, over medium heat. Drain off fat.
2 Transfer pork to a 3½- or 4-quart slow cooker. Add sweet peppers to cooker. Sprinkle with Cajun seasoning and top with undrained tomatoes.
3 Cover and cook on low-heat setting for 7 to 8 hours or on high-heat setting for 3½ to 4 hours.
4 If using low-heat setting, turn to high-heat setting. Stir in frozen okra. Cover and cook for 30 minutes more. Meanwhile, cook rice according to package directions. Serve pork mixture over rice. If desired, pass hot pepper sauce.

PER SERVING 233 calories; 8 g fat (3 g sat.); 25 g protein; 15 g carbohydrate; 4 g fiber; 444 mg sodium; 77 mg cholesterol

German in nature, this slow-cooked meal showcases pork ribs that are fall-apart tender.

Ribs & Kraut

Ribs & Kraut

MAKES 6 to 8 servings
PREP 20 minutes **COOK** 7 to 8 hours (low) or 3½ to 4 hours (high)

- **1 14-ounce can sauerkraut, drained**
- **2 cups sliced sweet onion (1 large)**
- **2 cups sliced, peeled and cored tart cooking apples (2 medium)**
- **2 pounds boneless pork country-style ribs**
- **1 cup apple juice**
- **Snipped fresh chives**

1 In a 4- or 4½-quart slow cooker combine drained sauerkraut, onion, and apples. Top with ribs. Pour apple juice over all in cooker.
2 Cover and cook on low-heat setting for 7 to 8 hours or on high-heat setting for 3½ to 4 hours. Use a slotted spoon to transfer ribs, onion, and apple to serving platter. Sprinkle each serving with chives.

PER SERVING 312 calories; 12 g fat (4 g sat.); 30 g protein; 19 g carbohydrate; 4 g fiber; 541 mg sodium; 96 mg cholesterol

Pulled Pork & Peaches 

MAKES 20 servings
PREP 20 minutes **COOK** 8 to 10 hours (low) or 4 to 5 hours (high)

- **1 3- to 4-pound boneless pork shoulder roast**
- **3 medium onions, cut into wedges**
- **½ teaspoon salt**
- **½ teaspoon black pepper**
- **6 cloves garlic, minced**
- **2 12- to 16-ounce packages frozen peaches**
- **1 cup ginger ale**
- **1 28-ounce can diced tomatoes with basil, garlic, and oregano, drained**
- **20 hamburger buns, split**
- **Lettuce leaves (optional)**
- **Sliced peaches (optional)**

1 Trim fat from pork. If necessary, cut pork to fit in a 5- to 6-quart slow cooker. Place onions in cooker. Place pork on onions in cooker. Sprinkle pork with salt and pepper. Add garlic, peaches, and ginger ale to cooker.
2 Cover and cook on low-heat setting for 8 to 10 hours or on high-heat setting for 4 to 5 hours.
3 Transfer pork to a cutting board. Using two forks, pull pork apart into bite-size pieces. Return pork to cooker. Add drained tomatoes. Stir to combine. Keep warm on warm setting, if available, or low setting.
4 If desired, line buns with lettuce leaves. Use a slotted spoon to spoon meat mixture on lettuce-lined buns. If desired, top with additional sliced peaches.

PER SERVING 339 calories; 14 g fat (5 g sat.); 17 g protein; 36 g carbohydrate; 2 g fiber; 517 mg sodium; 48 mg cholesterol

Wheelie Ham Salad 

MAKES 4 servings
PREP 25 minutes **CHILL** 2 to 24 hours

- **4 ounces dried wagon wheel pasta (1½ cups)**
- **4 ounces cooked lean ham, cut into bite-size pieces**
- **1 small zucchini, quartered lengthwise and sliced**
- **2 tablespoons sliced green onion (1) (optional)**
- **⅓ cup bottled reduced-fat ranch salad dressing**
- **2 tablespoons plain low-fat yogurt**
- **1 teaspoon dried basil, crushed**
- **¾ cup grape or cherry tomatoes, halved**

1 Cook pasta according to package directions; drain. Rinse pasta with cold water; drain again. In a large bowl combine cooked pasta, ham, zucchini, and, if desired, green onion.
2 In a small bowl stir together salad dressing, yogurt, and basil. Pour dressing over pasta mixture. Toss lightly to coat. Cover and chill for 2 to 24 hours. Before serving, gently stir tomatoes into pasta mixture.

PER SERVING 214 calories; 8 g fat (1 g sat.); 10 g protein; 27 g carbohydrate; 2 g fiber; 596 mg sodium; 23 mg cholesterol

Wheelie Ham Salad *(above)* is a great way to feed your kids the foods they love—pasta, ham, and ranch salad dressing—while sneaking in a veggie or two. If zucchini doesn't top their list of favorites, try sliced carrots, sliced mushrooms, peas, or sweet pepper strips.

Greens, Beans & Ham 

MAKES 4 servings
PREP 10 minutes **COOK** 8 minutes

- **2 15-ounce cans Great Northern beans**
- **6 cloves garlic, minced**
- **1 tablespoon olive oil**
- **2 cups cooked smoked ham, cut into bite-size strips**
- **3 cups chopped fresh spinach or one 10-ounce package frozen spinach, thawed and well drained**

1 Drain beans, reserving liquid. In a large nonstick skillet cook garlic in hot oil over medium heat for 1 minute. Add beans and ham to skillet. Cook about 5 minutes or until heated through, stirring occasionally. Stir in spinach; cover and cook for 2 to 5 minutes more or until fresh greens are wilted or frozen spinach is heated through. If desired, thin mixture with some of the reserved bean liquid.

PER SERVING 353 calories; 6 g fat (1 g sat.); 27 g protein; 51 g carbohydrate; 11 g fiber; 537 mg sodium; 12 mg cholesterol

Greens, Beans & Ham

Baked Ratatouille-Sausage Penne

MAKES 6 servings
PREP 30 minutes **BAKE** 35 minutes **OVEN** 350°F

- 3 uncooked turkey Italian sausage links (12 ounces total)
- 4 cloves garlic, minced
- 1 teaspoon olive oil
- 1 14.5-ounce can no-salt-added diced tomatoes, undrained
- 3 tablespoons snipped fresh parsley
- ¼ teaspoon crushed red pepper (optional)
- 1 pound eggplant, peeled and cut into ½-inch cubes
- 6 ounces dried whole wheat penne pasta (about 2¼ cups)
- ⅓ cup finely shredded Parmesan cheese
- Snipped fresh parsley (optional)

1 Place sausage links in an unheated skillet. Add ½ inch of water to the skillet. Bring to boiling; reduce heat. Simmer, covered, about 15 minutes or until juices run clear; drain off liquid. Cook sausages for 2 to 4 minutes more or until brown, turning occasionally. Remove from heat. When cool enough to handle, cut sausages in half lengthwise; bias-cut into ½-inch slices. Set aside.
2 In a large skillet cook garlic in hot oil over medium heat for 1 minute. Stir in undrained tomatoes, the 3 tablespoons parsley, and, if desired, the crushed red pepper. Bring to boiling. Stir in eggplant. Reduce heat. Simmer, covered, for 15 minutes.
3 Meanwhile, cook pasta according to package directions, cooking it for the minimum time listed; drain. Return pasta to hot pan. Stir in eggplant mixture and sausage. Spoon pasta mixture into a 2-quart rectangular baking dish.
4 Bake, covered, in a 350°F oven about 30 minutes or until heated through. Sprinkle with cheese. Uncover and bake about 5 minutes more or until cheese melts. If desired, sprinkle with additional parsley.

PER SERVING 251 calories; 8 g fat (2 g sat.); 17 g protein; 30 g carbohydrate; 6 g fiber; 559 mg sodium; 39 mg cholesterol

Baked Ratatouille-Sausage Penne

Crusty Pepperoni Pizza 

MAKES 8 servings
PREP 5 minutes **BAKE** 12 minutes **OVEN** 400°F

- 1 loaf Italian bread
- ½ cup jarred pizza sauce
- 2 cups shredded mozzarella cheese (8 ounces)
- 24 slices pepperoni

1 Slice Italian bread in half lengthwise, then cut in half crosswise to make four pieces. Cut each piece in half to make eight pieces total. Spread pizza sauce evenly on cut sides of bread pieces. Top each with ¼ cup cheese and 3 slices of pepperoni.
2 Bake, uncovered, in a 400°F oven about 12 minutes or until cheese melts. Serve immediately.

PER SERVING 214 calories; 11 g fat (6 g sat.); 11 g protein; 16 g carbohydrate; 1 g fiber; 487 mg sodium; 35 mg cholesterol

page 205

page 195

Make-'em-Main

Meatless Dishes

Roasting caramelizes the veggies

Orzo Risotto with Roasted Vegetables

to perfection.

Orzo Risotto with Roasted Vegetables

MAKES 4 servings
START TO FINISH 45 minutes **OVEN** 425°F

- **Nonstick cooking spray**
- **½ 2-pound butternut squash, peeled, seeded, and cut into ¾- to 1-inch cubes**
- **⅛ teaspoon black pepper**
- **3 cups halved button or cremini mushrooms (8 ounces)**
- **1 large onion, cut into thin wedges**
- **1 tablespoon snipped fresh rosemary or oregano or 1 teaspoon dried rosemary or oregano, crushed**
- **1 tablespoon olive oil**
- **2 14-ounce cans reduced-sodium chicken broth**
- **8 ounces dried whole wheat orzo (1⅓ cups)**
- **2 cloves garlic, minced**
- **¼ cup chopped walnuts, toasted**
- **¼ cup crumbled feta cheese (optional)**

1 Coat a 15×10×1-inch baking pan with cooking spray. Place squash pieces in pan. Sprinkle with pepper. Bake, covered, in a 425°F oven for 10 minutes. Uncover; add mushrooms, onion, rosemary, and oil; toss to coat. Roast, uncovered, for 15 to 20 minutes or until vegetables are tender and light brown, stirring once or twice.
2 Meanwhile, in a medium saucepan bring broth to boiling; reduce heat. Cover and simmer. Coat a large skillet with cooking spray. Cook orzo and garlic in hot skillet over medium heat for 2 to 3 minutes or until orzo is light brown, stirring frequently. Remove from heat.
3 Add ½ cup hot broth to orzo mixture. Return to heat. Cook, stirring frequently, over medium heat until liquid is absorbed. Continue adding broth to orzo mixture, ½ cup at a time, stirring frequently until liquid is absorbed before adding more. Cook and stir about 15 minutes or until orzo is tender and creamy.
4 Add roasted vegetables and walnuts to orzo mixture, stirring gently to combine. Sprinkle each serving with feta cheese.

PER SERVING 385 calories; 9 g fat (1 g sat.); 15 g protein; 64 g carbohydrate; 6 g fiber; 471 mg sodium; 0 mg cholesterol

Vegetable Curry

Vegetable Curry 

MAKES 4 servings
PREP 10 minutes **COOK** 8 minutes

- **1 16-ounce package frozen baby lima beans**
- **½ cup water**
- **1 15-ounce can tomato sauce with garlic and onion**
- **1½ teaspoons curry powder**
- **2 8.8-ounce pouches cooked Spanish-style rice**
- **¼ cup sliced green onion (2) or snipped fresh cilantro**
- **Olive oil (optional)**

1 In a medium saucepan combine beans and water. Bring to boiling; reduce heat. Simmer, covered, for 5 minutes. Stir in tomato sauce and curry powder. Return to boiling; reduce heat. Simmer, covered, for 3 minutes.
2 Meanwhile, heat rice according to package directions. Spoon rice on one side of four dinner plates; spoon bean mixture alongside rice. Sprinkle with green onion. Drizzle oil over all.

PER SERVING 385 calories; 3 g fat (0 g sat.); 14 g protein; 72 g carbohydrate; 9 g fiber; 939 mg sodium; 0 mg cholesterol

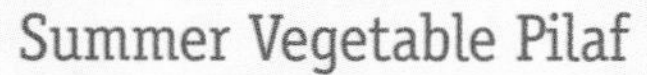

Summer Vegetable Pilaf

MAKES 4 servings
PREP 25 minutes **COOK** 20 minutes **STAND** 5 minutes

- **1 14-ounce can vegetable broth**
- **½ cup chopped onion (1 medium)**
- **½ cup dry lentils, rinsed and drained**
- **½ cup uncooked long grain white rice**
- **¼ cup water**
- **1 teaspoon finely shredded lemon peel**
- **1½ cups small fresh broccoli florets, sliced zucchini or yellow summer squash, and/or fresh snow or sugar snap pea pods**
- **1 medium carrot, cut into thin strips**
- **½ small eggplant, peeled and diced**
- **2 cloves garlic, minced**
- **2 teaspoons olive oil**
- **1 cup chopped roma tomato (3 medium)**
- **¼ cup snipped fresh basil**
- **¼ cup finely shredded Asiago or Parmesan cheese (1 ounce)**

1 In a large saucepan combine broth, onion, lentils, rice, water, and lemon peel. Bring to boiling; reduce heat. Simmer, covered, for 20 minutes, adding broccoli and carrot during the last 3 to 5 minutes of cooking.
2 Meanwhile, in a large skillet cook the eggplant and garlic in hot oil over medium heat about 5 minutes or until the eggplant is soft.
3 Remove lentil mixture from heat; let stand, covered, for 5 minutes. Carefully stir in the eggplant mixture, tomato, and basil. Sprinkle with Asiago cheese.

PER SERVING 275 calories; 6 g fat (2 g sat.); 12 g protein; 44 g carbohydrate; 11 g fiber; 495 mg sodium; 8 mg cholesterol

Chile Rellenos Casserole

MAKES 4 servings
PREP 20 minutes **BAKE** 15 minutes **STAND** 5 minutes
OVEN 450°F

- **2 large fresh poblano chile peppers, fresh Anaheim chile peppers, or green sweet peppers (8 ounces)**
- **1½ cups shredded reduced-fat Monterey Jack cheese with jalapeño peppers or reduced-fat Mexican-blend cheese**
- **¾ cup refrigerated or frozen egg product, thawed**
- **¼ cup fat-free milk**
- **⅓ cup all-purpose flour**
- **½ teaspoon baking powder**
- **¼ teaspoon cayenne pepper**
- **⅛ teaspoon salt**
- **Bottled picante sauce (optional)**
- **Light dairy sour cream (optional)**

1 Preheat oven to 450°F. Generously grease a 2-quart square baking dish; set aside. Quarter the chile peppers and remove seeds, stems, and veins.* Immerse quartered chile peppers into boiling water for 3 minutes; drain. Invert chile peppers on paper towels to drain well. Place chile peppers in prepared dish. Top with 1 cup of the cheese.
2 In a medium bowl beat egg product and milk with a rotary beater until well mixed. Add flour, baking powder, cayenne pepper, and salt. Beat with rotary beater until smooth. Pour egg mixture over quartered chile peppers and cheese.
3 Bake, uncovered, about 15 minutes or until a knife inserted into the egg mixture comes out clean. Sprinkle with the remaining ½ cup cheese. Let stand about 5 minutes or until cheese melts. If desired, serve with picante sauce and sour cream.
***Note:** Because chile peppers contain volatile oils that can burn your skin and eyes, avoid direct contact with them as much as possible. When working with chile peppers, wear plastic or rubber gloves. If your bare hands do touch the chile peppers, wash your hands and nails well with soap and warm water.

PER SERVING 207 calories; 9 g fat (6 g sat.); 18 g protein; 15 g carbohydrate; 1 g fiber; 569 mg sodium; 30 mg cholesterol

Southwestern Bean & Cheese Bake

Southwestern Bean & Cheese Bake

MAKES 8 servings
PREP 20 minutes **BAKE** 45 minutes **STAND** 15 minutes
OVEN 325°F

- **1 15-ounce can black beans, rinsed and drained**
- **¾ cup canned enchilada sauce**
- **2 4-ounce cans diced green chile peppers, drained**
- **½ cup thinly sliced green onion (4)**
- **Several dashes bottled hot pepper sauce (optional)**
- **2 cloves garlic, minced**
- **1 cup shredded sharp cheddar cheese and/or shredded Monterey Jack cheese with jalapeño chile peppers (4 ounces)**
- **3 egg whites**
- **3 egg yolks**
- **2 tablespoons all-purpose flour**
- **¼ teaspoon salt**
- **½ cup milk**
- **1 tablespoon snipped fresh cilantro**

1 Grease a 2-quart square baking dish. In the prepared dish, combine beans, enchilada sauce, drained chile peppers, green onion, pepper sauce (if desired), and garlic. Sprinkle with cheddar cheese.
2 In a medium bowl beat egg whites with an electric mixer on medium speed until soft peaks form (tips curl); set aside.
3 In a large bowl combine egg yolks, flour, and salt. Using a wire whisk, beat egg yolk mixture until combined (mixture will be stiff). Gradually whisk in milk until smooth. Fold the beaten egg whites and cilantro into egg yolk mixture. Pour the egg mixture over the bean mixture in the prepared baking dish.
4 Bake, uncovered, in a 325°F oven about 45 minutes or until egg mixture appears set when gently shaken. Let stand for 15 minutes before serving. If desired, garnish with *dairy sour cream* and *cilantro leaves.*

Tofu Stir-Fry
with Soba Noodles

Mushroom & Asparagus Fettuccine 

MAKES 4 servings
START TO FINISH 30 minutes

- **8 ounces dried whole wheat fettuccine or linguine pasta**
- **8 ounces fresh asparagus, trimmed and cut into 1½-inch pieces**
- **Nonstick cooking spray**
- **3 cups sliced fresh cremini, shiitake, or button mushrooms**
- **½ cup thinly sliced leek (1 medium) or ½ cup chopped onion (1 medium)**
- **3 cloves garlic, minced**
- **⅓ cup vegetable broth**
- **¼ cup evaporated fat-free milk**
- **1 tablespoon snipped fresh basil or 1 teaspoon dried basil, crushed**
- **1 tablespoon snipped fresh oregano or 1 teaspoon dried oregano, crushed**
- **¼ teaspoon salt**
- **⅛ teaspoon black pepper**
- **1 cup chopped roma tomato (3 medium)**
- **¼ cup pine nuts, toasted**
- **Finely shredded Parmesan cheese (optional)**

1 Cook pasta according to package directions, adding asparagus for the last 2 minutes of cooking; drain. Return pasta mixture to pan; cover and keep warm.
2 Meanwhile, coat an unheated large nonstick skillet with cooking spray. Cook mushrooms, leek, and garlic in hot skillet over medium-high heat for 4 to 5 minutes or until tender, stirring occasionally. Stir in broth, milk, dried basil (if using), dried oregano (if using), salt, and pepper. Bring to boiling; reduce heat. Boil gently, uncovered, for 4 to 5 minutes or until mushroom mixture is slightly thickened. Stir in tomato, fresh basil (if using), and fresh oregano (if using); heat through.
3 Spoon mushroom mixture over pasta mixture in pan; toss gently to combine. Sprinkle each serving with pine nuts and, if desired, cheese. Serve immediately.

PER SERVING 319 calories; 8 g fat (1 g sat.); 15 g protein; 54 g carbohydrate; 3 g fiber; 255 mg sodium; 1 mg cholesterol

Tofu Stir-Fry with Soba Noodles

MAKES 4 servings
START TO FINISH 1 hour

- **5 ounces soba noodles (buckwheat noodles)**
- **2 teaspoons toasted sesame oil**
- **2 cloves garlic, minced**
- **1 teaspoon grated fresh ginger**
- **1 large red sweet pepper, coarsely chopped**
- **12 ounces firm tub-style tofu (fresh bean curd), drained and cubed**
- **4 cups fresh baby spinach leaves**
- **3 tablespoons light teriyaki sauce**
- **1 tablespoon water**
- **3 tablespoons snipped fresh cilantro or basil**

1 Cook soba noodles according to package directions; drain and set aside. Meanwhile, in a large skillet heat sesame oil over medium-high heat. Add garlic and ginger; cook and stir for 30 seconds. Add sweet pepper; cook and stir for 2 minutes. Add tofu; cook and stir for 1 minute more.
2 Add spinach, teriyaki sauce, and the water; stir until spinach is wilted. Add cooked soba noodles and cilantro; heat through, stirring gently to coat.

PER SERVING 294 calories; 10 g fat (1 g sat.); 21 g protein; 36 g carbohydrate; 5 g fiber; 648 mg sodium; 0 mg cholesterol

Vegetable-Noodle Slaw 

MAKES 4 servings
START TO FINISH 25 minutes

- **6** **ounces dried multigrain spaghetti or soba (buckwheat) noodles**
- **⅓** **cup bottled peanut sauce**
- **⅓** **cup carrot juice**
- **1** **tablespoon finely chopped fresh ginger**
- **1** **tablespoon salad oil**
- **1** **16-ounce package shredded broccoli (broccoli slaw mix)**
- **¾** **cup shredded carrot (1 large)**

1 Cook pasta according to package directions; drain. Return pasta to pan. Using kitchen scissors, snip pasta into pieces. Cover and keep warm. In a small bowl whisk together peanut sauce and carrot juice; set aside.

2 In a wok or large nonstick skillet cook and stir ginger in hot oil over medium-high heat for 15 seconds. Add broccoli and carrot; cook and stir for 1 minute. Stir in peanut sauce mixture; cook and stir for 2 minutes more. Add pasta. Using tongs, toss to coat. Serve warm.

PER SERVING 285 calories; 7 g fat (1 g sat.); 12 g protein; 45 g carbohydrate; 7 g fiber; 318 mg sodium; 0 mg cholesterol

An interesting twist on

Pasta with Spicy Eggplant Sauce

MAKES 6 servings
PREP 20 minutes **COOK** 18 minutes

- **1½ pounds eggplant, ends trimmed and cut into ½-inch cubes**
- **1 medium onion, halved and thinly sliced**
- **3 cloves garlic, chopped**
- **1 teaspoon salt**
- **3 tablespoons olive oil**
- **1 28-ounce can diced tomatoes, undrained**
- **½ teaspoon red pepper flakes**
- **1 pound dried rotini pasta**
- **1 cup packed fresh basil, torn into pieces**
- **3 tablespoons snipped fresh chives**
- **1 tablespoon snipped fresh oregano**
- **6 tablespoons part-skim ricotta cheese**

1 In a large skillet cook eggplant, onion, garlic, and ½ teaspoon of the salt in hot oil over medium-high heat about 8 minutes or until eggplant softens, stirring occasionally. Add undrained tomatoes, red pepper flakes, and the remaining ½ teaspoon salt. Bring to boiling; reduce heat. Simmer, uncovered, about 10 minutes or until eggplant is very soft.
2 Meanwhile, cook pasta according to package directions; drain. Set aside.
3 Stir most of the basil, chives, and oregano into the eggplant mixture. Add pasta; toss to combine. Divide pasta mixture evenly among four shallow bowls. Top each serving with a spoonful of cheese and the reserved herbs.

PER SERVING 398 calories; 9 g fat (2 g sat.); 13 g protein; 67 g carbohydrate; 8 g fiber; 581 mg sodium; 5 mg cholesterol

Trattoria-Style Spinach Fettuccine 

MAKES 4 servings
START TO FINISH 15 minutes

- **1 9-ounce package refrigerated spinach fettuccine**
- **2 tablespoons chopped shallot or green onion**
- **1 tablespoon olive oil**
- **2 cups chopped red and/or yellow tomatoes (4)**
- **1 medium carrot, finely chopped**
- **¼ cup oil-packed dried tomatoes, drained and snipped**
- **½ cup crumbled garlic and herb feta cheese or peppercorn feta cheese (2 ounces)**

1 Using kitchen shears, snip fettuccine in half crosswise. Cook pasta according to package directions. Drain; return pasta to pan.
2 Meanwhile, in a large skillet cook shallot in hot oil over medium heat for 30 seconds. Stir in fresh tomatoes, carrot, and dried tomatoes. Cook, covered, for 5 minutes, stirring once. Spoon tomato mixture over cooked pasta; toss gently. Sprinkle each serving with feta cheese.

PER SERVING 318 calories; 12 g fat (4 g sat.); 13 g protein; 43 g carbohydrate; 2 g fiber; 294 mg sodium; 77 mg cholesterol

Ravioli with Spinach Pesto  

MAKES 4 servings
START TO FINISH 20 minutes

- **1 9-ounce package refrigerated four-cheese ravioli or tortellini**
- **12 ounces baby pattypan squash, halved, or yellow summer squash, halved lengthwise and sliced ½ inch thick**
- **3½ cups fresh baby spinach**
- **½ cup torn fresh basil**
- **¼ cup bottled Caesar Parmesan vinaigrette salad dressing**
- **2 tablespoons water**
- **Shaved Parmesan cheese (optional)**

1 Cook ravioli according to package directions, adding squash for the last 2 minutes of cooking; drain.
2 Meanwhile, for pesto, in a blender combine spinach, basil, dressing, and the water. Cover and blend until smooth, stopping to scrape down blender as needed.
3 Toss ravioli mixture with pesto. Sprinkle with cheese.

PER SERVING 218 calories; 6 g fat (2 g sat.); 11 g protein; 31 g carbohydrate; 3 g fiber; 525 mg sodium; 27 mg cholesterol

classic pesto sauce and a lot less fat.

Ravioli with Spinach Pesto

Linguine with
Zucchini Sauce

Penne with Ricotta
& Vegetables

Add some protein and fiber to your diet by using whole grain pasta instead of regular. Whole grain pasta is available in many traditional pasta shapes and has a slightly nutty flavor compared to the same old standby.

Linguine with Zucchini Sauce  

MAKES 6 servings
PREP 15 minutes **COOK** 5 minutes

- **1 pound dried linguine**
- **3 cloves garlic, peeled and thinly sliced**
- **2 tablespoons olive oil**
- **2 pounds zucchini, coarsely shredded**
- **½ teaspoon salt**
- **⅛ teaspoon black pepper**
- **1 cup shredded sharp cheddar cheese (4 ounces)**
- **½ cup jarred Alfredo sauce**
- **Fresh basil leaves (optional)**

1 Cook pasta according to package directions; drain. Return pasta to pan; cover and keep warm.
2 In a large skillet cook and stir garlic in hot oil over medium-high heat about 30 seconds or until light brown. Increase heat to high. Stir in zucchini, salt, and pepper. Cook and stir about 3 minutes or until tender. Stir in cheese and Alfredo sauce; heat through. Pour zucchini mixture over pasta in pan; toss to coat. If desired, garnish each serving with basil.

PER SERVING 378 calories; 15 g fat (6 g sat.); 16 g protein; 48 g carbohydrate; 4 g fiber; 593 mg sodium; 28 mg cholesterol

Penne with Ricotta & Vegetables 

MAKES 4 servings
START TO FINISH 25 minutes

- **6 ounces dried whole grain or regular ziti or penne pasta**
- **2½ cups broccoli florets**
- **1½ cups 1-inch pieces fresh asparagus or green beans**
- **1 cup light ricotta cheese**
- **¼ cup snipped fresh basil**
- **1 tablespoon snipped fresh thyme**
- **1 tablespoon balsamic vinegar**
- **1 tablespoon olive oil**
- **1 clove garlic, minced**
- **½ teaspoon salt**
- **½ teaspoon black pepper**
- **1⅓ cups chopped, seeded red and/or yellow tomatoes**
- **Shaved Parmesan or Romano cheese (optional)**
- **Fresh thyme sprigs (optional)**

1 Cook pasta according to package directions, adding green beans (if using) with pasta for the whole cooking time or adding broccoli and asparagus (if using) for the last 3 minutes of cooking. Drain well. Return to pan; cover and keep warm.
2 Meanwhile, in a large bowl combine ricotta cheese, basil, thyme, balsamic vinegar, oil, garlic, salt, and pepper. Gently stir in tomatoes.
3 Add drained pasta mixture to tomato mixture; toss gently to combine. If desired, top with Parmesan cheese and garnish with thyme sprigs.

PER SERVING 357 calories; 9 g fat (2 g sat.); 16 g protein; 55 g carbohydrate; 7 g fiber; 407 mg sodium; 17 mg cholesterol

Spinach & Cheese Roll-Ups

Spinach & Cheese Roll-Ups 

MAKES 4 servings
PREP 30 minutes **BAKE** 25 minutes **OVEN** 350°F

- **⅓ cup chopped onion (1 small)**
- **1 clove garlic, minced**
- **1 teaspoon olive oil or cooking oil**
- **1 14.5-ounce can diced tomatoes, undrained**
- **2 tablespoons tomato paste**
- **1½ teaspoons snipped fresh basil or ½ teaspoon dried basil, crushed**
- **¼ teaspoon sugar**
- **Dash salt**
- **Dash black pepper**
- **8 dried lasagna noodles**
- **¾ cup fat-free or reduced-fat ricotta cheese**
- **½ cup shredded part-skim mozzarella cheese (2 ounces)**
- **2 tablespoons finely shredded Parmesan cheese**
- **2 teaspoons snipped fresh basil or ½ teaspoon dried basil or Italian seasoning, crushed**
- **1 10-ounce package frozen chopped spinach, thawed and well drained**
- **1 egg white, lightly beaten**

1 For sauce, in a medium saucepan cook onion and garlic in hot oil over medium heat until onion is tender, stirring occasionally. Carefully stir in undrained tomatoes, tomato paste, the 1½ teaspoons basil, the sugar, salt, and pepper. Bring to boiling; reduce heat. Simmer, uncovered, about 5 minutes or until sauce is desired consistency, stirring occasionally.
2 Meanwhile, cook pasta according to package directions; drain. Rinse with cold water; drain again.
3 In a medium bowl stir together ricotta cheese, mozzarella cheese, Parmesan cheese, and the 2 teaspoons basil. Add spinach and egg white, stirring to combine.
4 To assemble, evenly spread about ¼ cup of the cheese mixture on each noodle. Roll up from one end. Place two rolls, seam sides down, into each of four individual casseroles. Top rolls evenly with sauce. Bake, covered, in a 350°F oven about 25 minutes or until heated through.

PER SERVING 231 calories; 3 g fat (0 g sat.); 20 g protein; 39 g carbohydrate; 2 g fiber; 425 mg sodium; 10 mg cholesterol

Vegetable Lo Mein 

MAKES 4 servings
START TO FINISH 35 minutes

- **1 cup dried shiitake mushrooms**
- **1 cup boiling water**
- **6 ounces dried udon or lo mein noodles**
- **2 egg whites**
- **1 egg**
- **2 teaspoons cooking oil**
- **2 teaspoons toasted sesame oil**
- **3 cloves garlic, minced**
- **2 teaspoons finely chopped fresh ginger**
- **½ teaspoon crushed red pepper (optional)**
- **1 red sweet pepper, cut into thin bite-size strips**
- **2 cups sugar snap peas or snow pea pods (strings and tips removed), halved**
- **¼ cup light teriyaki sauce**

1 In a small bowl combine mushrooms and boiling water. Cover and let stand for 20 minutes. Drain mushrooms, squeezing out excess liquid; reserve ½ cup liquid. Chop mushrooms and set aside. Meanwhile, cook noodles according to package directions for 5 minutes; drain. Return noodles to pan.

2 For egg strips, whisk together egg whites and egg. In a large nonstick skillet heat 1 teaspoon of the cooking oil and 1 teaspoon of the sesame oil over medium heat. Pour egg mixture into skillet. Lift and tilt the skillet to form a thin layer of egg on the bottom. Cook, without stirring, for 2 or 3 minutes or until just set. Slide egg mixture out onto a cutting board; cool slightly and cut into 2×½-inch-long strips. Set aside.

3 In the same skillet cook and stir mushrooms, garlic, ginger, and, if desired, crushed red pepper in the remaining 1 teaspoon cooking oil and 1 teaspoon sesame oil over medium-high heat for 1 minute. Add sweet pepper and peas; cook and stir for 2 minutes more. Add reserved mushroom-soaking liquid and the teriyaki sauce. Bring to boiling; reduce heat. Boil gently, uncovered, for 3 minutes. Add egg strips and vegetable mixture to noodles; toss to combine. Serve immediately.

PER SERVING 293 calories; 8 g fat (1 g sat.); 12 g protein; 44 g carbohydrate; 3 g fiber; 307 mg sodium; 94 mg cholesterol

Menu

Harvest Ravioli
[below]

Steamed green beans

Spinach salad with sliced red onion, dried cranberries, toasted walnuts, and balsamic vinaigrette

Harvest Ravioli 30

MAKES 6 servings
START TO FINISH 30 minutes

- **1 cup chopped onion (1 large)**
- **4 cloves garlic, minced**
- **1 tablespoon olive oil**
- **1 1-pound butternut squash, halved, seeded, peeled, and cut into 1-inch cubes (about 3 cups)**
- **1 14-ounce can chicken broth or vegetable broth**
- **1 tablespoon snipped fresh sage or 1 teaspoon dried sage, crushed**
- **½ cup apple cider or apple juice**
- **1 tablespoon cornstarch**
- **3 medium Granny Smith apples, cut into thin wedges**
- **1 20- to 24-ounce package frozen cheese-filled ravioli**
- **½ cup walnuts, toasted and chopped**
- **2 tablespoons grated Parmesan cheese**
- **¼ teaspoon cracked black pepper**
- **Snipped fresh sage (optional)**

1 In a very large skillet cook onion and garlic in hot oil over medium heat for 5 minutes or until tender, stirring occasionally. Add squash, broth, and dried sage, if using. Bring to boiling; reduce heat. Simmer, covered, for 10 minutes. Combine apple cider and cornstarch; add to skillet along with apples and fresh sage, if using. Cook, stirring gently, until thickened and bubbly. Cook, uncovered, 2 minutes more.
2 Meanwhile, cook ravioli according to package directions; drain. Add ravioli to hot apple mixture; toss gently to combine. To serve, top with walnuts, cheese, pepper, and, if desired, additional fresh sage.

PER SERVING 366 calories; 12 g fat (2 g sat.); 11 g protein; 57 g carbohydrate; 5 g fiber; 532 mg sodium; 31 mg cholesterol

Noodle Casserole

MAKES 6 servings
PREP 25 minutes **COOK** 7 to 8 hours (low) or 3½ to 4 hours (high) + 20 minutes on high

- **2½ cups water**
- **1 10.75-ounce can reduced-fat and reduced-sodium condensed cream of mushroom soup**
- **1 14.5-ounce can no-salt-added diced tomatoes, undrained**
- **1 cup sliced celery (2 stalks)**
- **1 cup sliced carrot (2 medium)**
- **1 cup chopped onion**
- **2 cloves garlic, minced**
- **1½ teaspoons dried Italian seasoning, crushed**
- **¼ teaspoon salt**
- **¼ teaspoon black pepper**
- **8 ounces dried extra-wide noodles**
- **1 16-ounce package extra-firm tub-style tofu (fresh bean curd), drained and cubed**
- **½ cup shredded reduced-fat cheddar cheese (2 ounces)**

1 In a 3½- or 4-quart slow cooker, whisk together the water and soup. Stir in undrained tomatoes, celery, carrot, onion, garlic, Italian seasoning, salt, and pepper.
2 Cover and cook on low-heat setting for 7 to 8 hours or high-heat setting for 3½ to 4 hours.
3 If using low-heat setting, turn to high-heat setting. Stir in noodles; cover and cook for 20 to 30 minutes more or until tender, stirring once halfway through cooking. Gently stir in tofu cubes. Sprinkle with cheese; cover and let stand until cheese is melted.

PER SERVING 316 calories; 8 g fat (2 g sat.); 17 g protein; 42 g carbohydrate; 4 g fiber; 447 mg sodium; 44 mg cholesterol

Garden Vegetables Lasagna

MAKES 8 servings
PREP 45 minutes **BAKE** 45 minutes **STAND** 10 minutes
OVEN 375°F

Nonstick cooking spray
- **9 dried white or whole grain lasagna noodles**
- **3 cups broccoli florets**
- **1 red sweet pepper, seeded and cut into bite-size strips (1 cup)**
- **1 medium zucchini, sliced (1¼ cups)**
- **1 medium yellow summer squash, sliced (about 1¼ cups)**
- **2 15-ounce cartons light ricotta cheese**
- **½ cup snipped fresh basil or 1 tablespoon dried basil, crushed**
- **1 tablespoon snipped fresh thyme or 1 teaspoon dried thyme, crushed**
- **3 cloves garlic, minced**
- **½ teaspoon salt**
- **¼ teaspoon black pepper**
- **¼ teaspoon bottled hot pepper sauce**
- **2 cups shredded part-skim mozzarella cheese (8 ounces)**

1 Lightly coat a 3-quart rectangular baking dish with cooking spray; set aside. In a 4-quart Dutch oven, cook lasagna noodles in a large amount of boiling water for 10 to 12 minutes or until tender but still firm. Drain noodles; rinse with cold water. Drain again.

2 Place a steamer basket in the 4-quart Dutch oven. Add water to just below the bottom of the steamer basket. Bring to boiling. Add broccoli, sweet pepper, zucchini, and yellow summer squash. Reduce heat. Cover and steam for 6 to 8 minutes or until vegetables are crisp-tender. Remove from heat.

3 In a large bowl stir together ricotta cheese, basil, thyme, garlic, salt, black pepper, and hot pepper sauce. Layer three of the cooked noodles in the prepared baking dish. Spread with one-third of the ricotta cheese mixture. Top with one-third of the vegetable mixture and ⅔ cup of the mozzarella cheese. Repeat layers twice.

4 Bake, covered, in a 375°F oven for 45 to 55 minutes or until heated through. Uncover; let stand for 10 minutes before serving.

PER SERVING 293 calories; 9 g fat (6 g sat.); 20 g protein; 30 g carbohydrate; 3 g fiber; 428 mg sodium; 44 mg cholesterol

Garden Vegetables Lasagna

Crispy Tofu & Vegetables

Crispy Tofu & Vegetables

MAKES 4 servings
PREP 25 minutes **MARINATE** 1 hour **COOK** 10 minutes

- **1 10.5-ounce package light extra-firm tofu (fresh bean curd), drained**
- **3 tablespoons reduced-sodium soy sauce**
- **8 green onions**
- **2 cups snow pea pods, strings and tips removed**
- **1 teaspoon grated fresh ginger or ½ teaspoon ground ginger**
- **1 clove garlic, minced**
- **1 tablespoon toasted sesame oil**
- **1 red sweet pepper, cut into long, thin strips**
- **1 yellow sweet pepper, cut into long, thin strips**
- **3 tablespoons yellow cornmeal**
- **1 tablespoon white or black sesame seeds, toasted (optional)**

1 Cut tofu crosswise into eight slices. Arrange slices in a single layer on a large plate or jelly-roll pan. Pour soy sauce over tofu; turn slices to coat and let stand for 1 hour.
2 Meanwhile, cut root ends off green onions. Cut off dark green portion of onions, leaving 3 inches of white and light green. Cut green onions in half lengthwise, making 16 long strips; set aside. Cut pea pods in half lengthwise; set aside.
3 In a large nonstick skillet cook and stir fresh ginger (if using) and garlic in hot oil over medium-high heat for 30 seconds. Add sweet peppers; cook and stir for 1 minute. Add green onion and pea pods; cook and stir for 2 to 3 minutes or until crisp-tender.
4 Drain tofu, reserving soy sauce. Stir reserved soy sauce and ground ginger (if using) into skillet. Transfer vegetable mixture to a serving platter; cover and keep warm. Carefully dip tofu slices in cornmeal to lightly coat both sides. Cook in the hot skillet about 6 minutes or until crisp and hot, using a spatula to carefully turn once. (Do not crowd the skillet. You may need to cook tofu in two batches.) Serve tofu with vegetables. If desired, sprinkle with sesame seeds.

PER SERVING 198 calories; 10 g fat (1 g sat.); 16 g protein; 14 g carbohydrate; 3 g fiber; 410 mg sodium; 0 mg cholesterol

Portobello Parmigiana 

MAKES 4 servings
PREP 15 minutes **BAKE** 15 minutes **OVEN** 450°F

- **Nonstick cooking spray**
- **½ cup grated Parmesan cheese**
- **¼ cup seasoned fine dry bread crumbs**
- **¼ teaspoon paprika**
- **⅛ teaspoon garlic powder**
- **⅛ teaspoon black pepper**
- **1 egg, lightly beaten**
- **1 tablespoon water**
- **4 4-inch-diameter fresh portobello mushrooms, stems removed**
- **½ cup pizza sauce**
- **½ cup bottled roasted sweet red peppers, drained and cut into strips**
- **½ cup shredded mozzarella cheese (2 ounces)**

1 Lightly coat a 15×10×1-inch baking pan with cooking spray; set aside. In a medium bowl stir together ¼ cup of the Parmesan cheese, the bread crumbs, paprika, garlic powder, and black pepper. In a small bowl whisk together egg and water. Set aside.
2 If desired, use a small spoon to scrape out mushroom gills. Dip mushrooms in egg mixture, turning to coat, then coat with bread crumb mixture (sprinkle with the crumb mixture as necessary to completely coat mushrooms). Place mushrooms, rounded sides down, in prepared baking pan. Bake in a 450°F for 10 minutes.
3 Top mushrooms evenly with pizza sauce and sweet peppers. Top sauce with mozzarella cheese and the remaining Parmesan cheese. Bake about 5 minutes more or until heated through and cheese melts.

PER SERVING 162 calories; 8 g fat (4 g sat.); 12 g protein; 13 g carbohydrate; 2 g fiber; 572 mg sodium; 69 mg cholesterol

Veggie-Cheese Sandwiches 

MAKES 4 sandwiches
PREP 20 minutes **COOK** 3 minutes

- **8 ½-inch slices country French white bread**
- **4 teaspoons olive oil**
- **2 tablespoons honey mustard**
- **4 ounces thinly sliced cheddar cheese**
- **½ cup thinly sliced cucumber**
- **½ cup fresh spinach leaves**
- **¼ cup thinly sliced red onion**

1 Brush one side of each bread slice with oil; brush the other side with mustard. Top mustard side of four slices with cheese, cucumber, spinach, and onion. Top with remaining bread slices, mustard side down.
2 Preheat indoor electric grill. Place sandwiches on grill. If using covered grill, close lid. Grill sandwiches until bread is golden. For covered grill, allow 3 to 5 minutes. For uncovered grill, allow 6 to 8 minutes, turning once halfway through grilling. Serve immediately.

PER SANDWICH 194 calories; 7 g fat (1 g sat.); 10 g protein; 22 g carbohydrate; 1 g fiber; 244 mg sodium; 0 mg cholesterol

If you don't have an indoor grill, use a large skillet or grill pan to toast these paninilike sandwiches. Heat the skillet or grill pan over medium heat, then add the sandwiches. Cook for 6 to 8 minutes or until the bread is toasted and golden, turning once halfway through cooking.

Cucumber and Apricot Sandwiches 

MAKES 4 sandwiches
START TO FINISH 15 minutes

- **1 large cucumber**
- **½ of an 8-ounce package reduced-fat cream cheese (Neufchâtel)**
- **2 tablespoons snipped fresh basil**
- **⅛ teaspoon salt (optional)**
- **8 slices firm-textured whole wheat bread**
- **2 large apricots or 1 nectarine, pitted and thinly sliced**
- **½ cup arugula leaves or cilantro sprigs**

1 Peel cucumber. Cut cucumber in half lengthwise and scoop out seeds. Thinly slice cucumber; set aside. In a small bowl stir together cream cheese, basil, and, if desired, salt.
2 Spread about 1 tablespoon cream cheese mixture on one side of each bread slice. Top four bread slices with cucumber, apricot, and arugula. Top with remaining bread slices, cream cheese side down. To serve, cut each sandwich in half diagonally.

PER SANDWICH 234 calories; 9 g fat (5 g sat.); 9 g protein; 32 g carbohydrate; 5 g fiber; 413 mg sodium; 21 mg cholesterol

Egg-Vegetable Salad Wraps

MAKES 6 wraps
START TO FINISH 35 minutes

- **6 hard-cooked eggs, chopped**
- **½ cup chopped cucumber**
- **½ cup chopped yellow summer squash or zucchini**
- **¼ cup shredded carrot**
- **2 tablespoons chopped red onion**
- **¼ cup mayonnaise or salad dressing**
- **2 tablespoons Dijon-style mustard**
- **1 tablespoon milk**
- **1 teaspoon snipped fresh tarragon or basil or ¼ teaspoon dried tarragon or basil, crushed**
- **¼ teaspoon salt**
- **⅛ teaspoon paprika**
- **6 leaf lettuce leaves**
- **6 6- to 7-inch low-carbohydrate multigrain or whole wheat flour tortillas or whole wheat flour tortillas**
- **2 plum tomatoes, thinly sliced**

1 In a large bowl combine eggs, cucumber, squash, carrot, and red onion. For dressing, in a small bowl stir together mayonnaise, mustard, milk, tarragon, salt, and paprika. Pour the dressing over egg mixture; toss gently to coat.

2 For each sandwich, place a lettuce leaf on a tortilla. Place 3 or 4 tomato slices on top of the lettuce, slightly off center. Spoon about ½ cup of the egg mixture on top of the tomato slices. Roll up tortilla; secure with wooden pick, if necessary. Cut the tortilla rolls in half crosswise.

PER WRAP 215 calories; 15 g fat (3 g sat.); 12 g protein; 15 g carbohydrate; 9 g fiber; 427 mg sodium; 218 mg cholesterol

Egg-Vegetable Salad Wraps

Roasted Veggie & Swiss Flats 

MAKES 4 sandwiches
PREP 15 minutes **ROAST** 10 minutes **BROIL** 3 minutes
OVEN 450°F

- **1 small zucchini, thinly sliced**
- **1 small yellow summer squash, thinly sliced**
- **1 medium onion, thinly sliced**
- **⅓ cup sliced fresh mushrooms**
- **½ of a red sweet pepper, cut into thin strips**
- **Olive oil nonstick cooking spray**
- **Salt**
- **Black pepper**
- **4 pita bread rounds**
- **4 teaspoons bottled vinaigrette or Italian salad dressing**
- **¾ cup shredded Swiss cheese (3 ounces)**

1 Place zucchini, squash, onion, mushrooms, and sweet pepper on a large baking sheet; lightly coat with cooking spray. Roast in a 450°F oven about 10 minutes or until vegetables are tender, stirring once. Season to taste with salt and pepper.

2 Divide roasted vegetables among pita bread rounds; drizzle with salad dressing. Top with shredded cheese. Place the pitas on the unheated rack of a broiler pan. Broil 4 inches from heat about 3 minutes or until cheese melts.

PER SANDWICH 269 calories; 7 g fat (4 g sat.); 12 g protein; 38 g carbohydrate; 1 g fiber; 453 mg sodium; 20 mg cholesterol

These crispy grilled burgers pack big, bold flavor. For fiery hot burgers, choose a hot salsa over a mild one and add an extra splash of salsa over the top when serving.

Bean Burgers 

MAKES 6 burgers
PREP 10 minutes **GRILL** 10 minutes

- **2 15.5-ounce cans pinto beans, rinsed and drained**
- **½ cup dry fine bread crumbs**
- **½ cup bottled salsa**
- **1 egg**
- **1 teaspoon chili powder**
- **½ teaspoon ground cumin**
- **½ cup coarsely crushed baked tortilla chips**
- **Nonstick cooking spray**
- **3 pita bread rounds, halved**
- **12 lettuce leaves**
- **12 slices tomato**
- **Bottled salsa**

1 Reserve 1 cup of the pinto beans. Place remaining beans in a food processor; process until smooth. (Or, if you do not have a food processor, use a potato masher to mash beans in a large bowl.)

2 In a large bowl combine the reserved 1 cup beans, the pureed beans, bread crumbs, the ½ cup salsa, the egg, chili powder, and cumin. Stir in crushed tortilla chips. Form bean mixture into six patties. Coat both sides of each patty with cooking spray.

3 For a charcoal grill, place burgers on the lightly greased grill rack directly over medium coals. Grill, uncovered, about 10 minutes or until an instant-read thermometer inserted in sides of burgers registers 160°F. (For a gas grill, preheat grill. Reduce heat to medium. Place burgers on grill rack over heat. Cover and grill as above.)

4 Serve burgers in pita pockets with lettuce and tomato slices. Serve with additional salsa.

Broiler Directions: Preheat broiler. Place burgers on the unheated lightly greased rack of a broiler pan. Broil 4 to 5 inches from heat about 10 minutes or until an instant-read thermometer inserted in sides of burgers registers 160°F, turning once halfway through broiling.

PER BURGER 234 calories; 3 g fat (1 g sat.); 10 g protein; 41 g carbohydrate; 5 g fiber; 994 mg sodium; 36 mg cholesterol

Open-Face Ratatouille Sandwiches

MAKES 4 servings
PREP 25 minutes **ROAST** 45 minutes **OVEN** 400°F

- **Nonstick cooking spray**
- **1 small eggplant, cut into 1-inch pieces**
- **1 small zucchini or yellow summer squash, cut into ¾-inch slices**
- **1 medium red sweet pepper, cut into strips**
- **½ of a small red onion, cut into ½-inch wedges**
- **1 tablespoon olive oil**
- **½ teaspoon herbes de Provence or dried thyme, crushed**
- **⅛ teaspoon each salt and black pepper**
- **2 medium roma tomatoes, each cut lengthwise into 6 wedges**
- **8 small ½-inch slices whole wheat or white French bread, toasted (about 8 ounces total)**
- **1 clove garlic, halved**
- **2 tablespoons balsamic vinegar**
- **Fresh thyme sprigs (optional)**

1 Coat a large shallow roasting pan with cooking spray. Add eggplant, zucchini, sweet pepper, and red onion to prepared pan. Drizzle on oil; sprinkle with herbes de Provence, salt, and pepper. Toss to coat. Roast, uncovered, in a 400°F oven for 30 minutes, tossing once. Add tomatoes to roasting pan. Roast for 15 to 20 minutes more or until vegetables are tender and some surfaces are light brown.

2 Meanwhile, rub toasted bread with cut sides of garlic clove. Place 2 bread slices on each of four serving plates. Sprinkle balsamic vinegar over vegetables; toss gently to coat. Spoon warm vegetables over bread. If desired, garnish with thyme sprigs.

PER SERVING 250 calories; 7 g fat (1 g sat.); 7 g protein; 43 g carbohydrate; 8 g fiber; 328 mg sodium; 0 mg cholesterol

3-Cheese White Pizza 

MAKES 8 servings
PREP 10 minutes **BAKE** 10 minutes **OVEN** 450°F

- **¾ cup ricotta cheese**
- **3 tablespoons grated Parmesan cheese**
- **1 bunch broccoli rabe (about 1 pound)**
- **3 cloves garlic, minced**
- **1 tablespoon olive oil**
- **¾ teaspoon salt**
- **½ teaspoon dried crushed rosemary**
- **¼ teaspoon red pepper flakes**
- **8 ounces fresh mozzarella cheese, cut into ¼-inch slices**
- **1 10-ounce prepared thin pizza crust (such as Boboli)**

1 In a small bowl stir together ricotta cheese and Parmesan cheese; set aside. Rinse broccoli rabe, removing outer leaves and thick stems; cut into 2-inch pieces. Set aside.
2 In a large skillet cook and stir garlic in hot oil over medium heat for 1 minute. Add broccoli rabe, salt, rosemary, and red pepper flakes; cook and stir about 9 minutes or until tender. Set broccoli rabe mixture aside.
3 Place mozzarella cheese slices evenly on pizza crust. Spread broccoli rabe mixture over cheese. Drop rounded tablespoons of ricotta mixture on top of pizza.
4 Bake in a 450°F oven about 10 minutes or until cheese melts. Cut into eight wedges and serve immediately.

PER SERVING 254 calories; 13 g fat (7 g sat.); 13 g protein; 21 g carbohydrate; 1 g fiber; 439 mg sodium; 34 mg cholesterol

Roasted Vegetable Pizzas

MAKES 8 servings
PREP 30 minutes **ROAST** 20 minutes **STAND** 15 minutes
BAKE 17 minutes **OVEN** 425°F

- **3 medium red, yellow, and/or green sweet peppers**
- **1 medium onion, cut into very thin wedges and separated into strips**
- **Olive oil nonstick cooking spray**
- **1 16-ounce loaf frozen whole wheat bread dough, thawed**
- **½ teaspoon crushed red pepper**
- **1 cup shredded part-skim mozzarella cheese (4 ounces)**
- **1 cup chopped red or yellow tomato (1 large)**
- **1 cup crumbled queso fresco or feta cheese (4 ounces)**
- **2 tablespoons snipped fresh basil or oregano**

1 Cut sweet peppers in half, removing stems, membranes, and seeds. Place sweet peppers, cut sides down, on a large baking sheet lined with foil. Lightly coat onion with cooking spray. Place onion around sweet peppers. Roast in a 425°F oven for 10 minutes. Remove onion from pan; set aside. Roast sweet peppers for 10 to 15 minutes more or until skin is blackened and blistered. Wrap sweet peppers in the foil; let stand for 15 to 20 minutes or until cool enough to handle. Using a paring knife, gently pull off the skin; discard skin. Cut sweet peppers into 1-inch-wide strips.
2 Meanwhile, lightly coat two 12-inch pizza pans with cooking spray. Divide bread dough in half. Pat dough halves into 11-inch circles in each pizza pan, building up edges slightly. Prick bottom of crusts with a fork. Do not let rise. Bake in the 425°F oven about 10 minutes or until brown. Remove from oven; cool on a wire rack.
3 Lightly coat crusts with cooking spray; sprinkle with crushed red pepper. Top with mozzarella cheese, sweet pepper, onion, and tomato. Sprinkle with queso fresco.
4 Bake in the 425°F oven about 7 minutes or until cheese melts and crusts are crisp. Sprinkle with basil.

PER SERVING 252 calories; 9 g fat (1 g sat.); 14 g protein; 32 g carbohydrate; 3 g fiber; 474 mg sodium; 21 mg cholesterol

Roasted Vegetable Pizzas

page 221
page 239
Satisfying

Soups & Stews

Vegetable Soup

If you like smooth, creamy soups, a handheld blender is a handy tool to have. It allows you to blend soup to the ultimate creaminess right in the pan. If you do not have one, you can use a food processor or regular blender to do the same job, but you will need to blend the soup in batches instead of all at once.

Caramelized Ginger-Carrot Soup

Vegetable Soup

MAKES 6 main-dish servings
PREP 20 minutes **COOK** 15 minutes

- **⅔ cup sliced leek (2 medium) or ½ cup chopped onion (1 medium)**
- **1 tablespoon olive oil or cooking oil**
- **8 ounces fresh mushrooms, quartered**
- **1 cup coarsely chopped yellow or red sweet pepper (1 large)**
- **4 cloves garlic, minced**
- **3 cups water**
- **1 28-ounce can whole Italian-style tomatoes, cut up and undrained**
- **1 19-ounce can cannellini (white kidney) beans, rinsed and drained**
- **¼ teaspoon salt**
- **¼ teaspoon black pepper**
- **4 cups fresh baby spinach leaves (about 8 ounces)**

1 In a Dutch oven cook leek in hot oil over medium heat until tender. Add mushrooms, sweet pepper, and garlic; cook and stir for 5 minutes.
2 Add the water, undrained tomatoes, beans, salt, and black pepper. Bring to boiling; reduce heat. Simmer, uncovered, for 5 minutes. Stir in spinach.

PER SERVING 139 calories; 3 g fat (0 g sat.); 9 g protein; 27 g carbohydrate; 8 g fiber; 522 mg sodium; 0 mg cholesterol

Caramelized Ginger-Carrot Soup

MAKES 12 side-dish servings
PREP 30 minutes **COOK** 50 minutes

- **2 tablespoons cooking oil**
- **3 cups thinly sliced onion**
- **2 tablespoons sugar**
- **⅛ teaspoon freshly ground black pepper**
- **2 tablespoons grated fresh ginger**
- **8 carrots (about 1¼ pounds)**
- **1 medium sweet potato**
- **6 cups chicken broth**
- **1 cup half-and-half or light cream**

1 For caramelized onions, in a large skillet heat oil over medium heat. Add onion, sugar, and pepper; reduce heat to low and cook, covered, for 30 minutes, stirring twice. Add ginger; cook, uncovered, 20 to 30 minutes more or until onion is golden brown, stirring occasionally. Divide in half.
2 Meanwhile, peel carrots and sweet potato and cut into 1-inch pieces. In a large saucepan combine broth, carrots, and sweet potato. Bring to boiling; reduce heat. Simmer, covered, for 40 minutes or until carrots and potatoes are very tender. Add half of the caramelized onions. Puree until nearly smooth with a handheld blender or process 2 cups at a time in a food processor. Add half-and-half; heat through. If desired, season to taste with *salt* and additional *pepper.* Garnish with remaining caramelized onions.

PER SERVING 105 calories; 5 g fat (2 g sat.); 2 g protein; 13 g carbohydrate; 2 g fiber; 524 mg sodium; 9 mg cholesterol

Carrot-Cucumber Gazpacho [right]

Grilled or roasted chicken breast

Grilled or roasted new potatoes

Salad of mesclun greens, fresh peach or nectarine slices, thinly sliced onion, and vinaigrette

Baby Vegetable Minestrone

MAKES 6 side-dish servings
PREP 20 minutes **COOK** 25 minutes

- **½ cup thinly sliced baby fennel**
- **½ cup sliced carrot, halved lengthwise (1 medium)**
- **2 large cloves garlic, minced**
- **¼ teaspoon lemon-pepper seasoning**
- **2 teaspoons olive oil**
- **2 14-ounce cans reduced-sodium chicken broth or 3½ cups homemade chicken broth**
- **½ cup dried ditalini or other small dried pasta**
- **6 ounces baby zucchini, halved lengthwise**
- **6 ounces baby yellow squash, halved lengthwise**
- **½ cup sliced green onion (4)**
- **¼ cup fresh basil leaves, thinly sliced**
- **6 ounces Parmigiana-Reggiano or Romano cheese, cut into 6 very thin wedges (optional)**

1 In a very large saucepan cook fennel, carrot, garlic, and lemon-pepper seasoning in hot oil over medium heat for 3 to 4 minutes or until carrot is slightly brown. Carefully stir in broth. Bring to boiling; reduce heat. Simmer, covered, about 8 minutes or until vegetables are just tender.
2 Add pasta. Simmer, covered, for 5 minutes. Add zucchini and squash. Return to boiling; reduce heat. Cover and simmer for 5 minutes more or until pasta is tender. Stir in green onion and basil.
3 If desired, place a wedge of cheese in each of six warmed bowls. Add hot soup. Let the cheese soften slightly before serving soup.

PER SERVING 77 calories; 2 g fat (0 g sat.); 4 g protein; 12 g carbohydrate; 2 g fiber; 376 mg sodium; 0 mg cholesterol

Carrot-Cucumber Gazpacho

MAKES 5 side-dish servings
PREP 25 minutes **CHILL** 1 to 24 hours

- **2 large tomatoes, quartered and seeded* (1 pound)**
- **1½ cups carrot juice**
- **2 tablespoons coarsely chopped fresh chives**
- **1½ cups coarsely chopped, seeded cucumber (1 medium)**
- **1½ cups fresh whole kernel corn (3 ears) (optional)**
- **1 cup chopped peeled jicama (¼ medium)**
- **½ cup arugula, shredded**
- **1 to 2 tablespoons prepared horseradish**
- **½ teaspoon salt**
- **4 large radishes, quartered or cut into chunks**
- **Shredded arugula (optional)**
- **Coarsely chopped radishes (optional)**
- **Fresh corn kernels (optional)**
- **Lime wedges (optional)**

1 In a blender or food processor combine tomatoes, carrot juice, and chives. Cover and blend until smooth. Transfer tomato mixture to a large bowl. Stir in cucumber, the 1½ cups corn (if desired), jicama, the ½ cup arugula, the horseradish, and salt. Cover and chill at least 1 hour or up to 24 hours before serving.
2 To serve, add the cut-up radishes to each serving. If desired, top with additional shredded arugula, chopped radishes, and corn. If desired, pass lime wedges.
***Note:** The color of gazpacho may vary with the ripeness and variety of the tomatoes used.

PER SERVING 66 calories; 0 g fat; 2 g protein; 15 g carbohydrate; 2 g fiber; 270 mg sodium; 0 mg cholesterol

Baby Vegetable Minestrone

Hearty Garlic & Snap Pea Soup

MAKES 8 side-dish servings or 4 main-dish servings
PREP 30 minutes **COOK** 19 minutes

- **4 cloves garlic, chopped**
- **2 tablespoons olive oil**
- **¼ cup chopped onion**
- **1 pound Yukon gold potatoes, quartered**
- **2 14-ounce cans reduced-sodium chicken broth**
- **1¾ cups water**
- **1 medium fennel bulb, thinly slivered (fronds reserved)**
- **1½ cups sugar snap peas, trimmed**
- **½ teaspoon salt**
- **¼ teaspoon black pepper**
- **1 tablespoon fresh snipped fennel fronds**
- **Plain yogurt (optional)**
- **Olive oil (optional)**

1 In a large saucepan cook garlic in the 2 tablespoons hot oil over medium heat for 1 minute. Add onion; cook and stir until tender. Add potatoes, broth, and the water. Bring to boiling; reduce heat. Simmer, covered, for 15 to 18 minutes or until potatoes are tender.

2 Place one-third of the potato mixture in a food processor or blender. Cover and process until smooth. Repeat with remaining potato mixture. Return all to saucepan. Add fennel and peas. Bring to boiling; reduce heat. Simmer, uncovered, for 3 minutes.
3 Stir in salt and pepper. Top with fennel fronds. If desired, top with yogurt and drizzle with oil.

PER SERVING 102 calories; 3 g fat (0 g sat.); 3 g protein; 15 g carbohydrate; 3 g fiber; 404 mg sodium; 0 mg cholesterol

Broccoli-Pea Soup

MAKES 8 main-dish servings
PREP 15 minutes **COOK** 27 minutes

- **¾ cup chopped green onion (6)**
- **2 tablespoons unsalted butter**
- **4 cups chopped broccoli (1 large bunch)**
- **1¼ cups finely chopped, peeled potato (1 large)**
- **4 cups water**
- **2 cups chicken broth**
- **1 10-ounce package frozen peas**
- **3 tablespoons prepared pesto**
- **½ cup shredded fontina cheese (2 ounces)**
- **½ cup whipping cream**
- **½ teaspoon salt**
- **¼ teaspoon black pepper**
- **6 teaspoons grated Parmesan cheese**

1 In a Dutch oven cook green onion in hot butter over medium heat about 3 minutes or until soft. Add broccoli, potato, the water, and the broth. Bring to boiling; reduce heat. Simmer, partially covered, for 20 minutes. Stir in peas and pesto; simmer, uncovered, about 4 minutes.
2 Place one-third of the broccoli mixture in a food processor or blender. Cover and process until very smooth. Repeat with remaining broccoli mixture. Return all to Dutch oven. Stir in fontina cheese, cream, salt, and pepper. Reheat soup over low heat, if necessary. Sprinkle each serving with Parmesan cheese.

PER SERVING 233 calories; 15 g fat (8 g sat.); 9 g protein; 18 g carbohydrate; 5 g fiber; 438 mg sodium; 40 mg cholesterol

Mulligatawny Soup

MAKES 6 main-dish servings
PREP 30 minutes **COOK** 20 minutes

- **1 cup chopped onion (1 large)**
- **1 cup coarsely chopped carrot (2 medium)**
- **1 cup sliced celery (2 stalks)**
- **1 tablespoon cooking oil**
- **1 large tart apple, chopped (1⅓ cups)**
- **2 to 3 teaspoons curry powder**
- **¼ teaspoon salt**
- **2 14-ounce cans reduced-sodium chicken broth**
- **2½ cups water**
- **1 14.5-ounce can stewed tomatoes, undrained**
- **2 cups chopped cooked chicken or turkey (about 10 ounces)**

1 In a Dutch oven cook onion, carrot, and celery in hot oil over medium heat about 10 minutes or until crisp-tender. Reduce heat to medium-low; add apple, curry powder, and salt. Cook, covered, for 5 minutes.
2 Stir in broth, the water, and undrained tomatoes. Bring to boiling; reduce heat. Simmer, uncovered, for 10 minutes. Stir in the cooked chicken; simmer for 10 minutes more.

PER SERVING 182 calories; 7 g fat (1 g sat.); 16 g protein; 15 g carbohydrate; 3 g fiber; 610 mg sodium; 42 mg cholesterol

Mulligatawny Soup

Potato-Lentil Soup

MAKES 6 main-dish servings
PREP 20 minutes **COOK** 40 minutes

- **1 cup chopped onion (1 large)**
- **6 cloves garlic, minced**
- **1 tablespoon olive oil**
- **1 tablespoon fajita seasoning**
- **6 cups water**
- **1¼ cups dry brown lentils (8 ounces)**
- **1½ teaspoons dried dill**
- **¼ teaspoon salt**
- **6 ounces round red potatoes, scrubbed and cut into ¾-inch pieces**
- **1 14.5-ounce can no-salt-added diced tomatoes, undrained**
- **1 6-ounce can no-salt-added tomato paste**
- **2 tablespoons canned diced green chile peppers, undrained**
- **1 tablespoon snipped fresh parsley**
- **Fresh dill sprigs (optional)**

1 In a Dutch oven cook onion and garlic in hot oil over medium heat about 4 minutes or until tender. Stir in fajita seasoning.
2 Add the water, the lentils, dried dill, and salt to the onion mixture. Bring to boiling; reduce heat. Simmer, covered, for 15 minutes. Stir in potatoes. Simmer, covered, for 10 to 15 minutes more or until potatoes and lentils are tender.
3 Add undrained tomatoes, tomato paste, and undrained chile peppers. Return to boiling; reduce heat. Simmer, uncovered, for 10 minutes. Stir in parsley. If desired, garnish each serving with fresh dill.

PER SERVING 242 calories; 3 g fat (0 g sat.); 13 g protein; 41 g carbohydrate; 16 g fiber; 259 mg sodium; 0 mg cholesterol

Most soups, stews, and chilies are good for stashing in the freezer for a hot meal on a cold day. If you plan to freeze soup, remember that hot foods bound for the freezer need to cool quickly. To do this, divide the soup into portions that are 2 to 3 inches deep and stir them while cooling. Arrange the containers in a single layer in the freezer until frozen; this allows air to circulate around the containers and thus the soup freezes faster.

Easy Egg-Drop Soup 

MAKES 4 main-dish servings
START TO FINISH 15 minutes

- **1 cup finely chopped cooked chicken**
- **2 teaspoons rice vinegar or white wine vinegar**
- **1½ teaspoons soy sauce**
- **⅛ teaspoon ground ginger**
- **1 14-ounce can chicken broth**
- **½ cup purchased shredded carrot**
- **¼ cup thinly sliced green onion (2)**
- **1 egg, beaten**

1 In a small bowl combine chicken, vinegar, soy sauce, and ginger; set aside.
2 In a medium saucepan combine broth, carrot, and green onion. Bring to boiling; reduce heat. Simmer, uncovered, about 2 minutes. Add chicken mixture; heat through.
3 Pour beaten egg into hot chicken mixture in a thin steady stream while stirring two or three times to create shreds. Remove from heat. Cover and let stand for 1 minute.

PER SERVING 102 calories; 4 g fat (1 g sat.); 13 g protein; 3 g carbohydrate; 1 g fiber; 582 mg sodium; 85 mg cholesterol

A hint of delicate dill puts a fresh twist on the earthy combo of potatoes and lentils.

Potato-Lentil Soup

Barley-Beef Soup

Barley-Beef Soup

MAKES 8 main-dish servings
PREP 25 minutes **COOK** 1¾ hours

- **12** **ounces beef stew meat, cut into 1-inch cubes**
- **1** **tablespoon cooking oil**
- **4** **14-ounce cans low-sodium beef broth**
- **1** **cup chopped onion (1 large)**
- **½** **cup chopped celery (1 stalk)**
- **1** **teaspoon dried oregano or basil, crushed**
- **2** **cloves garlic, minced**
- **¼** **teaspoon black pepper**
- **1** **bay leaf**
- **1** **cup frozen mixed vegetables**
- **1** **14.5-ounce can diced tomatoes, undrained**
- **1** **cup ½-inch slices peeled parsnip or ½-inch cubes peeled potato**
- **⅔** **cup quick-cooking barley**

1 In a Dutch oven brown beef in hot oil over medium heat. Stir in broth, onion, celery, oregano, garlic, pepper, and bay leaf. Bring to boiling; reduce heat. Simmer, covered, for 1½ hours.
2 Stir in frozen vegetables, undrained tomatoes, parsnip, and barley. Return to boiling; reduce heat. Simmer, covered, about 15 minutes more or until meat and vegetables are tender. Discard bay leaf.

PER SERVING 168 calories; 4 g fat (1 g sat.); 13 g protein; 20 g carbohydrate; 3 g fiber; 492 mg sodium; 25 mg cholesterol

Choose-a-Vegetable Chicken & Pasta Soup

Choose-a-Vegetable Chicken & Pasta Soup

MAKES 6 main-dish servings
START TO FINISH 40 minutes

- **2** **14-ounce cans reduced-sodium chicken broth**
- **2** **cups water**
- **¼** **teaspoon black pepper**
- **1** **cup dried twisted spaghetti or broken fusilli pasta**
- **3** **cups vegetable pieces (such as thinly sliced carrots, small broccoli florets, chopped green or red sweet pepper, and/or fresh or frozen whole kernel corn)**
- **1½** **cups cubed cooked chicken (about 8 ounces)**
- **1** **tablespoon snipped fresh basil**
- **¼** **cup finely shredded Parmesan cheese (1 ounce)**

1 In a Dutch oven combine the broth, the water, and black pepper. Bring to boiling; stir in the pasta. Return to boiling; reduce heat. Simmer, covered, for 5 minutes.
2 Stir in vegetables. Return to boiling; reduce heat. Simmer, covered, for 5 to 8 minutes more or until vegetables and pasta are tender. Stir in chicken and basil; heat through. To serve, sprinkle each serving with cheese.

PER SERVING 172 calories; 4 g fat (2 g sat.); 16 g protein; 18 g carbohydrate; 2 g fiber; 447 mg sodium; 35 mg cholesterol

Hot 'n' Spicy Fish Soup

Hot 'n' Spicy Fish Soup

MAKES 4 main-dish servings
START TO FINISH 35 minutes

- **4 6-ounce fresh or frozen halibut steaks, cut 1 inch thick**
- **½ teaspoon cumin seeds**
- **4 teaspoons cooking oil**
- **½ cup chopped onion (1 medium)**
- **3 to 4 teaspoons grated fresh ginger**
- **2 fresh serrano chile peppers, seeded and finely chopped***
- **½ cup chopped roma tomato (1 large)**
- **1½ cups water**
- **1 teaspoon ground coriander**
- **½ teaspoon ground turmeric**
- **½ teaspoon salt**

1 Thaw fish, if frozen. Rinse fish; pat dry with paper towels. Remove skin and bones. Cut into 1-inch pieces; set aside.
2 In a medium saucepan cook and stir cumin seeds in hot oil over medium heat about 1 minute or until toasted. Add onion; cook and stir for 4 to 5 minutes or until tender. Add ginger and serrano peppers; cook and stir for 1 minute. Add tomato; cook and stir for 2 to 3 minutes more or until tomato has softened. Stir in the water, the coriander, turmeric, and salt. Bring just to boiling; reduce heat. Stir in fish. Simmer, covered, about 5 minutes or just until fish flakes easily when tested with a fork. Serve immediately.
***Note:** Because chile peppers contain volatile oils that can burn your skin and eyes, avoid direct contact with them as much as possible. When working with chile peppers, wear plastic or rubber gloves. If your bare hands do touch the chile peppers, wash your hands and nails well with soap and warm water.

PER SERVING 252 calories; 9 g fat (1 g sat.); 36 g protein; 5 g carbohydrate; 1 g fiber; 392 mg sodium; 54 mg cholesterol

Curried Corn Soup

MAKES 4 main-dish servings
START TO FINISH 45 minutes

- **8 ounces fresh or frozen peeled and deveined medium shrimp**
- **1 cup finely chopped green and/or red sweet pepper**
- **¼ cup finely chopped onion**
- **2 teaspoons cooking oil**
- **2 teaspoons curry powder**
- **¼ teaspoon salt**
- **¼ teaspoon black pepper**
- **3 cups fresh corn kernels (6 ears) or one 16-ounce package frozen whole kernel corn, thawed**
- **1 cup reduced-sodium chicken broth**
- **3 cups fat-free milk or plain light soymilk**
- **2 tablespoons snipped fresh cilantro**
- **⅓ cup plain low-fat yogurt or plain soy yogurt**

1 Thaw shrimp, if frozen. Rinse shrimp; pat dry with paper towels. Set aside. In a large saucepan cook sweet pepper and onion in hot oil over medium-high heat about 4 minutes or until tender, stirring occasionally. Add curry powder, salt, and black pepper; cook and stir for 1 minute. Stir in corn and broth. Bring to boiling; reduce heat. Cook, covered, about 5 minutes or until corn is tender. Remove from heat and let stand for 10 minutes.
2 Transfer corn mixture to a blender or food processor.* Add ½ cup of the milk. Cover and blend until almost smooth. Return mixture to the saucepan. Stir in the remaining 2½ cups milk and the shrimp; heat through. (Do not boil.) Stir in snipped cilantro. To serve, top each serving with yogurt and *fresh cilantro sprigs.*
***Note:** If using a food processor, process mixture half at a time using ¼ cup of the milk with each half.

PER SERVING 271 calories; 5 g fat (1 g sat.); 24 g protein; 36 g carbohydrate; 4 g fiber; 528 mg sodium; 115 mg cholesterol

Curried Corn Soup

Hard to resist—succulent shrimp nestled in creamy chowderlike soup.

Vegetable Stew with
Cornmeal Dumplings

Easy Cassoulet

Vegetable Stew with Cornmeal Dumplings ✪

MAKES 6 main-dish servings
PREP 25 minutes **COOK** 8 to 10 hours (low) or 4 to 5 hours (high) + 50 minutes

- **3 cups peeled, cubed butternut or acorn squash, ½-inch cubes (1½ pounds)**
- **2 cups sliced fresh mushrooms**
- **2 14.5-ounce cans diced tomatoes, undrained**
- **1 15-ounce can Great Northern beans, rinsed and drained**
- **1 cup water**
- **4 cloves garlic, minced**
- **1 teaspoon dried Italian seasoning, crushed**
- **¼ teaspoon black pepper**
- **½ cup all-purpose flour**
- **⅓ cup yellow cornmeal**
- **2 tablespoons grated Parmesan cheese**
- **1 tablespoon snipped fresh parsley**
- **1 teaspoon baking powder**
- **¼ teaspoon salt**
- **1 egg**
- **2 tablespoons milk**
- **2 tablespoons cooking oil**
- **1 9-ounce package frozen Italian green beans or frozen cut green beans**
- **Paprika**

1 In a 3½- or 4-quart slow cooker stir together squash, mushrooms, undrained tomatoes, Great Northern beans, the water, the garlic, Italian seasoning, and pepper.
2 Cover and cook on low-heat setting for 8 to 10 hours or on high-heat setting for 4 to 5 hours.
3 For dumplings, in a medium bowl stir together flour, cornmeal, cheese, parsley, baking powder, and salt. In a small bowl whisk together egg, milk, and oil until combined. Add egg mixture to flour mixture; stir with a fork just until combined.
4 If using low-heat setting, turn to high-heat setting. Stir frozen green beans into stew. Drop the dumpling dough into six mounds on top of the stew. Sprinkle dough with paprika. Cover and cook for 50 minutes more.

PER SERVING 288 calories; 7 g fat (2 g sat.); 12 g protein; 45 g carbohydrate; 7 g fiber; 442 mg sodium; 37 mg cholesterol

Easy Cassoulet (30)

MAKES 5 main-dish servings
PREP 20 minutes **COOK** 8 minutes

- **Nonstick cooking spray**
- **6 ounces lean boneless pork, cut into bite-size pieces**
- **1 large onion, cut into thin wedges**
- **1 cup thinly sliced carrot (2 medium)**
- **½ cup reduced-sodium chicken broth**
- **2 cloves garlic, minced**
- **½ teaspoon dried thyme, crushed**
- **1 14.5-ounce can diced tomatoes, undrained**
- **¼ cup dry white wine or reduced-sodium chicken broth**
- **2 15-ounce cans Great Northern beans, rinsed and drained**
- **6 ounces fully cooked smoked turkey sausage, cut into bite-size pieces**
- **1 tablespoon snipped fresh parsley**

1 Lightly coat a large saucepan with cooking spray. Lightly brown pork in hot pan over medium heat for 2 to 3 minutes. Add onion, carrot, broth, garlic, and thyme. Bring to boiling; reduce heat. Simmer, covered, for 6 to 8 minutes or until pork and vegetables are just tender.
2 Stir in undrained tomatoes, wine, and beans; mash beans slightly. Stir in sausage. Bring just to boiling. To serve, sprinkle each serving with parsley.

PER SERVING 218 calories; 6 g fat (2 g sat.); 18 g protein; 24 g carbohydrate; 6 g fiber; 575 mg sodium; 37 mg cholesterol

Chicken & Duck Hunter Stew

MAKES 12 main-dish servings
PREP 1 hour **COOK** 45 minutes

- 12 chicken drumsticks
- 3 skinless, boneless duck breast halves
- ¼ cup olive oil
- 3 cups assorted sliced fresh mushrooms (such as cremini, shiitake, oyster, and/or button) (8 ounces)
- 2 medium onions, sliced
- 3 cloves garlic, minced
- 3 cups chopped, seeded tomato (6 medium)
- 3 medium green sweet peppers, cut into 1-inch pieces
- 1½ cups dry Marsala or beef broth
- 1 6-ounce can tomato paste
- ¾ cup pitted kalamata olives and/or green olives
- 2 tablespoons balsamic vinegar
- 1 teaspoon salt
- ¼ teaspoon black pepper
- ¼ cup snipped fresh oregano or marjoram
- 2 tablespoons snipped fresh rosemary
- 6 cups hot cooked Israeli couscous or couscous

1 If desired, skin drumsticks. Cut duck breast halves into quarters. In a 6-quart Dutch oven cook chicken and duck, half at a time, in hot oil over medium heat about 15 minutes or until light brown, turning to brown evenly. Remove chicken and duck from pan; set chicken aside. Cover and refrigerate duck while cooking vegetables and chicken.
2 Add mushrooms, onions, and garlic to drippings in pan. Cook and stir over medium heat about 5 minutes or until vegetables are just tender. Return chicken to pan.
3 Meanwhile, in a large bowl stir together the tomato, sweet peppers, Marsala, tomato paste, olives, vinegar, salt, and black pepper. Pour over chicken in pan. Bring to boiling; reduce heat. Simmer, covered, for 20 minutes. Add duck. Return to boiling; reduce heat. Simmer, uncovered, for 25 to 30 minutes more or until poultry is tender. Just before serving, stir in oregano and rosemary. Serve stew over hot cooked couscous.

PER SERVING 393 calories; 14 g fat (3 g sat.); 33 g protein; 28 g carbohydrate; 3 g fiber; 407 mg sodium; 129 mg cholesterol

Pumpkin-Cider Stew 

MAKES 8 main-dish servings
PREP 30 minutes **COOK** 1¾ hours

- 3 tablespoons all-purpose flour
- 2 teaspoons fennel seeds, crushed
- ¼ teaspoon salt
- ¼ teaspoon black pepper
- 1 2-pound boneless beef chuck roast, cut into 1-inch cubes
- 2 medium onions, halved and thinly sliced
- 2 tablespoons olive oil
- 1 14-ounce can lower-sodium beef broth
- 1½ cups apple cider
- ¼ cup cider vinegar
- 1 2- to 3-pound pie pumpkin or 2 pounds potatoes
- 4 medium parsnips and/or carrots, peeled and cut into 1-inch pieces
- 2 red apples, cored and cut into wedges

1 In a resealable plastic bag combine flour, fennel seeds, salt, and pepper. Add beef cubes, a few at a time, shaking to coat. In a Dutch oven cook half of the beef and onion in 1 tablespoon of the hot oil over medium heat until beef is brown. Using a slotted spoon, remove beef mixture from pan; set aside. Add remaining beef and onion to pan and cook in remaining 1 tablespoon hot oil until meat is brown. Return all beef and onion to pan. Add broth, cider, and vinegar. Bring to boiling; reduce heat. Simmer, covered, for 1¼ hours.
2 Meanwhile, if using pie pumpkin, peel, seed, and remove strings from pumpkin. Cut pumpkin into 1- to 2-inch chunks. If using potatoes, peel and cut potatoes into wedges.
3 Add pumpkin (or potatoes) and parsnips to meat mixture. Return to boiling; reduce heat. Simmer, covered, for 25 minutes. Add apple; simmer, covered, for 5 to 10 minutes more or until vegetables and apple are tender.

PER SERVING 279 calories; 8 g fat (2 g sat.); 26 g protein; 26 g carbohydrate; 3 g fiber; 247 mg sodium; 67 mg cholesterol

Pumpkin-Cider Stew

Golden raisins and their sweet goodness brighten this classic bowl.

Beef Stew with Red Wine Gravy

Beef Stew with Red Wine Gravy

MAKES 6 main-dish servings
PREP 30 minutes **COOK** 12 to 14 hours (low) or 6 to 7 hours (high)

- **¼ cup all-purpose flour**
- **2 teaspoons dried Italian seasoning**
- **1 teaspoon salt**
- **½ teaspoon freshly ground black pepper**
- **2 pounds boneless beef chuck roast, cut into 1-inch cubes**
- **2 tablespoons olive oil**
- **2 large onions, cut into thin wedges**
- **8 ounces parsnip, quartered lengthwise and halved**
- **8 ounces carrot, quartered lengthwise and halved**
- **8 ounces Jerusalem artichoke (sunchokes), peeled and coarsely chopped**
- **1 cup red wine (such as Cabernet Sauvignon) or beef broth**
- **½ cup beef broth**
- **¼ cup tomato paste**
- **Golden raisins and/or red wine vinegar**
- **Crusty bread (optional)**

1 In a plastic bag combine flour, Italian seasoning, salt, and pepper. Add beef cubes, a few at a time, shaking to coat. In a large skillet brown beef, half at a time, in hot oil over medium-high heat. Drain off fat.
2 In a 4½- to 6-quart slow cooker combine onions, parsnip, carrot, and artichoke; top with beef. Pour wine and broth over meat in cooker.
3 Cover and cook on low-heat setting for 12 to 14 hours or on high-heat setting for 6 to 7 hours. Stir in tomato paste. Top each serving with raisins and/or vinegar. If desired, serve with crusty bread.

PER SERVING 215 calories; 4 g fat (1 g sat.); 26 g protein; 7 g carbohydrate; 1 g fiber; 405 mg sodium; 64 mg cholesterol

French Beef Stew

MAKES 4 main-dish servings
PREP 25 minutes **COOK** about 2 hours

- **1 pound lean boneless beef round, cut into 1-inch cubes**
- **1 tablespoon olive oil**
- **⅓ cup chopped onion (1 small)**
- **1 cup dry white wine**
- **1 teaspoon dried herbes de Provence, crushed**
- **¼ teaspoon each salt and black pepper**
- **8 small new potatoes, halved or quartered**
- **8 pearl onions, peeled**
- **⅔ cup chopped, peeled, seeded tomato (1 large)**
- **¼ cup Niçoise olives, pitted, or pitted kalamata olives**
- **2 tablespoons drained capers**
- **8 ounces haricot verts or small green beans, trimmed and cut into 3-inch lengths**
- **1 tablespoon snipped fresh Italian parsley**

1 In a Dutch oven brown half the meat cubes in hot oil over medium heat. Using a slotted spoon, remove meat from pan; set aside. Add remaining meat cubes and chopped onion to drippings in pan. Cook for 3 to 5 minutes or until meat is brown and onion is tender. Drain off any fat. Return all meat to pan. Add wine, stirring to loosen any brown bits from bottom of pan. Add 2 cups *water,* the herbes de Provence, salt, and pepper. Bring to boiling; reduce heat. Simmer, covered, for 1¼ hours or until meat is nearly tender.
2 Add the potatoes and pearl onions. Return to boiling; reduce heat. Simmer, covered, about 30 minutes or until beef and vegetables are tender. Stir in tomato, olives, and drained capers; heat through.
3 Meanwhile, in a medium saucepan cook haricot verts, covered, in a small amount of boiling water for 5 to 7 minutes or until tender. To serve, divide stew among four bowls. Serve with haricot verts and garnish with parsley.

PER SERVING 289 calories; 8 g fat (2 g sat.); 28 g protein; 17 g carbohydrate; 4 g fiber; 399 mg sodium; 65 mg cholesterol

French Beef Stew

Curried Cider-Pork Stew

MAKES 6 main-dish servings
PREP 35 minutes **COOK** 1 hour

- **2 pounds boneless pork shoulder, cut into 1-inch cubes**
- **1 tablespoon cooking oil**
- **1⅓ cups chopped, peeled red and/or green tart cooking apple (2 medium)**
- **1 large onion, cut into thin wedges**
- **2 teaspoons curry powder**
- **1 14-ounce can chicken broth**
- **⅔ cup apple cider or apple juice**
- **¼ teaspoon each salt and black pepper**
- **12 ounces baby carrots with tops, trimmed, or packaged peeled baby carrots**
- **1 cup sliced celery (2 stalks)**
- **2 cups cubed, peeled butternut squash (1 pound)**
- **2 medium red and/or green tart cooking apples, cored and cut into ¼-inch wedges**
- **Sour cream, shredded orange peel, snipped fresh oregano, and/or freshly ground black pepper (optional)**

1 In a Dutch oven brown pork cubes, half at a time, in hot oil over medium-high heat. Return all pork to pan. Add chopped apple, the onion, and curry powder; cook and stir for 2 minutes. Add broth, cider, salt, and pepper. Bring to boiling; reduce heat. Simmer, covered, for 30 minutes, stirring occasionally.

2 Add carrots and celery to pan. Return to boiling; reduce heat. Simmer, covered, for 20 minutes, stirring occasionally. Add squash and apple wedges to pan. Simmer, covered, for 10 to 12 minutes or until pork and vegetables are tender. If desired, serve with sour cream, orange peel, oregano, and/or freshly ground black pepper.

PER SERVING 379 calories; 14 g fat (4 g sat.); 32 g protein; 31 g carbohydrate; 6 g fiber; 526 mg sodium; 102 mg cholesterol

Southwest Pork Salsa Stew

Southwest Pork Salsa Stew 

MAKES 4 main-dish servings
START TO FINISH 25 minutes

- **Nonstick cooking spray**
- **12 ounces boneless pork loin or sirloin, cut into bite-size strips**
- **1 14-ounce can reduced-sodium chicken broth**
- **1 6-ounce can no-salt-added tomato paste**
- **½ cup bottled cilantro-flavored salsa***
- **½ teaspoon ground cumin**
- **1 medium zucchini, halved lengthwise and thinly sliced (2 cups)**
- **1 cup frozen sweet soybeans (edamame) or baby lima beans**
- **½ cup chopped, pitted, peeled mango (1 small)**

1 Lightly coat a large saucepan with cooking spray. Cook and stir pork in hot pan over medium-high heat about 2 minutes or until brown. Stir in broth, tomato paste, salsa, and cumin. Stir in zucchini and soybeans. Bring to boiling; reduce heat. Simmer, covered, about 10 minutes or until vegetables are tender. To serve, top each serving with chopped mango.

***Note:** If you can't find cilantro-flavored salsa, use regular salsa and stir in 2 tablespoons snipped fresh cilantro.

PER SERVING 243 calories; 7 g fat (2 g sat.); 26 g protein; 19 g carbohydrate; 6 g fiber; 594 mg sodium; 47 mg cholesterol

Chicken & Sausage Gumbo

MAKES 8 main-dish servings
PREP 25 minutes **COOK** 6 to 7 hours (low) or 3 to 3½ hours (high)

- **⅓ cup all-purpose flour**
- **1 14-ounce can reduced-sodium chicken broth**
- **2 cups chopped cooked chicken breast or turkey breast (10 ounces)**
- **8 ounces smoked turkey sausage, quartered lengthwise and sliced**
- **2 cups sliced fresh okra or one 10-ounce package frozen cut okra, partially thawed**
- **1 cup water**
- **1 cup coarsely chopped onion (1 large)**
- **1 cup coarsely chopped red or green sweet pepper (1 large)**
- **½ cup sliced celery (1 stalk)**
- **4 cloves garlic, minced**
- **1 teaspoon dried thyme, crushed**
- **½ teaspoon black pepper**
- **¼ teaspoon cayenne pepper**
- **3 cups hot cooked brown rice**

1 For roux, in a medium heavy saucepan cook flour over medium heat about 6 minutes or until brown, stirring occasionally. Remove from heat; cool slightly. Gradually stir broth into flour. Cook and stir over medium heat until thickened and bubbly.

2 Pour flour mixture into a 3½- or 4-quart slow cooker. Add chicken, sausage, okra, the water, the onion, sweet pepper, celery, garlic, thyme, black pepper, and cayenne pepper.
3 Cover and cook on low-heat setting for 6 to 7 hours or on high-heat setting for 3 to 3½ hours. Skim off fat. Serve gumbo over hot cooked rice.

PER SERVING 230 calories; 5 g fat (1 g sat.); 19 g protein; 27 g carbohydrate; 3 g fiber; 425 mg sodium; 48 mg cholesterol

Chicken & Sausage Gumbo

Chicken Sausage Noodle Bowl 

MAKES 6 main-dish servings
PREP 10 minutes **COOK** 18 minutes

- **1 large onion, halved and thinly sliced**
- **3 cups sliced assorted fresh mushrooms (8 ounces)**
- **2 tablespoons olive oil**
- **2 14-ounce cans reduced-sodium chicken broth**
- **2 cups water**
- **1 12-ounce package teriyaki-flavored cooked chicken sausage, diagonally sliced ¼ inch thick**
- **1 1-pound bag peeled baby carrots, halved diagonally**
- **8 ounces snow peas, trimmed**
- **¼ teaspoon red pepper flakes**
- **¼ cup light teriyaki sauce**
- **2 tablespoons cornstarch mixed with 3 tablespoons water**
- **8 ounces dried angel hair pasta, broken into thirds**
- **Chives for garnish (optional)**

1 In a large saucepan cook onion and mushrooms in hot oil over medium-high heat about 7 minutes or until tender. Carefully add broth and the water; bring to boiling. Add sausage, carrots, snow peas, and red pepper flakes. Return to boiling; reduce heat. Simmer, uncovered, about 5 minutes or until vegetables are tender.
2 Stir in teriyaki sauce and the cornstarch mixture. Simmer, uncovered, about 2 minutes or until thickened. Stir in pasta; simmer about 4 minutes or until pasta is tender. If desired, garnish with chives.

PER SERVING 348 calories; 11 g fat (2 g sat.); 19 g protein; 47 g carbohydrate; 4 g fiber; 584 mg sodium; 63 mg cholesterol

Baby vegetables cry out for attention. They are little, cute, and downright delicious. When in season, look for them at farmers' markets. Or find them year-round in the produce section of many large supermarkets.

Moroccan Chicken Stew 

MAKES 4 main-dish servings
START TO FINISH 30 minutes

- **1 cup couscous**
- **12 ounces skinless, boneless chicken thighs or breast halves, cut into 1-inch pieces**
- **⅓ cup sliced shallot (2 large)**
- **3 cloves garlic, minced**
- **1 tablespoon olive oil**
- **½ teaspoon salt**
- **½ teaspoon paprika**
- **½ teaspoon ground cumin**
- **¼ teaspoon ground cinnamon**
- **¼ teaspoon ground saffron or ground turmeric**
- **⅛ teaspoon cayenne pepper**
- **6 ounces baby pattypan squash or 1½ cups sliced zucchini**
- **1 cup slender baby carrots, tops trimmed, or packaged peeled baby carrots**
- **1 cup reduced-sodium chicken broth**
- **¼ cup golden or dark raisins**
- **Fresh mint (optional)**

1 Cook couscous according to package directions, except omit the oil and salt; set aside and keep warm.
2 Meanwhile, in a large nonstick skillet cook chicken, shallot, and garlic in hot oil over medium-high heat for 2 minutes.
3 In a small bowl stir together salt, paprika, cumin, cinnamon, saffron, and cayenne pepper; sprinkle evenly over chicken mixture in skillet. Cook and stir for 2 minutes more or until chicken is no longer pink.
4 Cut any large pieces of squash and carrots in half; add to skillet along with broth and raisins. Bring to boiling; reduce heat. Simmer, covered, for 6 to 8 minutes or until vegetables are crisp-tender. Serve chicken mixture over couscous. If desired, garnish with fresh mint.

PER SERVING 363 calories; 7 g fat (1 g sat.); 24 g protein; 51 g carbohydrate; 9 g fiber; 496 mg sodium; 45 mg cholesterol

Use the broccoli-like clusters,

Tuscan Ravioli Stew

leaves, and stalks of the broccoli rabe.

Tuscan Ravioli Stew 

MAKES 4 main-dish servings
START TO FINISH 20 minutes

- ½ cup thinly sliced leek (1 large)
- 3 cloves garlic, minced
- 1 tablespoon olive oil
- 1 14-ounce can beef broth
- ¾ cup water
- ¼ teaspoon crushed red pepper (optional)
- 5 cups coarsely chopped broccoli rabe (6 ounces)
- 1 14.5-ounce can no-salt-added stewed tomatoes, undrained
- 1 9-ounce package refrigerated chicken-filled or cheese-filled ravioli
- 1 tablespoon snipped fresh rosemary or 1 teaspoon dried rosemary, crushed
- ¼ cup grated Asiago cheese

1 In a large saucepan cook leek and garlic in hot oil over medium heat for 5 minutes. Stir in broth, the water, and, if desired, the red pepper. Bring to boiling. Stir in broccoli rabe, undrained tomatoes, ravioli, and rosemary. Return to boiling; reduce heat. Simmer, covered, for 7 to 8 minutes or until broccoli rabe and ravioli are tender. To serve, top each serving with Asiago cheese.

PER SERVING 320 calories; 13 g fat (2 g sat.); 15 g protein; 38 g carbohydrate; 5 g fiber; 704 mg sodium; 65 mg cholesterol

Spiced Seafood Stew

Spiced Seafood Stew

MAKES 4 main-dish servings
PREP 30 minutes **SOAK** 45 minutes **COOK** 6 minutes

- 8 ounces fresh or frozen medium shrimp in shells
- 8 ounces fresh or frozen scallops
- 8 ounces (8 to 12) fresh mussels in shells
- 1 cup finely chopped onion (2 medium)
- 4 cloves garlic, minced
- 1 tablespoon olive oil
- 1 teaspoon ground cumin
- ½ teaspoon ground cinnamon
- ¼ teaspoon cayenne pepper
- 1 cup fish or vegetable broth
- 1 cup finely chopped tomato (2 medium)
- ¼ teaspoon salt
- ⅛ teaspoon ground saffron
- Hot cooked couscous (optional)
- Italian parsley (optional)

1 Thaw shrimp and scallops, if frozen. Peel and devein shrimp, leaving tails intact. Rinse shrimp and scallops; pat dry with paper towels. Set aside. Scrub mussels; remove beards. In a large bowl combine 2 cups *water* and 3 tablespoons *salt;* soak mussels in salt water for 15 minutes. Drain; rinse. Repeat twice. Set aside.

2 In a large saucepan cook onion and garlic in hot oil over medium heat until tender. Stir in cumin, cinnamon, and cayenne pepper; cook and stir for 1 minute. Carefully stir in broth, tomato, the ¼ teaspoon salt, and the saffron. Bring to boiling; add shrimp, scallops, and mussels. Return to boiling; reduce heat. Simmer, covered, about 5 minutes or until mussel shells open. If desired, serve over couscous and garnish with parsley.

PER SERVING 187 calories; 6 g fat (1 g sat.); 23 g protein; 12 g carbohydrate; 1 g fiber; 503 mg sodium; 116 mg cholesterol

Shrimp & Crab Gumbo

MAKES 8 main-dish servings
PREP 30 minutes **COOK** 30 minutes

- 1 pound fresh or frozen large shrimp in shells
- ⅓ cup all-purpose flour
- 2 cups chopped onion (2 large)
- 1½ cups chopped green or red sweet pepper (2 medium)
- 2 cups thinly sliced celery (4 stalks)
- 4 cloves garlic, minced
- 2 tablespoons cooking oil
- 2 14-ounce cans reduced-sodium beef broth
- 1 cup water
- 1 recipe Cajun Spice Mix
- 1 16-ounce package frozen cut okra
- 2 6-ounce cans crabmeat, drained, flaked, and cartilage removed
- 3 cups hot cooked long grain rice or brown rice
- Green onions (optional)
- Bottled hot pepper sauce (optional)

Shrimp & Crab Gumbo

1 Thaw shrimp, if frozen. Peel and devein shrimp, leaving tails intact. Rinse shrimp; pat dry with paper towels. Set aside. In a medium heavy saucepan cook flour over medium heat about 6 minutes or until brown, stirring occasionally. Place in a small bowl; set aside to cool.

2 In a Dutch oven cook onion, sweet pepper, celery, and garlic in hot oil over medium-high heat about 5 minutes or until vegetables are tender. Slowly whisk 1 can of the broth into brown flour. Add broth-flour mixture, remaining 1 can broth, the water, and the Cajun Spice Mix to pan. Stir in okra. Bring to boiling; reduce heat. Simmer, covered, for 15 minutes.

3 Add shrimp; cook for 2 to 3 minutes or until shrimp are opaque. Gently stir in crabmeat. Serve gumbo over rice. If desired, garnish each serving with green onions and pass hot pepper sauce.

Cajun Spice Mix: In a small bowl stir together ½ teaspoon dried thyme, crushed; ¼ teaspoon ground white pepper; ¼ teaspoon salt; ¼ teaspoon black pepper; and ¼ teaspoon crushed red pepper.

PER SERVING 263 calories; 5 g fat (1 g sat.); 22 g protein; 31 g carbohydrate; 4 g fiber; 510 mg sodium; 102 mg cholesterol

Chipotle Chili with Hominy & Beans (30)

MAKES 6 main-dish servings
START TO FINISH 30 minutes

- Nonstick cooking spray
- 8 ounces extra-lean ground beef or ground uncooked chicken or turkey breast
- 1 cup chopped onion (1 large)
- 1½ teaspoons ground cumin
- ½ teaspoon dried oregano, crushed
- 1 to 2 teaspoons chopped canned chipotle chile peppers in adobo sauce*
- 2 14.5-ounce cans no-salt-added stewed tomatoes, undrained
- 1 15-ounce can red beans, rinsed and drained
- 1 15-ounce can yellow hominy, rinsed and drained

- ½ **cup chopped green or red sweet pepper (1 small)**
- ½ **cup water**
- 6 **tablespoons shredded cheddar cheese (1½ ounces) (optional)**

1 Lightly coat a large saucepan with cooking spray. Cook beef and onion in hot pan over medium heat until meat is brown and onion is tender. If necessary, drain off fat.
2 Stir in cumin and oregano; cook and stir for 1 minute more. Add chipotle peppers, undrained tomatoes, beans, hominy, sweet pepper, and the water. Bring to boiling; reduce heat. Simmer, covered, for 5 minutes. If desired, sprinkle each serving with cheese.
***Note:** Because chile peppers contain volatile oils that can burn your skin and eyes, avoid direct contact with them as much as possible. When working with chile peppers, wear plastic or rubber gloves. If your bare hands do touch the chile peppers, wash your hands and nails well with soap and warm water.

PER SERVING 257 calories; 7 g fat (3 g sat.); 13 g protein; 35 g carbohydrate; 9 g fiber; 477 mg sodium; 26 mg cholesterol

Three-Bean Vegetarian Chili

MAKES 4 main-dish servings
PREP 20 minutes **COOK** 6 to 8 hours (low) or 3 to 4 hours (high)

- 1 **15-ounce can no-salt-added red kidney beans, rinsed and drained**
- 1 **15-ounce can small white beans, rinsed and drained**
- 1 **15-ounce can low-sodium black beans, rinsed and drained**
- 1 **14.5-ounce can diced tomatoes with green chile peppers, undrained**
- 1 **cup beer or chicken broth**
- 3 **tablespoons chocolate-flavored syrup**
- 1 **tablespoon chili powder**
- 2 **teaspoons Cajun seasoning**
- **Light dairy sour cream (optional)**
- **Shredded cheddar cheese (optional)**

1 In a 3½- or 4-quart slow cooker combine kidney beans, white beans, black beans, undrained tomatoes with green chile peppers, beer, chocolate syrup, chili powder, and Cajun seasoning.
2 Cover and cook on low-heat setting for 6 to 8 hours or on high-heat setting for 3 to 4 hours. If desired, top each serving with sour cream and cheese.

PER SERVING 308 calories; 1 g fat (0 g sat.); 21 g protein; 60 g carbohydrate; 21 g fiber; 569 mg sodium; 0 mg cholesterol

Hearty Beef Chili

Hearty Beef Chili 

MAKES 8 to 10 main-dish servings
PREP 20 minutes **COOK** 9 to 10 hours (low) or 4½ to 5 hours (high)

- **1½ pounds beef chuck pot roast, cut into 1-inch cubes**
- **2 cups low-sodium vegetable juice or tomato juice**
- **2 cups chopped onion (2 large)**
- **2 15- to 16-ounce cans black, red kidney, and/or garbanzo beans (chickpeas), rinsed and drained**
- **1 14.5-ounce can no-salt-added diced tomatoes, undrained**
- **1½ cups chopped green sweet pepper (2 medium)**
- **1 10-ounce can diced tomatoes with green chile peppers, undrained**
- **1 teaspoon ground chipotle chile pepper**
- **1 teaspoon ground cumin**
- **1 teaspoon dried oregano, crushed**
- **3 cloves garlic, minced**

1 In a 4½- to 6-quart slow cooker combine meat, vegetable juice, onion, beans, undrained tomatoes, sweet pepper, undrained tomatoes with chile peppers, chipotle chile pepper, cumin, oregano, and garlic.
2 Cover and cook on low-heat setting for 9 to 10 hours or on high-heat setting for 4½ to 5 hours.

PER SERVING 226 calories; 4 g fat (1 g sat.); 26 g protein; 27 g carbohydrate; 8 g fiber; 467 mg sodium; 50 mg cholesterol

Traditional Cincinnati Chili 

MAKES 8 main-dish servings
PREP 25 minutes **COOK** 45 minutes

- **5 bay leaves**
- **1 teaspoon whole allspice**
- **2 pounds lean ground beef**
- **2 cups chopped onion (2 large)**
- **1 clove garlic, minced**
- **2 tablespoons chili powder**
- **1 teaspoon ground cinnamon**
- **½ teaspoon cayenne pepper**
- **4 cups water**
- **1 15-ounce can red kidney beans, rinsed and drained**
- **1 8-ounce can tomato sauce**
- **1 tablespoon vinegar**
- **1 teaspoon Worcestershire sauce**
- **½ teaspoon salt**
- **¼ teaspoon black pepper**
- **Hot cooked spaghetti (optional)**

1 For spice bag, place bay leaves and allspice on a square of double thickness 100-percent-cotton cheesecloth. Bring up corners and tie with 100-percent-cotton string; set aside.
2 In a Dutch oven cook beef, onion, and garlic over medium heat until the beef is brown. Drain off fat. Stir in chili powder, cinnamon, and cayenne pepper; cook and stir for 1 minute. Stir in the water, the beans, tomato sauce, vinegar, Worcestershire sauce, salt, and black pepper. Add spice bag.
3 Bring to boiling; reduce heat. Simmer, covered, for 30 minutes. Uncover and simmer for 15 to 20 minutes more or until desired consistency. Discard spice bag. If desired, serve chili over spaghetti.

PER SERVING 256 calories; 11 g fat (4 g sat.); 25 g protein; 15 g carbohydrate; 5 g fiber; 435 mg sodium; 71 mg cholesterol

Take chili beyond the basic bowl by adding a tasty topper or two. Try chopped onion, shredded cheese, sliced ripe olives, chopped tomato, and/or a spoonful of sour cream.

Pineapple-Pork Chili 30

MAKES 4 main-dish servings
START TO FINISH 20 minutes

- **1 pound ground pork or beef**
- **1 16-ounce jar pineapple salsa***
- **1 15-ounce can red kidney beans, rinsed and drained**
- **1 8-ounce can tomato sauce**
- **1 tablespoon chili powder**
- **Pineapple slices (optional)**

1 In a large saucepan brown pork over medium heat. Drain off fat. Stir in salsa, beans, tomato sauce, and chili powder. Bring to boiling; reduce heat. Simmer, uncovered, for 10 minutes. If desired, serve with pineapple slices.

***Note:** If you can't find pineapple salsa, use regular salsa and stir in 1/3 to 1/2 cup crushed pineapple.

PER SERVING 329 calories; 9 g fat (4 g sat.); 22 g protein; 44 g carbohydrate; 11 g fiber; 852 mg sodium; 53 mg cholesterol

Pineapple-Pork Chili

Simply

Sides

Applesauce

MAKES 12 servings

PREP 15 minutes **COOK** 20 minutes **COOL** 1 hour

- **6 sprigs fresh thyme**
- **4 pounds cooking apples, cored and cut into chunks**
- **½ cup water**
- **½ to ¾ cup granulated sugar**
- **Brown sugar (optional)**
- **Fresh thyme sprigs (optional)**

1 Bundle thyme sprigs and tie with 100-percent-cotton kitchen string. In an 8-quart Dutch oven combine apples, thyme, and the water. Bring to boiling; reduce heat. Simmer, covered, about 20 minutes or until apples are just beginning to break up, stirring occasionally. Discard thyme. With a potato masher or large spoon, mash apples slightly.* Stir in granulated sugar to taste.

2 Serve warm or spoon into airtight containers. Cover and refrigerate for up to 3 weeks.** Stir before serving. If desired, garnish with a sprinkle of brown sugar and thyme.

***Note:** For a smoother, slightly thinner applesauce, process apple mixture, half at a time, in a food processor.

****Note:** Applesauce may be frozen for up to 6 months. Thaw in the refrigerator before serving.

PER SERVING 111 calories; 0 g fat; 0 g protein; 29 g carbohydrate; 4 g fiber; 2 mg sodium; 0 mg cholesterol

Cranberry Sauce with Lime & Ginger

Baked Apples with Feta & Thyme

MAKES 6 servings
PREP 20 minutes **BAKE** 30 minutes **COOK** 10 minutes
OVEN 350°F

- **3 small to medium cooking apples**
- **2 teaspoons snipped fresh thyme**
- **1 cup apple cider or apple juice**
- **⅓ cup raisins and/or dried cherries**
- **½ cup crumbled feta cheese (2 ounces)**
- **2 teaspoons olive oil**
- **Apple cider or apple juice**

1 Cut apples in half lengthwise; cut out the cores to make deep wells.* Sprinkle cut sides of apples evenly with 1 teaspoon of the thyme. Place apple halves, cut sides down, in a 2-quart rectangular baking dish. Pour the 1 cup apple cider over apples. Bake, covered, in a 350°F oven for 25 minutes. Remove from oven and turn apples, cut sides up. Spoon cider in bottom of the dish over the apples.
2 Meanwhile, combine the raisins, feta cheese, and the remaining 1 teaspoon thyme. Drizzle oil over top; toss to coat. Spoon raisin mixture into centers of apple halves, mounding as needed. Bake, uncovered, about 5 minutes more or until filling is just heated through.
3 Transfer apple halves to serving platter. If desired, strain juices from dish through a strainer lined with 100-percent-cotton cheesecloth. Measure juices. If necessary, add enough of the apple cider to make ¾ cup total liquid. Place juices in a small saucepan and bring to boiling over high heat. Continue boiling about 10 minutes or until liquid is reduced to ¼ cup. Spoon liquid over apple halves to serve.
***Note:** Use a melon baller to make a deep well in the apple halves.

PER SERVING 111 calories; 4 g fat (2 g sat.); 2 g protein; 19 g carbohydrate; 2 g fiber; 107 mg sodium; 8 mg cholesterol

Cranberry Sauce with Lime & Ginger 

MAKES 12 servings
START TO FINISH 25 minutes

- **½ cup sugar**
- **½ cup pure maple syrup or maple-flavored syrup**
- **½ cup water**
- **1½ teaspoons finely shredded lime peel**
- **1 tablespoon lime juice**
- **1 12-ounce package fresh cranberries**
- **1 teaspoon grated fresh ginger**
- **Thin lime wedges (optional)**

1 In a medium heavy saucepan stir together sugar, maple syrup, the water, the lime peel, and lime juice. Bring to boiling; reduce heat. Simmer, uncovered, about 3 minutes or until sugar dissolves.
2 Stir in cranberries. Simmer, uncovered, for 5 minutes, stirring occasionally. Stir in ginger. Simmer, uncovered, about 6 minutes more or until cranberries have popped and mixture starts to thicken, stirring occasionally. Let cool. If desired, garnish with lime wedges.
Make-Ahead Directions: Prepare as directed; let cool. Transfer cranberry sauce to an airtight container. Cover and chill for up to 3 days. Let stand at room temperature for 30 minutes before serving.

PER SERVING 79 calories; 0 g fat; 0 g protein; 21 g carbohydrate; 1 g fiber; 2 mg sodium; 0 mg cholesterol

Orange & Pineapple Salad

Orange Dream Fruit Salad  

MAKES 4 to 6 servings
START TO FINISH 15 minutes

- **1 cup chopped, peeled, and seeded mango or papaya (1 medium)**
- **1 11-ounce can mandarin orange sections, drained**
- **1 cup seedless red and/or green grapes, halved**
- **½ cup orange-flavored yogurt**
- **¼ teaspoon poppy seeds**

1 In a medium bowl combine mango, drained mandarin orange sections, and grapes. In a small bowl stir together the yogurt and poppy seeds. Add yogurt mixture to fruit mixture; stir to coat.

PER SERVING 136 calories; 1 g fat (0 g sat.); 2 g protein; 32 g carbohydrate; 2 g fiber; 26 mg sodium; 2 mg cholesterol

Honeydew & Apple Salad  

MAKES 6 servings
START TO FINISH 15 minutes

- **2 cups coarsely chopped, peeled, and seeded honeydew melon**
- **2 cups thinly sliced, pitted nectarine or peach (2 medium)**
- **1⅓ cups coarsely chopped cored tart apple (2 medium)**
- **¼ cup vanilla low-fat yogurt**
- **3 tablespoons apricot jam**
- **¼ teaspoon ground ginger or ground nutmeg**
- **1 cup fresh red raspberries**

1 In a large bowl combine melon, nectarine, and apple. For dressing, in a small bowl stir together yogurt, jam, and ginger.
2 To serve, spoon fruit mixture into dishes or glasses. Drizzle with dressing. Top with raspberries. Serve immediately.

PER SERVING 109 calories; 1 g fat (0 g sat.); 1 g protein; 27 g carbohydrate; 3 g fiber; 16 mg sodium; 1 mg cholesterol

Orange & Pineapple Salad 

MAKES 4 servings
PREP 10 minutes **CHILL** 2 to 24 hours

- **1 8-ounce can pineapple chunks (juice pack), drained**
- **½ cup miniature marshmallows**
- **½ cup light dairy sour cream**
- **1 11-ounce can mandarin orange sections, drained**
- **1 tablespoon coconut, toasted**

1 In a medium bowl stir together drained pineapple, marshmallows, and sour cream. Gently fold in drained mandarin orange sections. Cover and chill for 2 to 24 hours. Before serving, sprinkle with coconut.

PER SERVING 138 calories; 3 g fat (2 g sat.); 3 g protein; 26 g carbohydrate; 1 g fiber; 33 mg sodium; 10 mg cholesterol

Menu

Grilled turkey burgers or hamburgers

Green Bean Salad
[page 256]

Honeydew & Apple Salad [opposite]

Iced tea or lemonade

Honeydew & Apple Salad

Double delight—sweet dressing over

Summer Strawberry Salad

sweet fruit.

Summer Strawberry Salad 

MAKES 6 to 8 servings
START TO FINISH 20 minutes

- **6 cups chopped romaine lettuce (½ of a large head)**
- **3 cups sliced fresh strawberries**
- **2 cups cubed fresh pineapple (½ of a small)**
- **¾ cup sliced banana (1 medium)**
- **¼ cup water**
- **¼ cup cream of coconut**
- **2 tablespoons lemon juice**
- **1 tablespoon yellow mustard**
- **½ teaspoon ground ginger**
- **¼ cup sliced almonds, toasted (optional)**

1 In a very large bowl toss together the lettuce, strawberries, pineapple, and banana. If desired, cover and refrigerate for up to 1 hour.
2 For dressing, in a small bowl whisk together the water, the cream of coconut, lemon juice, mustard, and ginger. If desired, cover and refrigerate. To serve, toss greens mixture with dressing to coat. If desired, sprinkle with almonds.

PER SERVING 111 calories; 4 g fat (3 g sat.); 2 g protein; 20 g carbohydrate; 4 g fiber; 35 mg sodium; 0 mg cholesterol

Ginger Ale Salad 

MAKES 12 servings
PREP 20 minutes **CHILL** 6¾ hours

- **Nonstick cooking spray**
- **1 cup water**
- **1 6-ounce package lemon-flavored gelatin**
- **2 cups ginger ale**
- **2 cups assorted chopped fruit (such as drained canned pineapple [do not use fresh pineapple]; fresh strawberries; fresh or canned peaches; fresh or canned pears; fresh apple; or fresh grapes)**
- **½ cup chopped celery (1 stalk) or toasted nuts**
- **2 tablespoons finely chopped crystallized ginger**

1 Coat a 6-cup nonreactive mold with cooking spray; set aside. In a medium saucepan combine the water and gelatin; heat and stir until gelatin dissolves. Stir in ginger ale. Refrigerate gelatin mixture about 30 minutes or until partially set (the consistency of unbeaten egg whites).

Ginger Ale Salad

Just like Grandma used to make, this jiggly salad is full of fruit. Make it company special with a spoonful of whipped dessert topping and a sprinkling of nuts.

2 Fold fruit, celery, and ginger into gelatin mixture. Pour into the prepared mold. Cover the mold with plastic wrap and refrigerate about 6 hours or until firm.
3 When ready to unmold, dip the mold briefly (10 seconds or less) into very hot water. Invert the mold onto a serving dish to release the salad.

PER SERVING 100 calories; 0 g fat; 1 g protein; 25 g carbohydrate; 0 g fiber; 46 mg sodium; 0 mg cholesterol

Rice & Veggie Salad

MAKES 8 servings
PREP 55 minutes **CHILL** 4 to 24 hours

- **⅔ cup uncooked regular brown rice**
- **1 teaspoon finely shredded lemon peel**
- **2 tablespoons lemon juice**
- **2 tablespoons water**
- **2 tablespoons olive oil**
- **1 teaspoon Dijon-style mustard**
- **2 tablespoons snipped fresh parsley**
- **2 tablespoons snipped fresh dill**
- **⅛ teaspoon black pepper**
- **1 small yellow summer squash, halved lengthwise and sliced (1 cup)**
- **1 cup broccoli florets**
- **½ cup chopped red sweet pepper (1 small)**
- **¼ cup thinly sliced green onion (2)**

1 Cook rice according to package directions. Place cooked rice in a colander; rinse with cold water. Drain and set aside.
2 Meanwhile, in a large bowl stir together the lemon peel, lemon juice, the water, the oil, mustard, parsley, dill, and black pepper. Stir in the squash, broccoli, sweet pepper, and green onion. Add the rice; toss to coat. Cover and chill in the refrigerator for 4 to 24 hours.

PER SERVING 99 calories; 4 g fat (1 g sat.); 2 g protein; 15 g carbohydrate; 2 g fiber; 156 mg sodium; 0 mg cholesterol

Asparagus Slaw

Asparagus Slaw 30

MAKES 8 to 10 servings
START TO FINISH 30 minutes

- **1 pound fresh asparagus spears**
- **4 cups shredded green cabbage**
- **1 cup shredded radicchio or red cabbage**
- **½ cup finely shredded carrot (1 medium)**
- **¼ cup snipped fresh mint**
- **¼ cup snipped fresh parsley**
- **¼ of a small red onion, thinly sliced**
- **2 tablespoons olive oil**
- **2 tablespoons balsamic vinegar**
- **½ teaspoon finely shredded lemon peel**
- **1 tablespoon lemon juice**
- **1 clove garlic, minced**
- **½ teaspoon black pepper**
- **¼ cup shredded Parmesan cheese (1 ounce)**

1 Snap off and discard woody bases from asparagus. If desired, scrape off scales from asparagus. In a medium saucepan bring 1 inch of water to boiling. Place asparagus in a steamer basket. Cover and steam asparagus over the boiling water for 4 to 6 minutes or until crisp-tender. Drain. Gently rinse asparagus with cold water.
2 Meanwhile, in a large bowl toss together cabbage, radicchio, carrot, mint, parsley, and onion. Divide asparagus among salad plates; top with cabbage mixture.
3 In a screw-top jar combine oil, vinegar, lemon peel, lemon juice, garlic, and pepper. Cover and shake well. Pour over cabbage mixture. Sprinkle each serving with cheese.

PER SERVING 76 calories; 5 g fat (1 g sat.); 3 g protein; 6 g carbohydrate; 2 g fiber; 56 mg sodium; 3 mg cholesterol

Asian Broccoli Slaw

Asian Broccoli Slaw

MAKES 12 servings
PREP 10 minutes **CHILL** 2 hours or overnight

- **2 12-ounce bags shredded broccoli (broccoli slaw mix)**
- **1 cup shredded carrot (2 medium)**
- **⅔ cup sliced green onion (6)**
- **1 8-ounce can sliced water chestnuts, drained**
- **6 tablespoons cooking oil**
- **6 tablespoons rice wine vinegar**
- **5 tablespoons light soy sauce**
- **1 tablespoon sugar**
- **4 teaspoons sesame oil**
- **2 teaspoons grated fresh ginger**
- **½ teaspoon salt**

1 In a large bowl stir together broccoli, carrot, green onion, and drained water chestnuts. In a medium bowl whisk together oil, vinegar, soy sauce, sugar, sesame oil, ginger, and salt. Pour over broccoli mixture; toss to coat. Cover and chill for 2 hours or overnight.

PER SERVING 117 calories; 9 g fat (1 g sat.); 2 g protein; 9 g carbohydrate; 3 g fiber; 332 mg sodium; 0 mg cholesterol

Green Bean Salad

A slaw that's

Ginger-Spiced Cucumbers

MAKES 4 to 6 servings
PREP 15 minutes **MARINATE** 30 minutes

- **¼ cup seasoned rice vinegar**
- **¼ cup mirin (sweet cooking rice wine)**
- **¼ cup packed brown sugar**
- **2 teaspoons grated fresh ginger**
- **1 large English cucumber (about 12 ounces), peeled if desired, and thinly sliced**
- **¼ cup thinly sliced red onion**

1 In a medium bowl combine vinegar, mirin, brown sugar, and ginger. Stir in cucumber and onion. Cover and chill for 30 minutes. Serve with a slotted spoon.

PER SERVING 115 calories; 0 g fat; 1 g protein; 30 g carbohydrate; 1 g fiber; 173 mg sodium; 0 mg cholesterol

Apple & Cabbage Slaw 

MAKES 12 servings
PREP 20 minutes **CHILL** 2 to 48 hours

- **⅔ cup light mayonnaise dressing**
- **3 tablespoons cider vinegar**
- **1 tablespoon snipped fresh dill or 1 teaspoon dried dill**
- **½ teaspoon salt**
- **½ teaspoon coarsely ground black pepper**
- **7 cups shredded green cabbage (1 medium)**
- **3 medium apples, cored and thinly sliced**
- **1 cup chopped sweet onion (1 large)**
- **Fresh dill sprig (optional)**

1 For dressing, in a very large bowl stir together the mayonnaise dressing, vinegar, dill, salt, and pepper. Add cabbage, apples, and onion; toss to coat. Cover and chill for 2 hours to 48 hours. If desired, garnish with fresh dill sprigs.

PER SERVING 78 calories; 5 g fat (1 g sat.); 1 g protein; 10 g carbohydrate; 2 g fiber; 195 mg sodium; 5 mg cholesterol

Green Bean Salad

MAKES 6 servings
PREP 15 minutes **CHILL** 1 to 2 hours

- **12 ounces fresh green beans, trimmed**
- **8 ounces yellow and/or red cherry tomatoes, halved**
- **½ of a small red onion, thinly sliced**
- **1 recipe Basil-Tomato Vinaigrette**

1 In a medium saucepan cook green beans, covered, in a small amount of boiling lightly salted water about 8 minutes or just until crisp-tender. Drain; rinse with cold water and drain again.
2 In a large bowl combine green beans, cherry tomatoes, and onion. Drizzle with Basil-Tomato Vinaigrette; toss gently to coat. Cover and chill for 1 to 2 hours before serving.
Basil-Tomato Vinaigrette: In a small bowl stir together ⅓ cup snipped fresh basil; 3 tablespoons red wine vinegar; 2 tablespoons snipped dried tomatoes;* 1 tablespoon olive oil; 2 cloves garlic, minced; ¼ teaspoon salt; and ¼ teaspoon black pepper.
***Note:** To soften dried tomatoes for the vinaigrette, soak them in enough boiling water to cover for 5 minutes; drain.

PER SERVING 53 calories; 2 g fat (0 g sat.); 2 g protein; 8 g carbohydrate; 3 g fiber; 126 mg sodium; 0 mg cholesterol

red and green, and holiday spectacular.

Apple & Cabbage Slaw

Menu

Roasted turkey or chicken

Baked sweet potatoes with a sprinkling of brown sugar

Steamed broccoli

Really Red Coleslaw
[right]

Really Red Coleslaw 

MAKES 8 servings
START TO FINISH 15 minutes

- **1 10-ounce package shredded red cabbage (about 6 cups)**
- **1 cup slivered red onion (1 medium)**
- **½ cup dried tart red cherries**
- **½ cup bottled red raspberry vinaigrette salad dressing**
- **1 tablespoon seedless red raspberry preserves**

1 In a large bowl combine cabbage, onion, and cherries; set aside. In a small bowl stir together vinaigrette and preserves; pour over cabbage mixture. Toss gently to coat. Serve immediately or cover and chill for up to 6 hours.

PER SERVING 108 calories; 6 g fat (1 g sat.); 1 g protein; 12 g carbohydrate; 1 g fiber; 5 mg sodium; 0 mg cholesterol

Really Red Coleslaw

Cabbage & Fennel Salad

MAKES 8 servings
PREP 15 minutes **CHILL** 2 to 24 hours

- **1 medium fennel bulb**
- **⅓ cup olive oil**
- **⅓ cup white balsamic or white wine vinegar**
- **1 tablespoon snipped fresh parsley**
- **1 tablespoon coarse-grain brown mustard**
- **1 to 2 teaspoons sugar**
- **½ teaspoon salt**
- **¼ teaspoon freshly ground black pepper**
- **8 cups thinly sliced savoy cabbage (about 1 small head) or one 16-ounce package (8 cups) shredded cabbage with carrot (coleslaw mix)**
- **1 small zucchini cut into thin bite-size strips**

1 Remove and discard upper stalks from fennel. Discard any wilted outer layers; cut off a thin slice from base of bulb. Quarter fennel bulb lengthwise; slice very thinly. Set aside.
2 For vinaigrette, in a small screw-top jar with a tight-fitting lid combine oil, vinegar, parsley, mustard, sugar, salt, and pepper. Cover and shake well. Set aside.
3 In a very large serving bowl combine the sliced fennel, cabbage, and zucchini. Pour the vinaigrette over cabbage mixture; toss lightly to coat. Cover; chill for 2 to 24 hours.

PER SERVING 125 calories; 9 g fat (1 g sat.); 2 g protein; 10 g carbohydrate; 3 g fiber; 208 mg sodium; 0 mg cholesterol

If you have a mandoline, use it to cut the fennel into very thin slices.

Cabbage & Fennel Salad

Summer's Best BBQ Beans

Summer's Best BBQ Beans

MAKES 10 servings
PREP 15 minutes **COOK** 25 minutes **STAND** 5 minutes

- **Nonstick cooking spray**
- **½ cup thinly sliced halved onion (1 medium)**
- **¾ cup chopped green or red sweet pepper (1 medium)**
- **2 cups chopped tomato (2 large)**
- **3 15- to 16-ounce cans light red kidney beans, rinsed and drained**
- **1 8-ounce can tomato sauce**
- **1 8-ounce can crushed pineapple, undrained**
- **1 tablespoon Worcestershire sauce**
- **1 tablespoon molasses**
- **Italian parsley sprigs (optional)**

1 Lightly coat a large saucepan or Dutch oven with cooking spray. Cook onion and sweet pepper in hot pan over medium heat for 5 to 10 minutes or until tender, stirring occasionally. Stir in tomato, beans, tomato sauce, undrained pineapple, Worcestershire sauce, and molasses. Bring to boiling; reduce heat. Simmer, covered, for 10 minutes. Uncover and simmer for 10 minutes more.

2 Transfer to a serving bowl. Let stand for 5 to 10 minutes before serving. Sauce will thicken as it stands. If desired, garnish with parsley.

PER SERVING 140 calories; 0 g fat; 10 g protein; 32 g carbohydrate; 8 g fiber; 351 mg sodium; 0 mg cholesterol

Gorgeous green never tasted so good.

Garlic & Parsley Green Beans

MAKES 6 to 8 servings
PREP 25 minutes **COOK** 10 minutes

- **1 tablespoon salt**
- **1½ pounds fresh green beans, trimmed**
- **3 tablespoons unsalted butter**
- **4 cloves garlic, minced with a pinch of salt**
- **2 tablespoons snipped fresh parsley**
- **Salt and freshly ground black pepper**
- **Snipped fresh parsley (optional)**

1 Fill a large pot with water and bring to boiling. Add the 1 tablespoon salt and the beans. Cook, uncovered, for 5 to 8 minutes or until beans are just tender but still vibrantly green. Drain the beans and immediately submerge in a bowl of lightly salted ice water; drain well.
2 In a large skillet heat butter over medium-high heat until melted and foaming. Add the beans; cook and stir until heated through. Add the garlic, parsley, salt, and pepper to taste; cook and stir for 1 minute longer. Sprinkle with additional parsley. Serve immediately.

PER SERVING 90 calories; 6 g fat (4 g sat.); 2 g protein; 9 g carbohydrate; 4 g fiber; 80 mg sodium; 15 mg cholesterol

Green Beans with Lime 

MAKES 4 servings
START TO FINISH 30 minutes

- **1 pound fresh green beans, trimmed**
- **1 tablespoon cooking oil or olive oil**
- **1 lime**
- **Salt**

1 In a large skillet cook green beans in hot oil over medium heat for 18 to 20 minutes or until crisp-tender and lightly brown, stirring occasionally.
2 Meanwhile, shred 1 teaspoon of lime peel. Cut lime in half. Add lime peel to beans. Cook and stir for 1 minute more. Lightly season beans with salt, drizzle with lime juice, and serve immediately.

PER SERVING 66 calories; 4 g fat (0 g sat.); 2 g protein; 9 g carbohydrate; 4 g fiber; 67 mg sodium; 0 mg cholesterol

Green Beans with Lime

Caramelized Brussels Sprouts

3 Carefully add the water and salt. Bring to boiling; add the Brussels sprouts. Return to boiling; reduce heat. Simmer, covered, for 6 minutes. Uncover and cook about 15 minutes more or until most of the liquid has been absorbed and the Brussels sprouts are coated with a golden glaze, gently stirring occasionally.

PER SERVING 76 calories; 3 g fat (2 g sat.); 2 g protein; 11 g carbohydrate; 2 g fiber; 155 mg sodium; 8 mg cholesterol

Honey-Glazed Carrots 

MAKES 12 servings
START TO FINISH 30 minutes

- **6 cups water**
- **3 pounds baby carrots with tops trimmed to 2 inches, peeled or scrubbed, or 3 pounds packaged peeled baby carrots**
- **2 tablespoons butter**
- **3 to 4 tablespoons honey**
- **1 teaspoon finely shredded lemon peel**
- **½ teaspoon crushed red pepper**
- **½ teaspoon salt**
- **Crushed red pepper (optional)**

1 In a very large skillet bring water to boiling. Add carrots. Return to boiling; reduce heat. Cover and simmer for 8 to 10 minutes or until carrots are just tender. Drain carrots. Pat dry with paper towels.
2 In the same skillet combine butter, honey, lemon peel, the ½ teaspoon crushed red pepper, and salt. Stir constantly over medium heat until butter melts and mixture bubbles. Carefully add carrots. Toss gently for 2 to 3 minutes or until carrots are well coated with glaze and heated through.
3 To serve, transfer carrots to shallow bowl or platter. Drizzle with any remaining glaze from pan. If desired, sprinkle with additional crushed red pepper.
Make-Ahead Directions: Prepare carrots as directed through Step 1. Cool cooked carrots, then cover and refrigerate for up to 1 day. Bring to room temperature before glazing (takes about 1 hour). Heat carrots in glaze for 4 to 5 minutes.

PER SERVING 75 calories; 2 g fat (1 g sat.); 1 g protein; 14 g carbohydrate; 3 g fiber; 180 mg sodium; 5 mg cholesterol

Caramelized Brussels Sprouts

MAKES 16 servings
PREP 25 minutes **COOK** 21 minutes

- **10 cups small, fresh Brussels sprouts (about 2¾ pounds)**
- **½ cup sugar**
- **¼ cup butter**
- **½ cup red wine vinegar**
- **¾ cup water**
- **¾ teaspoon salt**

1 Prepare the Brussels sprouts by peeling off two or three of the dark outer leaves from each Brussels sprout; trim the stem ends.
2 In a Dutch oven or very large skillet heat the sugar over medium-high heat until sugar begins to melt, shaking the pan occasionally to heat sugar evenly. Once sugar starts to melt, reduce heat and cook until sugar begins to turn brown. Add butter; stir until melted. Add vinegar; cook and stir for 1 minute.

Wine-Poached Beets

MAKES 8 to 10 servings
PREP 25 minutes **COOK** 45 minutes

- ¾ cup dry red wine such as Merlot or Shiraz, or apple juice
- ½ cup water
- 1 tablespoon packed brown sugar
- 2½ pounds beets, peeled, and quartered*
- Salt and black pepper
- Honey (optional)
- 1 tablespoon snipped fresh parsley
- Lemon wedges (optional)

1 In a large saucepan combine ½ cup of the wine, the water, and the brown sugar. Bring to boiling, stirring to dissolve sugar. Add beets. Return to boiling; reduce heat. Simmer, covered, about 45 minutes or until beets are tender enough to pierce with a fork, stirring occasionally. Drain.

2 Transfer beets to a serving bowl. Season to taste with salt and pepper. Splash beets with remaining ¼ cup wine and, if desired, drizzle with honey. Sprinkle with parsley. If desired, serve with lemon wedges.

***Note:** You can avoid staining your hands with beet juice if you wear plastic gloves while peeling and cutting the beets. Trim beet tops or leave tops on.

PER SERVING 54 calories; 0 g fat; 1 g protein; 9 g carbohydrate; 2 g fiber; 119 mg sodium; 0 mg cholesterol

Wine-Poached Beets

Lemony Sugar Snap Pea Stir-Fry (30)

MAKES 4 servings
START TO FINISH 20 minutes

- **¼ lemon, cut into thin slices**
- **1 to 2 tablespoons olive oil**
- **2½ cups sugar snap peas**
- **⅓ cup sliced leek (1 medium)**
- **1 tablespoon snipped fresh dill (optional)**
- **Salt and black pepper**

1 In a large skillet cook and stir lemon slices in hot oil over medium-high heat for 4 minutes, turning once. Remove lemon from skillet; set aside. Add sugar snap peas and leek to skillet; cook and stir for 3 to 4 minutes or until crisp-tender. Stir in dill, if desired, and the lemon slices. Season to taste with salt and pepper.

PER SERVING 73 calories; 3 g fat (0 g sat.); 2 g protein; 10 g carbohydrate; 3 g fiber; 87 mg sodium; 0 mg cholesterol

Beet Greens with Walnuts & Blue Cheese

If beet greens are not available, substitute spinach or Swiss chard. Always rinse the greens under cold running water to remove any dirt or sand. Be sure to dry them on paper towels before cooking.

Kale Sauté 30

MAKES 4 servings
START TO FINISH 15 minutes

- **12 ounces dinosaur kale or regular kale, cut or torn into 1- to 2-inch pieces (about 12 cups)**
- **¼ cup soft sourdough or French loaf bread crumbs**
- **6 teaspoons olive oil**
- **⅛ teaspoon black pepper**
- **1 teaspoon Worcestershire sauce for chicken**
- **Lemon wedges (optional)**

1 Rinse kale leaves thoroughly under cold running water. Drain well; set aside.
2 In a small skillet cook and stir bread crumbs in 2 teaspoons of the oil over medium heat for 1 to 2 minutes or until brown. Season with pepper; set aside.
3 In a large nonstick skillet heat the remaining 4 teaspoons oil. Add kale; cover and cook for 1 minute. Uncover. Cook and stir about 1 minute more or just until wilted.
4 Transfer kale to a serving dish. Drizzle with Worcestershire sauce. Sprinkle with the bread crumbs. If desired, serve with lemon wedges.

PER SERVING 89 calories; 5 g fat (1 g sat.); 3 g protein; 9 g carbohydrate; 4 g fiber; 53 mg sodium; 0 mg cholesterol

Beet Greens with Walnuts & Blue Cheese 30

MAKES 4 servings
START TO FINISH 15 minutes

- **8 ounces fresh beet greens**
- **2 tablespoons chopped walnuts**
- **2 teaspoons cooking oil**
- **1 tablespoon crumbled blue cheese**
- **¼ teaspoon black pepper**

1 Cut beet greens into 1-inch strips. In a large skillet cook and stir walnuts in hot oil over medium-high heat for 2 minutes. Add beet greens. Cook and stir about 1 minute or just until wilted. Top each serving with crumbled blue cheese and pepper.

PER SERVING 55 calories; 5 g fat (1 g sat.); 2 g protein; 3 g carbohydrate; 2 g fiber; 109 mg sodium; 0 mg cholesterol

Blue Cheese-Stuffed Summer Squash

MAKES 8 servings
PREP 25 minutes **BAKE** 20 minutes **OVEN** 400°F

- **4** medium yellow summer squash or zucchini
- **½** of an 8-ounce package reduced-fat cream cheese (Neufchâtel), softened
- **½** cup shredded carrot (1 medium)
- **⅓** cup crumbled blue cheese (1½ ounces)
- **⅓** cup thinly sliced green onion (3)
- **⅓** cup fine dry bread crumbs
- **¼** cup fat-free or light dairy sour cream
- **⅛** teaspoon black pepper
- **2** tablespoons chopped walnuts

1 Grease a 3-quart rectangular baking dish; set aside.
2 Halve the squash lengthwise. Using a spoon, remove seeds, leaving a shell about ¼ inch thick. Place squash halves, cut sides down, in the prepared baking dish. Bake, uncovered, in a 400°F oven for 10 minutes. Turn squash halves cut sides up.
3 Meanwhile, in a medium bowl stir together cream cheese, carrot, blue cheese, green onion, ¼ cup of the bread crumbs, the sour cream, and pepper. (Mixture will be stiff.) Spoon mixture evenly into squash halves. Sprinkle with walnuts and the remaining bread crumbs. Bake, uncovered, about 10 minutes more or until squash is tender and filling is heated through.

PER SERVING 107 calories; 6 g fat (3 g sat.); 5 g protein; 8 g carbohydrate; 1 g fiber; 178 mg sodium; 15 mg cholesterol

Blue Cheese-Stuffed Summer Squash

Menu

Roasted pork loin

Cheesy Squash Bake
[below]

Spinach salad with sliced pears, thinly sliced sweet onion, golden raisins, and balsamic vinaigrette

Rye rolls

Cheesy Squash Bake

Cheesy Squash Bake 

MAKES 6 servings
PREP 20 minutes **BAKE** 25 minutes **OVEN** 350°F

- **3 cups thinly sliced yellow summer squash (2 large)**
- **½ cup chopped onion (1 medium)**
- **1 tablespoon reduced-fat margarine**
- **1 tablespoon all-purpose flour**
- **½ cup fat-free milk**
- **½ cup shredded reduced-fat cheddar cheese (2 ounces)**
- **¼ teaspoon black pepper**
- **⅛ teaspoon salt**
- **Nonstick cooking spray**
- **½ cup soft whole wheat bread crumbs, toasted**

1 In a large saucepan cook squash and onion in a small amount of boiling water for 5 to 10 minutes or until tender. Drain and set aside.
2 Meanwhile, in a medium saucepan melt margarine over medium heat. Stir in flour until well mixed. Gradually stir in milk; cook and stir until thickened and bubbly. Remove from heat. Stir in cheese, pepper, and salt until cheese melts. Add squash mixture; toss to coat.
3 Coat a 1- to 1½-quart baking dish with cooking spray. Spoon squash mixture into prepared dish. Sprinkle top evenly with bread crumbs. Bake, uncovered, in a 350°F oven about 25 minutes or until golden brown and heated through.

PER SERVING 72 calories; 3 g fat (1 g sat.); 5 g protein; 8 g carbohydrate; 1 g fiber; 169 mg sodium; 7 mg cholesterol

Tomatoes with Crispy Bread Topping

MAKES 4 servings
PREP 20 minutes **BAKE** 15 minutes **OVEN** 400°F

- 8 **roma tomatoes (1⅓ pounds), cored and halved lengthwise**
- **Kosher salt and freshly ground black pepper**
- ½ **cup soft whole wheat bread crumbs**
- ¼ **cup thinly sliced green onion (2)**
- 2 **tablespoons snipped fresh thyme**
- 1 **tablespoon snipped fresh Italian parsley**
- 1 **tablespoon snipped fresh tarragon**
- 1 **tablespoon grated Parmesan cheese (optional)**
- 1 **tablespoon olive oil**
- 2 **cloves garlic, minced**

1 Sprinkle cut sides of tomatoes with salt and pepper. Arrange tomatoes, cut sides up, in a shallow baking pan.
2 In a small bowl stir together bread crumbs, green onion, thyme, parsley, tarragon, cheese (if desired), oil, and garlic. Sprinkle on tomato halves. Bake, uncovered, in a 400°F oven for 15 to 20 minutes or until the tomatoes are heated through and bread crumbs are brown and crisp.

PER SERVING 75 calories; 4 g fat (1 g sat.); 2 g protein; 9 g carbohydrate; 3 g fiber; 152 mg sodium; 0 mg cholesterol

Sage-Grilled Root Vegetables

MAKES 4 servings
PREP 25 minutes **GRILL** 6 minutes

- 1 **tablespoon honey**
- 1 **tablespoon balsamic vinegar**
- 2 **teaspoons Dijon-style mustard**
- 2 **teaspoons snipped fresh sage or 1 teaspoon dried sage, crushed**
- 16 **baby carrots or 4 medium carrots, cut into 2-inch pieces**
- 8 **tiny new potatoes or 2 medium red or Yukon gold potatoes, quartered**
- 8 **pearl onions, peeled, or 1 small onion, cut into small wedges**

1 In a small bowl combine honey, vinegar, mustard, and sage; set aside. In a large saucepan combine carrots and potatoes; add enough water to cover. Bring to boiling. Add onions. Cover and simmer for 3 to 5 minutes or until potatoes, carrots, and onions are just tender. Drain vegetables; let stand until cool enough to handle.
2 On four metal skewers, alternately thread carrots, potatoes, and onions, leaving a ¼-inch space between each.
3 For a charcoal grill, place kabobs on the grill rack directly over medium coals. Grill, uncovered, for 6 to 8 minutes or until potatoes are tender, turning once halfway through grilling and brushing frequently with honey-sage mixture. (For a gas grill, preheat grill. Reduce heat to medium. Place kabobs on grill rack over heat. Cover and grill as above.)

PER SERVING 108 calories; 0 g fat; 2 g protein; 24 g carbohydrate; 2 g fiber; 77 mg sodium; 0 mg cholesterol

Roasted Vegetable Medley

MAKES 8 servings
PREP 15 minutes **ROAST** 25 minutes **OVEN** 425°F

- 2 **medium red onions, cut into eighths**
- 2 **small yellow summer squash, cut into ½-inch slices**
- 2 **small zucchini, cut into ½-inch slices**
- 3 **red, yellow, and/or green sweet peppers, cut into ½-inch-wide strips**
- 4 **cloves garlic, thinly sliced**
- 2 **tablespoons snipped fresh parsley**
- 2 **tablespoons balsamic vinegar**
- 1 **tablespoon olive oil**
- 1 **teaspoon dried oregano, crushed**
- ½ **teaspoon salt**
- ¼ **teaspoon black pepper**

1 In a 13×9×2-inch baking pan combine onions, squash, zucchini, sweet peppers, and garlic.
2 In a screw-top jar, combine parsley, vinegar, oil, oregano, salt, and black pepper; cover and shake well. Pour over the vegetables; toss gently to coat.
3 Roast, uncovered, in a 425°F oven about 25 minutes or until vegetables are crisp-tender, stirring twice.

PER SERVING 50 calories; 2 g fat (0 g sat.); 1 g protein; 8 g carbohydrate; 2 g fiber; 150 mg sodium; 0 mg cholesterol

Easy as can be...mixed in the pan and roasted in the oven.

Roasted Vegetable Medley

Brown Sugar
Sweet Potato Wedges

Brown Sugar Sweet Potato Wedges 

MAKES 8 servings
PREP 10 minutes **MICROWAVE** 10 minutes **GRILL** 15 minutes

- **6 small sweet potatoes (about 6 ounces each), with skins, scrubbed and pierced with a fork**
- **¼ cup walnuts, chopped**
- **¼ cup plus 2 tablespoons packed light brown sugar**
- **2 tablespoons cider vinegar**
- **½ teaspoon salt**
- **¼ teaspoon black pepper**
- **¼ teaspoon ground allspice**
- **1 tablespoon butter**

1 Place potatoes on paper towels in a microwave oven. Microwave on 100-percent power (high) 10 minutes or until partially cooked but still very firm, turning over halfway through cooking. Cool slightly. Cut lengthwise into quarters.

2 Meanwhile, in small skillet cook and stir walnuts, brown sugar, vinegar, salt, pepper, and allspice in hot butter over medium heat about 2 minutes or until brown sugar melts. Remove from heat. Brush cut sides of sweet potatoes with the brown sugar mixture, leaving the walnuts in the skillet.

3 For a charcoal grill, place potatoes, cut sides down, on the grill rack directly over medium coals. Grill, uncovered, for 5 minutes. Turn potatoes so the second cut sides of wedges are down on grill rack. Grill for 5 minutes more. Turn wedges so skin sides are down; brush cut sides with brown sugar mixture. Grill about 5 minutes more or until sweet potatoes are tender. (For a gas grill, preheat grill. Reduce heat to medium. Place potatoes on grill rack over heat. Cover; grill as above.) Transfer sweet potatoes to a serving platter. Spoon remaining brown sugar mixture with nuts over top.

Stovetop Method: Heat a stovetop grill pan over medium-high heat. Cook potato wedges in grill pan as directed above.

PER SERVING 173 calories; 4 g fat (1 g sat.); 2 g protein; 33 g carbohydrate; 4 g fiber; 159 mg sodium; 4 mg cholesterol

Roasted Potato Mash 

MAKES 8 servings
PREP 25 minutes **ROAST** 40 minutes **OVEN** 450°F

- **6 medium baking potatoes (2 pounds total), peeled and cut into eighths**
- **1 cup coarsely chopped onion (1 large)**
- **½ cup water**
- **2 tablespoons olive oil or cooking oil**
- **1 to 2 tablespoons snipped fresh herbs such as parsley, chives, and/or thyme**
- **½ teaspoon salt**
- **¼ teaspoon black pepper**
- **1 to 1¼ cups buttermilk**
- **Olive oil (optional)**
- **Salt and black pepper**

1 In a greased 3-quart rectangular baking dish combine potatoes and onion. In a small bowl combine the water, the 2 tablespoons oil, the herbs, the ½ teaspoon salt, and the ¼ teaspoon pepper; drizzle over potatoes and onion.
2 Roast, uncovered, in a 450°F oven for 40 to 45 minutes or until the vegetables are tender and brown, stirring twice.
3 Transfer vegetables to a large mixing bowl. Mash with a potato masher or beat with an electric mixer on low speed. Gradually beat in enough buttermilk to make potato mixture smooth and fluffy. If desired, drizzle with additional oil. Season to taste with additional salt and pepper.

PER SERVING 155 calories; 5 g fat (1 g sat.); 4 g protein; 24 g carbohydrate; 2 g fiber; 185 mg sodium; 1 mg cholesterol

Roasted Chestnut & Andouille Sausage Stuffing

MAKES 16 servings
PREP 30 minutes **BAKE** 30 minutes **OVEN** 325°F

- **1 10-ounce can whole peeled chestnuts, drained**
- **8 ounces cooked andouille or smoked sausage, chopped**
- **3 cups soft bread crumbs**
- **3 cups crumbled corn bread**
- **2 tablespoons snipped fresh parsley**
- **1 tablespoon snipped fresh thyme**
- **½ teaspoon salt**
- **¼ to ½ teaspoon black pepper**
- **½ cup finely chopped shallot (4 medium)**
- **¼ cup butter**
- **¼ to ½ cup water**

1 Place drained chestnuts in a very large bowl. Coarsely mash with a potato masher. Stir in sausage, bread crumbs, corn bread, parsley, thyme, salt, and pepper; set aside.
2 In a small skillet cook shallot in hot butter over medium heat for 4 to 5 minutes or until tender, stirring occasionally. Add shallot mixture to chestnut mixture; toss to combine. Add the water to make stuffing of desired moistness.
3 Use chestnut mixture to stuff a whole broiler-fryer *chicken*, *turkey*, or *pork chops*. Place extra stuffing in a casserole. Bake, covered, along with poultry or meat in a 325°F oven for 30 to 45 minutes or until heated through.

PER SERVING 116 calories; 5 g fat (2 g sat.); 5 g protein; 14 g carbohydrate; 0 g fiber; 324 mg sodium; 24 mg cholesterol

Roasted Potato Mash

Red Lentil, Quinoa & Flaxseed Pilaf

MAKES 5 servings
PREP 15 minutes **COOK** 28 minutes **STAND** 5 minutes

- **⅓ cup dry red lentils**
- **⅓ cup uncooked quinoa**
- **⅓ cup finely chopped shallot (2 large) or onion (1 small)**
- **2 cloves garlic, minced**
- **1 tablespoon olive oil**
- **2 tablespoons flaxseeds**
- **1 14-ounce can reduced-sodium chicken broth**
- **1 cup chopped red or green sweet pepper (1 large)**
- **1 teaspoon snipped fresh thyme or ¼ teaspoon dried thyme, crushed**
- **Fresh thyme sprigs (optional)**

1 Rinse and drain lentils and quinoa separately. In a medium saucepan cook and stir shallot and garlic in hot oil over medium heat for 3 minutes. Add quinoa and flaxseeds; cook and stir about 5 minutes or until quinoa is light brown. Add lentils and broth. Bring to boiling; reduce heat. Cover and simmer for 15 minutes.

2 Stir in sweet pepper and the 1 teaspoon thyme. Cover and cook about 5 minutes more or until quinoa and lentils are tender. Let stand, covered, for 5 minutes. If desired, garnish with thyme sprigs.

PER SERVING 152 calories; 5 g fat (1 g sat.); 7 g protein; 20 g carbohydrate; 4 g fiber; 198 mg sodium; 0 mg cholesterol

Couscous with Seven Vegetables

MAKES 10 servings
PREP 30 minutes **COOK** 15 minutes

- 1½ cups slivered yellow onion (2 medium)
- 2 cloves garlic, minced
- 1 tablespoon olive oil
- 1 cup sliced carrot (1 large)
- 1 cup peeled, cubed sweet potato (1 small)
- 2 teaspoons ground turmeric
- 2 teaspoons ground cumin
- ½ teaspoon salt
- ¾ cup water
- 1 cup sliced yellow summer squash
- 1 cup sliced zucchini
- 1 cup chopped green sweet pepper (1 large)
- 1 large tomato, seeded and chopped
- 1 10-ounce package quick-cooking couscous
- ½ cup snipped fresh mint

1 In a 4-quart Dutch oven cook onion and garlic in hot oil over medium heat until tender. Add carrot, sweet potato, turmeric, cumin, and salt. Add the water. Bring to boiling; reduce heat. Cook, covered, for 5 minutes, stirring occasionally. Add squash, zucchini, and sweet pepper. Cover and cook 5 minutes more or until vegetables are tender. Stir in tomato.
2 Meanwhile, prepare couscous according to package directions, adding optional salt. Transfer couscous to a very large bowl. Add vegetable mixture; stir gently. Stir in mint. Serve immediately.

PER SERVING 159 calories; 2 g fat (0 g sat.); 5 g protein; 31 g carbohydrate; 3 g fiber; 134 mg sodium; 0 mg cholesterol

Bulgur-Mushroom Pilaf

Bulgur-Mushroom Pilaf

MAKES 6 servings
PREP 15 minutes **COOK** 45 minutes **STAND** 5 minutes

- ½ cup chopped onion (1 medium)
- 1 tablespoon olive oil
- 1 14-ounce can chicken broth
- 1 cup apple juice
- ½ cup uncooked wild rice, rinsed
- 2 cups quartered or sliced shiitake mushrooms, stemmed, cremini mushrooms, or button mushrooms
- ½ cup bulgur
- ¾ cup chopped red or green sweet pepper (1 medium)
- ½ cup snipped fresh Italian (flat-leaf) parsley
- ¼ cup chopped walnuts, toasted
- Freshly ground black pepper
- ¼ cup crumbled feta cheese (1 ounce)

1 In a large saucepan cook onion in hot oil over medium heat about 5 minutes or until tender, stirring occasionally. Carefully add broth, apple juice, and wild rice. Bring to boiling; reduce heat. Simmer, covered, for 30 minutes.
2 Stir in the mushrooms and bulgur. Cover and simmer for 10 to 15 minutes more or until rice and bulgur are tender and most of the liquid is absorbed. Stir in sweet pepper; remove from heat. Cover and let stand for 5 minutes. Stir in parsley and walnuts. Season to taste with black pepper. Sprinkle with cheese.

PER SERVING 197 calories; 7 g fat (1 g sat.); 7 g protein; 29 g carbohydrate; 5 g fiber; 328 mg sodium; 5 mg cholesterol

Parmesan-Cornmeal Pancakes 

MAKES about 16 pancakes
PREP 15 minutes **COOK** 2 to 4 minutes per batch

- **1 cup all-purpose flour**
- **¾ cup yellow cornmeal**
- **⅓ cup grated Parmesan cheese**
- **1 tablespoon sugar (optional)**
- **1 teaspoon baking soda**
- **½ teaspoon salt**
- **1¾ cups buttermilk or sour milk***
- **2 eggs, lightly beaten**
- **⅓ cup finely chopped green onion (3)**
- **2 tablespoons cooking oil**

1 In a medium bowl stir together flour, cornmeal, Parmesan cheese, sugar (if desired), baking soda, and salt. In another medium bowl use a fork to combine the buttermilk, eggs, onion, and oil. Add buttermilk mixture all at once to flour mixture. Stir just until moistened (batter should be slightly lumpy).
2 For each pancake, pour about 1/4 cup batter onto a hot, lightly greased griddle or heavy skillet, spreading batter if necessary. Cook over medium heat for 1 to 2 minutes on each side or until pancakes are golden brown, turning to second side when pancakes have bubbly surfaces and edges are slightly dry.
***Note:** To make sour milk, place 2 tablespoons lemon juice or vinegar in a 2-cup glass measuring cup. Add enough milk to make 1 3/4 cups total liquid; stir. Let mixture stand for 5 minutes before using.

PER PANCAKE 92 calories; 3 g fat (1 g sat.); 4 g protein; 12 g carbohydrate; 1 g fiber; 216 mg sodium; 29 mg cholesterol

Upside-Down Tomato Cornbread Muffins

MAKES 12 muffins
PREP 25 minutes **ROAST** 45 minutes **BAKE** 25 minutes
COOL 10 minutes **OVEN** 350°F/400°F

- **6 medium tomatoes**
- **1 cup chopped onion (1 large)**
- **3 tablespoons olive oil**
- **1 teaspoon sea salt or ¾ teaspoon salt**
- **1 teaspoon freshly ground black pepper**
- **1 teaspoon garlic powder**
- **1 8.5-ounce package corn muffin mix**
- **1 cup shredded smoked cheddar cheese (4 ounces)**
- **1 cup frozen whole kernel corn, thawed**
- **1 4-ounce can diced green chile peppers, drained**
- **¼ cup milk**
- **¼ cup dairy sour cream**
- **1 egg, lightly beaten**
- **Nonstick cooking spray**

1 Trim ends off tomatoes and remove cores. Cut the tomatoes in half horizontally to make 12 slices. Line a 15×10×1-inch baking pan with parchment paper. Place tomato slices and onion in the prepared pan. Drizzle with oil. Sprinkle with salt, black pepper, and garlic powder. Roast, uncovered, in a 350°F oven for 45 minutes. Remove from oven. Increase oven temperature to 400°F.
2 Meanwhile, in a large bowl combine corn muffin mix, cheese, corn, drained chile peppers, milk, sour cream, and egg. Stir just until combined. Set aside.
3 Coat twelve 3 1/4- to 3 1/2-inch muffin cups with cooking spray. Place a tomato slice and some of the onion in the bottom of each muffin cup. Spoon corn mixture over onion and tomato slices, filling muffin cups nearly full.
4 Bake for 25 to 30 minutes or until tops are golden brown and a wooden toothpick inserted in centers comes out clean. Let muffins cool in pan on a wire rack for 10 minutes. Remove from muffin cups. Serve warm.

PER MUFFIN 100 calories; 5 g fat (2 g sat.); 3 g protein; 11 g carbohydrate; 1 g fiber; 241 mg sodium; 15 mg cholesterol

Chive Batter Bread 

MAKES 12 rolls
PREP 30 minutes **RISE** 20 minutes **BAKE** 18 minutes
STAND 15 minutes **OVEN** 350°F

- **1 tablespoon yellow cornmeal**
- **2 cups all-purpose flour**
- **1 package fast-rising active dry yeast**
- **¼ teaspoon black pepper**
- **1 cup milk**
- **2 tablespoons sugar**
- **3 tablespoons butter**
- **½ teaspoon salt**
- **1 egg**
- **½ cup snipped fresh chives or ¼ cup finely chopped green onion (green tops only)**
- **⅓ cup yellow cornmeal**

1 Grease the bottom and sides of twelve 2½-inch muffin cups. Sprinkle bottoms of cups evenly with the 1 tablespoon cornmeal; set aside. In a large mixing bowl stir together 1¼ cups of the flour, the yeast, and the pepper; set aside.
2 In a small saucepan combine milk, sugar, butter, and salt; heat and stir over medium heat just until mixture is warm (120°F to 130°F) and butter almost melts. Add milk mixture and egg to flour mixture. Beat with an electric mixer on low to medium speed for 30 seconds, scraping bowl constantly. Beat on high speed for 3 minutes. Stir in chives and the ⅓ cup cornmeal. Stir in remaining flour. (The batter will be soft and sticky.) Cover and let rest in a warm place for 10 minutes.
3 Preheat oven to 350°F. Spoon batter into prepared muffin cups. Cover loosely with plastic wrap. Let rise in a warm place for 20 minutes.
4 Bake about 18 minutes or until rolls sound hollow when tapped. Cool in muffin cups on a wire rack for 5 minutes. Remove from muffin cups; serve warm.

PER ROLL 140 calories; 4 g fat (2 g sat.); 4 g protein; 21 g carbohydrate; 1 g fiber; 144 mg sodium; 28 mg cholesterol

Chive Batter Bread

for a topping to top
poppy seed, and sesame seed

Pretzel Bread Houses

them all, try a sea salt, combo instead of plain salt.

Pretzel Bread Houses 

MAKES 24 pretzels

PREP 1 hour **BAKE** 12 minutes per batch **OVEN** 425°F

- **4 to 4½ cups all-purpose flour**
- **1 package active dry yeast**
- **1 tablespoon fennel seeds or coriander seeds, crushed**
- **1 tablespoon sugar**
- **1 teaspoon salt**
- **1½ cups warm water (120°F to 130°F)**
- **2 tablespoons cooking oil**
- **1 egg white**
- **1 tablespoon water**
- **Coarse sea salt**
- **1 recipe each Herbed Dijon Mustard, Ball Park Mustard, and/or Horseradish Honey Mustard**

1 In a large mixing bowl stir together 1¾ cups of the flour, the yeast, fennel seeds, sugar, and 1 teaspoon salt. Add the 1½ cups warm water and the oil. Beat with an electric mixer on low to medium speed for 30 seconds, scraping the sides of the bowl. Beat on high speed for 3 minutes. Using a wooden spoon, stir in as much of the remaining flour as you can.

2 Turn dough out onto a lightly floured surface. Knead in enough of the remaining flour to make a moderately stiff dough that is smooth and elastic (6 to 8 minutes total). Shape dough into a ball. Divide in half. Cover and let stand for 10 minutes. Preheat oven to 425°F. Lightly grease baking sheets; set aside.

3 On a lightly floured surface, roll each dough half into a 13-inch square. Using a 3½×3¼-inch house-shape cookie cutter, cut 12 houses from each square.* Arrange cutouts about 2 inches apart on the prepared baking sheets. In a small bowl whisk together egg white and the 1 tablespoon water. Brush cutouts with egg white mixture and sprinkle with coarse salt.

4 Bake about 12 minutes or until golden brown. Transfer pretzels to a wire rack and let cool. Serve pretzels with desired mustard.

Herbed Dijon Mustard: In a small bowl stir together one 8-ounce jar Dijon-style mustard (¾ cup), 3 tablespoons packed brown sugar, 2 tablespoons dry white wine, and 1 tablespoon snipped fresh marjoram. Makes about 1 cup.

Ball Park Mustard: In a small bowl stir together one 8-ounce jar yellow mustard (¾ cup) and ¼ cup packed brown sugar. Before serving, stir in ⅓ cup chopped peanuts.

Horseradish Honey Mustard: In a small bowl stir together ¾ cup honey mustard and ¼ cup horseradish sauce.

***Note:** Gather dough scraps and gently pull dough to shape into a ball. Cover and let rest for 10 to 15 minutes. Roll out dough until ¼ inch thick and cut out additional houses as above. Or, divide ball into 8 pieces. Roll each piece into a 12-inch-long rope. Shape each rope into a pretzel by crossing one rope end over the other about 4 inches from each end, forming a circle. Twist once. Bring ends up and over the top of the circle. Press ends just under the top of circle to seal. Brush, sprinkle, and bake as above.

To store: Place pretzels in an airtight container. Cover and store at room temperature for up to 3 days.

PER PRETZEL 84 calories; 1 g fat (0 g sat.); 2 g protein; 15 g carbohydrate; 1 g fiber; 117 mg sodium; 0 mg cholesterol

These versatile rolls are the perfect accompaniments to countless meals so save a few for another day. Simply cool the rolls completely, wrap them in foil packets, and put them in the freezer. Just before serving, reheat the rolls in the foil packets in a 350°F oven about 20 minutes or until warm.

Parmesan Dinner Rolls 

MAKES 24 rolls
PREP 25 minutes **RISE** 30 minutes **BAKE** 12 minutes
OVEN 400°F

- **1 16-ounce package hot roll mix**
- **¼ cup finely shredded Parmesan cheese (1 ounce)**
- **2 tablespoons snipped fresh basil or 1 teaspoon dried basil, crushed**
- **2 tablespoons sugar**
- **1 tablespoon milk**
- **2 tablespoons finely shredded Parmesan cheese**

1 In a large mixing bowl prepare hot roll mix according to package directions through the resting step, stirring the ¼ cup Parmesan cheese, the basil, and sugar into the flour mixture. Divide dough in half.
2 Grease twenty-four 1¾-inch muffin cups. Divide each dough half into 12 pieces. Gently pull each piece into a ball, tucking edges under to make smooth tops. Place in the prepared muffin cups. Cover; let rise in a warm place until nearly double (about 30 minutes).
3 Preheat oven to 400°F. Brush tops of rolls with milk; sprinkle with the 2 tablespoons Parmesan cheese. Bake rolls for 12 to 15 minutes or until tops are golden brown. Remove rolls from muffin cups and serve warm.

PER ROLL 89 calories; 2 g fat (0 g sat.); 3 g protein; 15 g carbohydrate; 0 g fiber; 145 mg sodium; 9 mg cholesterol

Home Run Garlic Rolls 

MAKES 24 rolls
PREP 20 minutes **RISE** 1½ hours **BAKE** 15 minutes **OVEN** 350°F

- **1 16-ounce loaf frozen white or whole wheat bread dough, thawed**
- **1 tablespoon butter, melted**
- **2 cloves garlic, minced**
- **2 tablespoons grated Parmesan cheese**

1 Lightly grease a 13×9×2-inch baking pan; set aside. Shape dough into 24 balls. Place balls in the prepared pan. Cover; let rise in a warm place until nearly double (1½ to 2 hours).
2 Preheat oven to 350°F. In a small bowl stir together melted butter and garlic. Brush top of rolls with butter mixture; sprinkle rolls with cheese. Bake rolls for 15 to 20 minutes or until golden. Remove rolls from pan and cool slightly on a wire rack. Serve warm.

PER 2 ROLLS 55 calories; 1 g fat (0 g sat.); 1 g protein; 9 g carbohydrate; 0 g fiber; 99 mg sodium; 2 mg cholesterol

page 288

page 307

Sweet

Somethings

Reserve a few

Peanut Butter Macaroons 

MAKES about 30 cookies
PREP 20 minutes **BAKE** 10 minutes per batch **STAND** 15 minutes
OVEN 300°F

- 2 egg whites
- ⅛ teaspoon cream of tartar
- Dash salt
- ½ cup sugar
- ½ cup creamy peanut butter
- 2 cups chocolate-flavored crisp rice cereal
- ⅓ cup chopped honey-roasted peanuts

1 Preheat oven to 300°F. Lightly grease two cookie sheets or line with parchment paper; set aside.
2 In a medium mixing bowl beat egg whites, cream of tartar, and salt with an electric mixer on high speed until soft peaks form (tips curl). Gradually add sugar, 1 tablespoon at a time, beating until stiff peaks form (tips stand straight). Gently fold in peanut butter. Fold in cereal. Drop mixture by rounded teaspoons 2 inches apart onto the prepared cookie sheets. Sprinkle with chopped peanuts.
3 Bake for 10 minutes. Turn oven off and let cookies stand in oven with door closed for 15 minutes. Transfer to a wire rack and let cool.

PER COOKIE 57 calories; 3 g fat (1 g sat.); 2 g protein; 7 g carbohydrate; 0 g fiber; 50 mg sodium; 0 mg cholesterol

Malted Milk Ball Cookies 

MAKES about 60 cookies
PREP 35 minutes **BAKE** 8 minutes per batch **COOL** 2 minutes
OVEN 375°F

- ¾ cup butter, softened
- 1¼ cups packed brown sugar
- 1 cup granulated sugar
- 1½ teaspoons baking soda
- ½ teaspoon salt
- 3 eggs
- ¼ cup cooking oil
- 1½ teaspoons vanilla
- 3½ cups all-purpose flour
- 1½ cups whole bran cereal
- 3 cups malted milk balls, crushed (12 ounces)

1 Preheat oven to 375°F. In a large mixing bowl beat butter with an electric mixer on medium to high speed for 30 seconds. Add brown sugar, granulated sugar, baking soda, and salt. Beat until combined, scraping sides of bowl occasionally. Beat in eggs, oil, and vanilla. Beat in as much of the flour as you can with the mixer. Stir in any remaining flour and the cereal. If desired, reserve ½ cup crushed candies to sprinkle on top. Stir remaining candies into dough.
2 Shape dough into 1½-inch balls. Place balls 2 inches apart on an ungreased cookie sheet. Bake for 8 to 10 minutes or until golden. Place cookie sheet on a wire rack. If desired, immediately sprinkle tops of warm cookies with reserved crushed candies. Let cool on cookie sheet for 2 minutes. Transfer to a wire rack and cool completely.

PER COOKIE 122 calories; 5 g fat (2 g sat.); 1 g protein; 19 g carbohydrate; 1 g fiber; 100 mg sodium; 17 mg cholesterol

crushed candies to sprinkle on top.

Malted Milk Ball Cookies

Snickerdoodles

MAKES about 48 cookies
PREP 25 minutes **BAKE** 10 minutes per batch **CHILL** 1 to 2 hours
OVEN 375°F

- **⅓ cup butter, softened**
- **1 cup sugar**
- **1 teaspoon baking powder**
- **½ teaspoon ground nutmeg**
- **¼ teaspoon baking soda**
- **⅓ cup fat-free dairy sour cream**
- **1 egg, lightly beaten**
- **1 teaspoon vanilla**
- **2 cups all-purpose flour**
- **Nonstick cooking spray**
- **2 tablespoons sugar**
- **2 teaspoons unsweetened cocoa powder (optional)**

1 In a large mixing bowl beat butter with an electric mixer on medium to high speed for 30 seconds. Add the 1 cup sugar, the baking powder, nutmeg, and baking soda; beat until combined. Beat in sour cream, egg, and vanilla until combined. Beat in as much of the flour as you can with the mixer. Stir in any remaining flour. Cover and chill for 1 to 2 hours or until dough is easy to handle.

2 Preheat oven to 375°F. Lightly coat cookie sheets with cooking spray; set aside. In a small bowl stir together the 2 tablespoons sugar and, if desired, the cocoa powder.

3 Shape dough into 1-inch balls. Roll balls in sugar mixture to coat. Place 2 inches apart on prepared cookie sheets. Bake for 10 to 11 minutes or until edges are golden brown. Transfer to a wire rack and let cool.

PER COOKIE 53 calories; 1 g fat (1 g sat.); 0 g protein; 9 g carbohydrate; 0 g fiber; 25 mg sodium; 8 mg cholesterol

Oaty Doodle Hearts 

MAKES about 60 cookies
PREP 30 minutes **BAKE** 8 minutes per batch
COOL 1 minute **OVEN** 400°F

- **2 cups rolled oats**
- **1½ cups all-purpose flour**
- **½ cup whole wheat flour**
- **4 teaspoons ground cinnamon**
- **1 teaspoon baking soda**
- **½ teaspoon cream of tartar**
- **¼ teaspoon salt**
- **½ cup butter, softened**
- **½ cup butter-flavored shortening**
- **1½ cups sugar**
- **2 eggs**
- **1 teaspoon vanilla**
- **⅓ cup sugar**

1 Preheat oven to 400°F. Line cookie sheets with parchment paper or foil; set aside. In a food processor process oats until finely ground. In a medium bowl stir together ground oats, the flours, the cinnamon, baking soda, cream of tartar, and salt; set aside.
2 In a large mixing bowl beat butter and shortening with an electric mixer on medium to high speed for 30 seconds. Add the 1½ cups sugar and beat until combined, scraping sides of bowl. Beat in eggs and vanilla until combined. Beat in as much of the flour mixture as you can with the mixer. Stir in any remaining flour mixture.
3 Using a heaping teaspoon for each, shape dough into balls. Roll balls in the ⅓ cup sugar. Place 2 inches apart on the prepared cookie sheets. Flatten balls to a little less than ½ inch thick. Use your fingers to shape into hearts by forming a point and two rounded shapes. Bake for 8 to 10 minutes or until set and light brown. Cool on cookie sheets for 1 minute. Transfer to a wire rack and let cool.

PER COOKIE 82 calories; 4 g fat (1 g sat.); 1 g protein; 11 g carbohydrate; 1 g fiber; 45 mg sodium; 11 mg cholesterol

Triple-Chocolate Raspberry Fudgies

MAKES about 72 cookies
PREP 40 minutes **CHILL** 1 hour **BAKE** 8 to 10 minutes per batch
OVEN 350°F

- **2 cups all-purpose flour**
- **2 teaspoons baking powder**
- **¼ teaspoon salt**
- **½ cup shortening**
- **¼ cup butter, softened**
- **1⅓ cups sugar**
- **2 eggs**
- **2 ounces unsweetened chocolate, melted and cooled slightly**
- **⅓ cup seedless raspberry preserves**
- **⅓ cup miniature semisweet chocolate pieces**
- **½ cup powdered sugar**
- **1 tablespoon unsweetened cocoa powder**

1 In a medium bowl stir together flour, baking powder, and salt; set aside. In a large mixing bowl beat shortening, butter, and sugar with an electric mixer on medium to high speed until combined. Beat in eggs and then melted unsweetened chocolate until combined. Add flour mixture alternately with preserves, beating well after each addition. Stir in chocolate pieces. Cover and chill dough for 1 to 2 hours or until easy to handle.
2 Preheat oven to 350°F. Grease cookie sheets; set aside. Sift together powdered sugar and cocoa powder. Shape dough into 1-inch balls. Roll balls in powdered sugar mixture to coat. Place 2 inches apart on prepared cookie sheets. Bake for 8 to 10 minutes or until puffed and tops are slightly cracked. Transfer to a wire rack and let cool.

PER COOKIE 61 calories; 3 g fat (1 g sat.); 1 g protein; 8 g carbohydrate; 0 g fiber; 29 mg sodium; 8 mg cholesterol

Choco-Cran Cut-Ups 

MAKES 32 bars
PREP 20 minutes **MICROWAVE** about 4 minutes **CHILL** 1 hour

- **1 16-ounce package toasted honey-flavored corn and wheat cereal flakes with oats (8 cups)**
- **¾ cup chopped peanuts**
- **⅔ cup dried cranberries**
- **1 cup semisweet chocolate pieces**
- **¼ cup honey**
- **3 tablespoons butter**
- **5 cups miniature marshmallows**
- **2 teaspoons shortening**

1 Line a 13×9×2-inch pan with foil, extending the foil over the edges of the pan. Grease foil; set aside.
2 In a very large bowl stir together cereal, peanuts, cranberries, and ½ cup of the chocolate pieces; set aside.
3 In a large microwave-safe bowl combine honey and butter. Microwave on 100-percent power (high) for 1 minute. Stir until butter melts. Add marshmallows; toss to coat. Microwave on 100-percent power (high) for 1½ minutes. Stir until melted and smooth. Add marshmallow mixture to cereal mixture; toss to coat. Press cereal mixture firmly into the prepared pan.
4 In a small bowl combine the remaining chocolate pieces and the shortening. Microwave on 50-percent power (medium) for 1 minute or until melted, stirring once. Drizzle chocolate mixture over bars.
5 Chill for 1 hour or until set. Use foil to lift from pan. Cut into bars. Store in an airtight container at room temperature for up to 3 days.

PER BAR 144 calories; 5 g fat (2 g sat.); 2 g protein; 24 g carbohydrate; 1 g fiber; 94 mg sodium; 3 mg cholesterol

Marbled Brownies 

MAKES 48 brownies
PREP 20 minutes **BAKE** 25 minutes **OVEN** 350°F

- **Nonstick cooking spray**
- **1 15- to 22-ounce package brownie mix**
- **1 8-ounce package cream cheese, softened**
- **¾ cup milk**
- **¾ cup powdered sugar**
- **1 package 1-layer-size white cake mix**
- **2 tablespoons water**

1 Preheat oven to 350°F. Coat a 15×10×1-inch baking pan with cooking spray; set aside. Prepare brownie mix according to package directions. Spread batter evenly in prepared pan.
2 In a medium mixing bowl beat cream cheese with an electric mixer on medium speed for 30 seconds. Gradually beat in the milk and powdered sugar until combined. Add cake mix and the water; beat well. Spoon the white batter on top of brownie batter. Using a butter knife or spatula, gently lift and fold brownie batter to marble into the white batter.
3 Bake for 25 to 30 minutes or until a wooden toothpick inserted near the center comes out clean. Cool in pan on a wire rack. Using a wet knife, cut into bars. Store bars, covered, in the refrigerator for up to 3 days.

PER BROWNIE 109 calories; 4 g fat (1 g sat.); 1 g protein; 17 g carbohydrate; 0 g fiber; 115 mg sodium; 6 mg cholesterol

Looks can be deceiving. This decadent bar actually features convenience products, brownie mix and cake mix. Store these chewy treats in the refrigerator to keep them fresh.

Marbled Brownies

Ginger Squares

Ginger Squares ✪

MAKES about 48 cookies
PREP 25 minutes **FREEZE** 30 minutes **BAKE** 8 minutes per batch
OVEN 375°F

- ⅓ **cup molasses**
- ⅓ **cup butter**
- 2 **cups all-purpose flour**
- ⅓ **cup packed brown sugar**
- 1½ **teaspoons ground ginger**
- ½ **teaspoon baking soda**
- ½ **teaspoon ground cinnamon**
- ¼ **teaspoon salt**
- ¼ **teaspoon black pepper (optional)**
- ⅛ **teaspoon ground cloves**
- 1 **egg, lightly beaten**
- **Powdered sugar (optional)**

1 In a saucepan combine molasses and butter. Cook and stir over low heat until butter melts. Pour molasses mixture into a large bowl; cool to room temperature. In another large bowl stir together flour, brown sugar, ginger, baking soda, cinnamon, salt, pepper (if desired), and cloves. Stir egg into molasses mixture. Stir in flour mixture until combined.
2 Divide dough in half; shape into two 5½×1½-inch square logs. Wrap in plastic wrap or waxed paper. Chill in freezer about 30 minutes or until dough is firm enough to slice.
3 Preheat oven to 375°F. Cut logs into ⅛-inch slices (reshaping logs as necessary). Place slices 1 inch apart on an ungreased cookie sheet. Prick slices several times each with a fork. Bake for 8 to 10 minutes or until edges are firm and light brown. Transfer to a wire rack and let cool. If desired, sprinkle cooled cookies with powdered sugar.

PER COOKIE 44 calories; 1 g fat (1 g sat.); 1 g protein; 7 g carbohydrate; 0 g fiber; 37 mg sodium; 8 mg cholesterol

Pistachio-Apple Baklava

Apple Puffed Oven Pancake 

MAKES 6 servings
PREP 25 minutes **BAKE** 20 minutes **OVEN** 400°F

- **1 tablespoon butter**
- **¾ cup refrigerated or frozen egg product, thawed, or 3 eggs**
- **½ cup all-purpose flour**
- **½ cup fat-free milk**
- **¼ teaspoon apple pie spice**
- **⅛ teaspoon salt**
- **Nonstick cooking spray**
- **2 cups thinly sliced cooking apple (2 medium)**
- **2 tablespoons packed brown sugar**
- **2 teaspoons water**
- **1 recipe Caramel Sauce or ½ cup purchased sugar-free caramel-flavored ice cream topping**
- **Powdered sugar (optional)**

1 Preheat oven to 400°F. Place butter in a 10-inch ovenproof skillet with flared sides. Place skillet in oven for 3 to 5 minutes or until butter melts. Meanwhile, for batter, in a medium bowl whisk together egg product, flour, milk, apple pie spice, and salt until mixture is smooth. Immediately pour batter into the hot skillet. Bake for 20 to 25 minutes or until puffed and brown.
2 Meanwhile, lightly coat an unheated medium saucepan with cooking spray. Preheat pan over medium heat. Add apple slices, brown sugar, and the water. Cook for 4 to 6 minutes or until apple is golden brown and tender, stirring occasionally.
3 Spoon apple mixture into baked pancake; drizzle with Caramel Sauce. If desired, sprinkle edges with powdered sugar. Cut into wedges.
Caramel Sauce: In a small saucepan stir together 2 tablespoons packed brown sugar and 1½ teaspoons cornstarch. Stir in ½ cup water. Bring to boiling over medium heat, stirring constantly. Boil gently, uncovered, for 3 minutes; remove from heat. Stir in 1 teaspoon butter and ½ teaspoon vanilla. Serve warm.

PER SERVING 145 calories; 3 g fat (2 g sat.); 5 g protein; 25 g carbohydrate; 1 g fiber; 138 mg sodium; 7 mg cholesterol

Pistachio-Apple Baklava

MAKES 18 servings
PREP 35 minutes **BAKE** 40 minutes **OVEN** 325°F

- **2 cups finely chopped cooking apple (2 large)**
- **½ teaspoon finely shredded lemon peel**
- **1 tablespoon lemon juice**
- **1 tablespoon honey**
- **¼ teaspoon ground allspice**
- **¾ cup lightly salted pistachio nuts, finely chopped**
- **½ cup snipped dried cranberries**
- **Butter-flavored nonstick cooking spray**
- **20 sheets (½ of a 16-ounce package) frozen phyllo dough (14×9-inch rectangles), thawed**

1 Preheat oven to 325°F. In a large bowl combine apple, lemon peel, lemon juice, honey, and allspice. Stir in pistachio nuts and cranberries. Set aside.
2 Coat a 2-quart square baking dish with cooking spray. Unroll phyllo dough. With kitchen shears or a long knife, cut the whole stack of phyllo in half crosswise to make forty 9×7-inch sheets. Keep phyllo covered with plastic wrap, removing sheets as you need them.
3 Using one sheet of the phyllo dough at a time, layer 10 phyllo sheets in the dish, coating the top of each sheet with cooking spray and folding over any extra. Turn every other sheet a quarter turn to make even layers. Spread about 1 cup of the apple mixture over phyllo in dish. Repeat layers twice. Layer remaining 10 phyllo dough sheets over apple mixture, coating the top of each sheet with cooking spray.
4 Using a sharp knife, cut through phyllo and apple layers to make nine squares; cut each square in half diagonally. (Do not remove the pieces from dish.) Bake for 40 to 45 minutes or until golden brown. Cool completely on a wire rack.

PER SERVING 88 calories; 3 g fat (0 g sat.); 2 g protein; 14 g carbohydrate; 1 g fiber; 85 mg sodium; 0 mg cholesterol

A popoverlike batter bakes into a golden shell and cradles sweet apple filling.

Apple Puffed Oven Pancake

Tropical Fruit Pavlova

Tropical Fruit Pavlova

MAKES 8 servings
PREP 30 minutes **BAKE** 35 minutes **COOL** 1½ hours
CHILL overnight **OVEN** 300°F

- 1 recipe Mango Cream
- 3 egg whites
- ¼ teaspoon cream of tartar
- ⅔ cup sugar
- 2 cups cut-up, seeded, pitted fresh mango; sliced kumquats; cut-up, peeled kiwifruit; and/or halved fresh strawberries

1 Prepare Mango Cream. In a medium mixing bowl let egg whites stand at room temperature for 30 minutes. Meanwhile, line a baking sheet with parchment paper or foil. Using a pencil, draw eight 3-inch circles on the paper or foil (or draw one 8-inch circle); set aside.
2 Preheat oven to 300°F. For meringue shells, add cream of tartar to egg whites. Beat with an electric mixer on medium speed until soft peaks form (tips curl). Add the sugar, 1 tablespoon at a time, beating on high speed until stiff peaks form (tips stand straight).
3 Spoon egg white mixture into a pastry bag. Pipe the meringue over the circles (or large circle) on the paper, building up the sides to form shells. (Or use the back of a spoon to spread meringue over circles, building up the sides.)
4 Bake for 35 minutes for the 3-inch shells or for 40 minutes for the 8-inch shell. Turn off the oven; let meringues dry in oven with door closed for 1 hour. Lift meringues off paper. Transfer to a wire rack; cool completely.
5 To serve, place meringue shells on dessert dishes. Spoon Mango Cream into shells. Top with fruit. (To serve, cut large shell into wedges.)
Mango Cream: For yogurt cheese, line a sieve or small colander with three layers of 100-percent-cotton cheesecloth or a clean paper coffee filter. Suspend strainer over a large bowl. Spoon 2½ cups plain low-fat or fat-free yogurt* into the strainer; cover with plastic wrap. Refrigerate for 24 hours. Discard liquid in bowl.

In a blender or food processor, place 1 cup cut-up, seeded, peeled fresh mango. Cover and blend until smooth. Transfer mango puree to a medium bowl. Stir in the yogurt cheese, 1 tablespoon powdered sugar, and ½ teaspoon finely shredded orange peel. Cover and chill for up to 3 days.
***Note:** Be sure to use a brand of yogurt that contains no gums, gelatin, or fillers. These ingredients may prevent the whey from separating from the curd to make yogurt cheese.

PER SERVING 164 calories; 1 g fat (1 g sat.); 6 g protein; 31 g carbohydrate; 2 g fiber; 76 mg sodium; 5 mg cholesterol

Luscious Lemon Triangles

Luscious Lemon Triangles 

MAKES 18 triangles
PREP 25 minutes **BAKE** 35 minutes **COOL** 1 hour **OVEN** 350°F

- Nonstick cooking spray
- ¾ cup all-purpose flour
- 3 tablespoons granulated sugar
- ¼ cup butter
- 1 egg
- 1 egg white
- ⅔ cup granulated sugar
- 2 tablespoons all-purpose flour
- 1 teaspoon finely shredded lemon peel
- 2 tablespoons lemon juice
- 1 tablespoon water
- ¼ teaspoon baking powder
- Powdered sugar (optional)

1 Preheat oven to 350°F. Lightly coat an 8×8×2-inch baking pan with cooking spray; set aside. In a small bowl stir together the ¾ cup flour and the 3 tablespoons granulated sugar. Using a pastry blender, cut in butter until flour mixture resembles coarse crumbs. Press flour mixture into the bottom of the prepared pan. Bake for 15 minutes.
2 Meanwhile, for filling, in a small mixing bowl combine the egg and egg white. Beat with an electric mixer on medium speed until frothy. Add the ⅔ cup granulated sugar, the 2 tablespoons flour, the lemon juice, the water, and baking powder. Beat on medium speed 3 minutes or until slightly thickened. Stir in lemon peel. Pour mixture over hot crust.
3 Bake for 20 to 25 minutes more or until edges are light brown and center is set. Cool on a wire rack. Cut into 9 squares; cut each square diagonally to make a triangle. If desired, sift powdered sugar over top of triangles.

PER TRIANGLE 85 calories; 3 g fat (2 g sat.); 1 g protein; 14 g carbohydrate; 0 g fiber; 40 mg sodium; 19 mg cholesterol

Oatmeal-Banana Bread Pudding

Apple peels of red or green brighten this nutty favorite. However, if you prefer a skinless dish, use a small knife or vegetable peeler to remove the peels before slicing the apples.

Apples 'n' Peanut Butter Crisp

Oatmeal-Banana Bread Pudding

MAKES 9 servings
PREP 25 minutes **BAKE** 35 minutes **OVEN** 350°F

- **2 eggs, lightly beaten**
- **2 cups fat-free milk**
- **3 tablespoons packed brown sugar**
- **1 teaspoon vanilla**
- **½ teaspoon pumpkin pie spice or ground cinnamon**
- **5 cups dry oatmeal bread cubes***
- **2 medium bananas, halved lengthwise and sliced**
- **½ cup chopped walnuts or pecans, toasted (optional)**

1 Preheat oven to 350°F. In a medium bowl whisk together eggs, milk, brown sugar, vanilla, and pumpkin pie spice; set aside. In an ungreased 2-quart square baking dish toss together bread cubes, banana, and, if desired, walnuts. Pour egg mixture evenly over bread mixture; toss until bread is moistened.
2 Bake, uncovered, for 35 to 40 minutes or until a knife inserted near the center comes out clean. Cool slightly.
***Note:** For 5 cups dry bread cubes, spread 8½ cups fresh bread cubes (11 slices oatmeal bread) in a shallow baking pan. Bake in a 350°F oven for 10 to 15 minutes or until bread cubes are dry, stirring twice; cool.

PER SERVING 167 calories; 3 g fat (1 g sat.); 6 g protein; 30 g carbohydrate; 2 g fiber; 239 mg sodium; 48 mg cholesterol

Apples 'n' Peanut Butter Crisp 

MAKES 8 servings
PREP 20 minutes **BAKE** 30 minutes **OVEN** 375°F

- **6 cups thinly sliced, peeled (if desired) red and/or green cooking apple (6 medium)**
- **2 tablespoons all-purpose flour**
- **1 tablespoon packed brown sugar**
- **⅔ cup quick-cooking rolled oats**
- **2 tablespoons all-purpose flour**
- **2 tablespoons packed brown sugar**
- **¼ cup peanut butter**
- **2 tablespoons chopped peanuts**

1 Preheat oven to 375°F. Place apple in a 2-quart oval or square baking dish; set aside. In a small bowl stir together the 2 tablespoons flour and the 1 tablespoon brown sugar. Sprinkle flour mixture over apple slices in dish; toss to coat.
2 Cover and bake for 15 minutes. Meanwhile, in a medium bowl stir together oats, the remaining 2 tablespoons flour, and the 2 tablespoons brown sugar. Using a fork, stir in peanut butter until coarse crumbs. Stir in peanuts.
3 Uncover apple mixture; sprinkle with oat mixture. Bake, uncovered, for 15 to 20 minutes more or until apple is tender and topping is golden. Serve warm.

PER SERVING 174 calories; 6 g fat (1 g sat.); 4 g protein; 28 g carbohydrate; 4 g fiber; 51 mg sodium; 0 mg cholesterol

Apple-Cranberry Crisp

MAKES 6 servings
PREP 15 minutes **BAKE** 30 minutes **OVEN** 375°F

- **5 cups thinly sliced, peeled cooking apple (5 medium)**
- **1 cup fresh cranberries**
- **2 tablespoons granulated sugar**
- **1 teaspoon apple pie spice or ground cinnamon**
- **½ cup quick-cooking rolled oats**
- **3 tablespoons packed brown sugar**
- **2 tablespoons all-purpose flour**
- **2 tablespoons butter**

1 Preheat oven to 375°F. In a 2-quart square baking dish stir together apple and cranberries. In a small bowl, stir together granulated sugar and ½ teaspoon of the apple pie spice. Sprinkle sugar mixture over fruit mixture; toss to coat.
2 For topping, in a small bowl stir together oats, brown sugar, flour, and the remaining ½ teaspoon apple pie spice. Using a pastry blender, cut in butter until mixture resembles coarse crumbs. Sprinkle topping over fruit mixture.
3 Bake, uncovered, for 30 to 35 minutes or until apple is tender. Serve warm.

PER SERVING 189 calories; 5 g fat (3 g sat.); 2 g protein; 37 g carbohydrate; 4 g fiber; 45 mg sodium; 11 mg cholesterol

Apple-Cranberry Crisp

Pear-Rhubarb Crisp

MAKES 9 servings
PREP 25 minutes **BAKE** 40 minutes **COOL** 30 minutes
OVEN 375°F

- **4 cups thinly sliced Bartlett pear or cooking apple (4 medium)**
- **2 cups sliced fresh rhubarb or frozen unsweetened sliced rhubarb***
- **¼ cup all-purpose flour**
- **¼ cup honey**
- **2 tablespoons apple juice or apple cider**
- **1 cup oat square cereal, crushed**
- **¼ cup whole bran cereal, crushed**
- **¼ cup sliced almonds or chopped pecans**
- **2 tablespoons butter, melted**
- **1 tablespoon honey**
- **½ of an 8-ounce container frozen light whipped dessert topping, thawed (optional)**

1 Preheat oven to 375°F. In a large bowl combine pear, rhubarb, and flour. Add the ¼ cup honey and the apple juice; toss gently to coat. Transfer fruit mixture to a 2-quart square baking dish. Cover and bake for 30 to 40 minutes or just until pear is tender.
2 Meanwhile, for topping, in a medium bowl stir together crushed cereals and almonds. Add melted butter and the 1 tablespoon honey; toss to coat. Sprinkle cereal mixture over partially baked fruit mixture. Bake, uncovered, about 10 minutes more or until fruit is very tender and topping is light brown.
3 Cool on a wire rack for 30 minutes. Serve warm. If desired, top with whipped topping.
***Note:** If using frozen rhubarb, measure while still frozen. Allow rhubarb to thaw in a large bowl about 1 hour or until the fruit is partially thawed but still icy; do not drain rhubarb. Continue as directed.

PER SERVING 169 calories; 5 g fat (2 g sat.); 2 g protein; 32 g carbohydrate; 4 g fiber; 55 mg sodium; 7 mg cholesterol

The expected crunch from an unexpected source: Oat and whole bran cereal squares make for a nontraditional fruit crisp topper.

Pear-Rhubarb Crisp

Peachy Berry Cobbler

Individual cobblers are both cute and easy to serve and require 6-ounce custard cups or small casseroles. To make a large cobbler instead, transfer hot filling to a 2-quart square baking dish. Drop topping from a spoon into eight mounds on top of hot filling. Bake about 20 minutes or until a wooden toothpick inserted into topping comes out clean.

Peachy Berry Cobbler

MAKES 8 servings
PREP 35 minutes **BAKE** 15 minutes **OVEN** 400°F

- **1 cup all-purpose flour**
- **1½ teaspoons baking powder**
- **¼ teaspoon ground ginger or ground cinnamon**
- **⅛ teaspoon salt**
- **2 tablespoons butter**
- **¼ cup sugar**
- **4 teaspoons cornstarch**
- **⅓ cup water**
- **3 cups fresh or frozen unsweetened peach slices**
- **2 cups fresh or frozen unsweetened raspberries**
- **⅓ cup plain fat-free yogurt**
- **1 egg, lightly beaten**
- **Ground ginger or ground cinnamon (optional)**

1 Preheat oven to 400°F. For topping, in a medium bowl stir together flour, baking powder, the ¼ teaspoon ginger, and the salt. Using a pastry blender, cut in butter until flour mixture resembles coarse crumbs. Set aside.
2 For filling, in a large saucepan stir together sugar and cornstarch. Stir in the water. Add peach slices and raspberries. Cook and stir until thickened and bubbly. Keep filling hot while finishing topping.
3 To finish topping, stir together yogurt and egg. Add yogurt mixture to flour mixture, stirring just until moistened.
4 Spoon filling evenly into eight 6-ounce custard cups or four 10- to 12-ounce casseroles. Drop the topping from a spoon onto hot filling. (Drop one mound into each custard cup or two mounds into each casserole.) Place custard cups on a baking sheet.
5 Bake, uncovered, for 15 to 20 minutes or until a wooden toothpick inserted into topping comes out clean. Cool slightly. If desired, sprinkle with additional ground ginger. Serve warm.

PER SERVING 160 calories; 4 g fat (2 g sat.); 4 g protein; 28 g carbohydrate; 4 g fiber; 120 mg sodium; 35 mg cholesterol

Gingered Sho

MAKES 12 bites

PREP 25 minutes B

Nonstick c
1 cup all-pu
2 tablespoo
1½ teaspoons
½ teaspoo
1 teaspoon
⅛ teaspoon
2 tablespoo
½ cup butte
¾ cup frozer
¼ cup fat-fr
¼ teaspoon
1 cup chopp
blueberrie
Finely cho

1 Preheat oven t
cooking spray; se
sugar, the 1½ tea
powder, and soda

Cider-Glazed Fig-Apple Cupcakes

MAKES 6 cupcakes

PREP 20 minutes **BAKE** 15 minutes **COOL** 10 minutes

OVEN 400°F

- **Nonstick cooking spray**
- **½ cup yellow cornmeal**
- **⅓ cup whole wheat flour**
- **2 tablespoons sugar**
- **1½ teaspoons finely shredded lemon peel**
- **1 teaspoon baking powder**
- **⅛ teaspoon baking soda**
- **⅔ cup buttermilk or sour milk***
- **⅔ cup shredded red cooking apple (1 medium)**
- **2 egg whites, lightly beaten**
- **3 tablespoons finely chopped dried figs (about 5 figs)**
- **1 small red cooking apple**
- **⅔ cup apple juice or apple cider**

1 Preheat oven to 400°F. Lightly coat six 3¼- to 3½-inch muffin cups with cooking spray. Set aside. In a medium bowl combine cornmeal, flour, sugar, lemon peel, baking powder, baking soda, and ⅛ teaspoon *salt;* set aside. In another medium bowl combine buttermilk, shredded apple, egg whites, and figs. Add apple mixture all at once to cornmeal mixture. Stir just until moistened. Set aside.

2 Core whole apple. Cut apple crosswise into six ¼-inch rings. Place one ring in each muffin cup, cutting slices to fit if necessary. Spoon cornmeal batter evenly into muffin cups over apple slices, filling each about half full.

3 Bake for 15 to 20 minutes or until tops are golden brown and a wooden toothpick inserted in centers comes out clean.

4 Meanwhile, in a small saucepan bring apple juice to boiling; reduce heat. Boil gently, uncovered, for 7 to 9 minutes or until reduced to ⅓ cup.

5 Let cupcakes cool in muffin cups on a wire rack for 10 minutes. Loosen edges of cupcakes. Invert pan onto a baking sheet; remove pan. While hot, drizzle cupcakes with apple juice reduction. Transfer to a platter. Serve warm.

***Note:** To make sour milk, place 2 teaspoons lemon juice in a glass measuring cup. Add enough fat-free milk to make ⅔ cup; stir. Let mixture stand 5 minutes before using.

PER CUPCAKE 139 calories; 1 g fat (0 g sat.); 4 g protein; 30 g carbohydrate; 3 g fiber; 170 mg sodium; 1 mg cholesterol

Cider-Glazed Fig-Apple Cupcakes

Grab a spoon to serve

Citrus Angel Cake with Peach & Plum Salsa

MAKES 12 servings
PREP 25 minutes **BAKE** 35 minutes **COOK** 5 minutes
COOL 1 hour **CHILL** 24 hours **OVEN** 350°F

- **1¼ cups egg whites (8 to 10 large)**
- **1 cup sifted cake flour or sifted all-purpose flour**
- **½ cup powdered sugar**
- **1¼ teaspoons cream of tartar**
- **½ teaspoon vanilla**
- **⅔ cup granulated sugar**
- **1 tablespoon finely shredded orange peel, lemon peel, and/or lime peel**
- **1 recipe Peach & Plum Salsa**
- **Fresh mint leaves and/or orange peel, lemon peel, or lime peel strips (optional)**

1 In a very large mixing bowl let egg whites stand at room temperature for 30 minutes. Meanwhile, sift flour and powdered sugar together three times; set aside.
2 Adjust baking rack to the lowest position in oven. Preheat oven to 350°F. Add cream of tartar and vanilla to egg whites. Beat with an electric mixer on medium speed until soft peaks form (tips curl). Gradually add granulated sugar, 2 tablespoons at a time, beating until stiff peaks form (tips stand straight).
3 Sift about one-fourth of the flour mixture over beaten egg whites. Sprinkle with orange peel; fold in gently. Repeat, folding in remaining flour mixture by fourths. Spoon batter into an ungreased 10-inch tube pan. Using a narrow metal spatula or knife, gently cut through batter to remove any large air pockets.
4 Bake on the lowest oven rack for 35 to 40 minutes or until top springs back when lightly touched. Immediately invert cake; cool thoroughly in the inverted pan. Loosen side of cake from pan; remove cake.
5 To serve, slice cake. Spoon Peach & Plum Salsa over each serving. If desired, garnish with fresh mint leaves and/or citrus peel strips.
Peach & Plum Salsa: In a small saucepan combine 1/3 cup orange juice and 3 tablespoons white or regular balsamic vinegar. Bring to boiling; boil gently, uncovered, for 5 to 7 minutes or until reduced to 1/4 cup. Remove from heat; cool completely. In a medium bowl combine 1 1/2 cups each coarsely chopped plum (3 medium) and peach (2 medium). Add orange juice mixture; toss gently to coat. Cover and chill for up to 24 hours. Just before serving, stir in 2 to 3 teaspoons snipped fresh mint, cilantro, or basil.

PER SERVING 127 calories; 0 g fat (0 g sat.); 4 g protein; 28 g carbohydrate; 1 g fiber; 43 mg sodium; 0 mg cholesterol

Triple Fruit Pie

MAKES 10 servings
PREP 30 minutes **BAKE** 40 minutes **COOL** 1 hour **OVEN** 375°F

- **1 recipe Oil Pastry Dough**
- **¼ cup packed brown sugar**
- **1 tablespoon all-purpose flour**
- **1 teaspoon apple pie spice**
- **4 cups thinly sliced red and/or green cooking apple (4 medium)**
- **1 cup thinly sliced pear (1 medium)**
- **1 15-ounce can unpeeled apricot halves in light syrup, rinsed, drained, and sliced, or 1 cup fresh blueberries**

1 Preheat oven to 375°F. Prepare Oil Pastry Dough. Cover and set aside.
2 In a very large bowl stir together brown sugar, flour, and apple pie spice. Add apple, pear, and apricot. Toss gently to coat. Transfer fruit mixture to a 9-inch pie plate.
3 On a floured surface, use your hands to slightly flatten the pastry dough. Roll dough from center to edge into a 12-inch circle. Use 1- to 1 1/2-inch cookie cutters to cut out shapes from the crust. To transfer pastry, wrap it around the rolling pin. Unroll pastry on top of fruit mixture. Trim pastry to 1/2 inch beyond edge of pie plate. Fold under extra pastry; crimp edge as desired.
4 Place pie plate on a foil-lined baking sheet. To prevent overbrowning, cover edge of pie with foil. Bake for 30 minutes; remove foil. Bake for 10 to 15 minutes more or until apples are tender and filling is bubbly. Cool about 1 hour. Serve slightly warm.
Oil Pastry Dough: In a medium bowl stir together 3/4 cup all-purpose flour, 1/4 cup whole wheat pastry flour or whole wheat flour, and 1/4 teaspoon salt. Add 1/4 cup fat-free milk and 3 tablespoons cooking oil all at once to the flour mixture. Stir lightly with a fork until moistened. Form dough into a ball.

PER SERVING 164 calories; 4 g fat (1 g sat.); 2 g protein; 31 g carbohydrate; 3 g fiber; 65 mg sodium; 0 mg cholesterol

this pandowdy-style pie.

Triple Fruit Pie

Glazed Tropical Fruit Pie

Glazed Tropical Fruit Pie

MAKES 10 servings
PREP 25 minutes **COOL** 30 minutes **CHILL** 3 to 4 hours

- **1 cup pineapple-orange juice**
- **1 tablespoon cornstarch**
- **2 cups pitted, peeled mango (1-inch pieces)**
- **2 cups seeded, peeled papaya (1-inch pieces)**
- **1½ cups peeled kiwifruit slices (halved slices)**
- **1 purchased reduced-fat graham cracker crumb pie shell**
- **Frozen light whipped dessert topping, thawed (optional)**

1 In a small saucepan combine juice and cornstarch. Cook and stir over medium heat until thickened and bubbly; cook and stir for 2 minutes more. Transfer to a large bowl. Cover surface of juice mixture with plastic wrap; cool for 30 minutes. Divide mixture among three small bowls.
2 Fold a different fruit into each of the bowls of fruit juice mixture. Spoon fruit into pie shell, arranging as desired. Cover and chill for 3 to 4 hours. If desired, serve with whipped topping.

PER SERVING 144 calories; 3 g fat (1 g sat.); 2 g protein; 28 g carbohydrate; 2 g fiber; 83 mg sodium; 0 mg cholesterol

Berry Pie with Creamy Filling

MAKES 10 servings
PREP 20 minutes **BAKE** 10 minutes **COOL** 1 hour
CHILL 24 hours; 3 to 6 hours **OVEN** 350°F

- **1 16-ounce carton plain fat-free or low-fat yogurt***
- **2 tablespoons powdered sugar**
- **½ teaspoon vanilla**
- **Nonstick cooking spray**
- **1⅓ cups finely crushed zwieback (about 17 slices)**
- **2 tablespoons packed brown sugar**
- **1 egg white, lightly beaten**
- **2 tablespoons butter, melted**
- **¾ cup low-calorie cranberry-raspberry drink**
- **1 tablespoon cornstarch**
- **6 cups fresh raspberries, blackberries, blueberries, and/or halved strawberries**
- **Fresh mint sprigs (optional)**

1 For yogurt cheese, line a yogurt strainer, sieve, or a small colander with three layers of 100-percent-cotton cheesecloth or a clean paper coffee filter. Suspend lined strainer over a large bowl. Spoon yogurt into the strainer; cover with plastic wrap. Refrigerate for 24 hours. Discard liquid in bowl. In a small bowl, combine yogurt cheese, powdered sugar, and vanilla. Cover and chill until ready to use.
2 Preheat oven to 350°F. Coat a 9-inch pie plate with cooking spray. In a medium bowl stir together zwieback and brown sugar. Add egg white and melted butter; mix well. Press mixture evenly onto bottom and up sides of prepared pie plate. Bake for 10 to 12 minutes or until edge is brown. Cool crust completely on a wire rack.
3 Meanwhile, for glaze, in a small saucepan stir together cranberry-raspberry drink and cornstarch. Cook and stir over medium heat until thickened and bubbly; cook and stir for 2 minutes more. Remove from heat. Transfer to a small bowl. Cover surface with plastic wrap; let stand at room temperature for 1 to 2 hours or until cool.
4 Spread yogurt cheese mixture in crust. In a large bowl combine berries and cooled glaze, tossing gently. Spoon fruit over yogurt mixture. Cover and chill for 3 to 6 hours. If desired, garnish with fresh mint.
***Note:** Be sure to use a brand of yogurt that contains no gums, gelatin, or fillers. These ingredients may prevent the whey from separating from the curd to make yogurt cheese.

PER SERVING 160 calories; 4 g fat (2 g sat.); 5 g protein; 27 g carbohydrate; 3 g fiber; 87 mg sodium; 10 mg cholesterol

Shimmering Strawberry Pie 

MAKES 8 servings
PREP 1 hour **BAKE** 9 minutes **CHILL** 3 to 4 hours **OVEN** 450°F

- **½ of a 15-ounce package rolled refrigerated unbaked piecrust (1 crust)**
- **6 cups strawberries, halved**
- **1 cup water**
- **¼ cup sugar**
- **2 tablespoons cornstarch**

1 Preheat oven to 450°F. Let piecrust stand according to package directions. Unroll; transfer to a 9-inch pie plate, easing pastry into pie plate. Trim pastry to ½ inch beyond edge of plate. Fold under extra pastry; crimp edge. Prick bottom and sides with the tines of a fork. Bake for 9 to 11 minutes or until golden. Cool crust on a wire rack.
2 In a blender combine 1 cup of the strawberries and the water. Blend until smooth. Transfer berry puree to a small saucepan. Bring to boiling; reduce heat. Simmer, uncovered, for 2 minutes. In a medium saucepan stir together sugar and cornstarch; stir in berry puree. Cook and stir over medium heat until thickened and bubbly. Cook and stir for 2 minutes more. Remove from heat. If desired, stir in enough *red food coloring* to tint a rich red color. Cool to room temperature.
3 Fold the remaining 5 cups strawberries into the cooled berry mixture; transfer to baked crust. Cover; chill for 3 to 4 hours. If desired, serve with *frozen light whipped dessert topping,* thawed.

PER SERVING 184 calories; 7 g fat (3 g sat.); 1 g protein; 29 g carbohydrate; 2 g fiber; 110 mg sodium; 5 mg cholesterol

Berry Pie with Creamy Filling

Temptation...it's hard to resist a second helping of this double-berry-filled goody.

Easy Berry Tarts

Easy Berry Tarts

MAKES 4 servings
PREP 25 minutes **BAKE** 8 minutes **OVEN** 375°F

- **Nonstick cooking spray**
- **2 tablespoons sugar**
- **1 teaspoon cornstarch**
- **⅛ teaspoon cayenne pepper**
- **¼ cup water**
- **1 cup fresh blueberries**
- **1 cup fresh raspberries**
- **1 tablespoon sugar**
- **¼ teaspoon ground cinnamon**
- **4 sheets frozen phyllo dough (14×9-inch rectangles), thawed**

1 Preheat oven to 375°F. Lightly coat four 4×2×½-inch rectangular tart pans with removable bottoms with cooking spray; set aside. In a small saucepan stir together the 2 tablespoons sugar, the cornstarch, and cayenne pepper. Stir in the water and half of the blueberries. Cook and stir over medium heat until mixture is thickened and bubbly. Fold in the remaining blueberries and raspberries; set aside.
2 In a small bowl stir together the 1 tablespoon sugar and the cinnamon. Place one sheet of phyllo on a cutting board. Lightly coat with cooking spray; sprinkle with about 1 teaspoon sugar mixture. Repeat layering with remaining phyllo and sugar mixture, ending with cooking spray. Using a sharp knife, cut phyllo stack in half lengthwise then crosswise, forming four rectangles. Ease rectangles into prepared tart pans.
3 Bake for 8 minutes or until phyllo is golden brown. Cool slightly; remove shells from pans. Just before serving, spoon fruit mixture into shells.

PER TART 131 calories; 1 g fat (0 g sat.); 2 g protein; 29 g carbohydrate; 3 g fiber; 93 mg sodium; 0 mg cholesterol

Pudding Tartlets

Pudding Tartlets

MAKES 15 tartlets
START TO FINISH 15 minutes

- **2 individual oblong creme-filled sponge cakes, or fifteen ½-inch cubes frozen pound cake, thawed**
- **1 2.1-ounce package baked miniature phyllo dough shells (15 shells)**
- **½ cup premade desired-flavor pudding**
- **Whipped cream or frozen whipped dessert topping, thawed**
- **Unsweetened cocoa powder**

1 Slice sponge cakes in half lengthwise then crosswise into about 1-inch pieces. Place one cake piece in each phyllo cup (may have a piece or two left over). Spoon pudding mixture over cake pieces. Cover and chill for 5 minutes. Before serving, top with whipped cream and sprinkle with cocoa powder.

PER TARTLET 54 calories; 2 g fat (0 g sat.); 1 g protein; 8 g carbohydrate; 0 g fiber; 47 mg sodium; 3 mg cholesterol

Crepes are like pancakes—with a few staple ingredients, you can make great ones from scratch in a matter of minutes. But for a really quick fix, look for ready-made crepes in the produce section of your supermarket.

Brownie-Fruit Pizza 

MAKES 12 servings
PREP 15 minutes **BAKE** 20 minutes **OVEN** 350°F

- **Nonstick cooking spray**
- ½ **cup sugar**
- 3 **tablespoons butter, softened**
- ¼ **cup refrigerated or frozen egg product, thawed**
- ¾ **cup chocolate-flavored syrup**
- ⅔ **cup all-purpose flour**
- 3 **cups assorted fruit (such as sliced, peeled kiwifruit; mandarin orange sections; sliced banana; sliced, peeled peach; sliced nectarine; strawberries; raspberries; and/or blueberries)**
- ½ **cup chocolate-flavored syrup**

1 Preheat oven to 350°F. Lightly coat a 12-inch pizza pan with cooking spray; set aside.
2 For crust, in a medium mixing bowl beat sugar and butter with an electric mixer on medium speed until creamy. Add the egg product; beat well. Alternately add the ¾ cup chocolate-flavored syrup and the flour, beating on low speed after each addition until combined. Spread batter in the prepared pizza pan.
3 Bake about 20 minutes or until top springs back when lightly touched. Cool in pan on a wire rack.
4 To serve, cut the brownie into 12 wedges. Top each wedge with fruit and drizzle evenly with the ½ cup chocolate-flavored syrup.

PER SERVING 187 calories; 3 g fat (2 g sat.); 2 g protein; 39 g carbohydrate; 2 g fiber; 61 mg sodium; 8 mg cholesterol

Peanut Butter-Banana Crepes  

MAKES 9 servings
START TO FINISH 30 minutes

- 1 **egg, lightly beaten**
- ¾ **cup fat-free milk**
- ½ **cup all-purpose flour**
- 1 **teaspoon cooking oil**
- ⅛ **teaspoon salt**
- 1 **cup Peanut Butter Dip**
- 3 **medium bananas, sliced**

1 In a medium bowl whisk together egg, milk, flour, oil, and salt. Heat a lightly oiled small nonstick skillet with flared sides over medium heat. Remove from heat. Spoon about 2 tablespoons of the crepe batter into hot skillet; lift and tilt skillet to spread batter. Return to heat; cook for 30 to 45 seconds or until top is set and dry. (Or cook on a crepe maker according to manufacturer's directions.) Invert skillet over paper towels to remove crepe. Repeat with remaining batter, oiling skillet occasionally to make 9 crepes.
2 Spread Peanut Butter Dip down center of crepes. Top with banana. Fold sides of crepes up over bananas.
Peanut Butter Dip: In a blender or food processor combine one 8-ounce carton light dairy sour cream, one 8-ounce package reduced-fat cream cheese (Neufchâtel), ½ cup creamy peanut butter, and 1 teaspoon vanilla. Cover and blend until smooth. Blend in 2 to 4 tablespoons fat-free milk to reach desired consistency.

PER SERVING 266 calories; 17 g fat (7 g sat.); 10 g protein; 21 g carbohydrate; 2 g fiber; 234 mg sodium; 52 mg cholesterol

Chocolate Crepes with Banana-Pecan Topping

MAKES 8 servings
START TO FINISH 35 minutes

- ⅓ cup white whole wheat flour or all-purpose flour
- 2 tablespoons packed brown sugar
- 2 tablespoons unsweetened cocoa powder
- ⅛ teaspoon salt
- ⅔ cup fat-free milk
- ¼ cup refrigerated or frozen egg product, thawed, or 1 egg, lightly beaten
- 1 teaspoon cooking oil
- ½ teaspoon vanilla
- 4 medium bananas
- Nonstick cooking spray
- ¼ cup sugar-free caramel-flavored ice cream topping
- ¼ teaspoon rum extract
- ¼ cup chopped pecans, toasted

1 For crepe batter, in a medium bowl stir together flour, brown sugar, cocoa powder, and salt. Add milk, egg product, oil, and vanilla; whisk until combined.

2 Heat a lightly oiled small nonstick skillet with flared sides over medium heat. Remove from heat. Spoon about 2 tablespoons of the crepe batter into hot skillet; lift and tilt skillet to spread batter. Return to heat; cook for 30 to 45 seconds or until top is set and dry. (Or cook on a crepe maker according to manufacturer's directions.) Invert skillet over paper towels to remove crepe. Repeat with remaining batter, oiling skillet occasionally to make 8 or 9 crepes. Set crepes aside.

3 Peel bananas; halve lengthwise, then crosswise. Lightly coat a nonstick grill pan or large nonstick skillet with cooking spray. Preheat pan over medium heat for 1 to 2 minutes. Grill bananas for 3 to 4 minutes or until brown and soft, turning once. Remove bananas from pan.

4 Meanwhile, in a small saucepan heat ice cream topping over low heat until heated through. Remove from heat; stir in rum extract.

5 To serve, divide crepes among eight dessert plates, folding crepes as desired. Top crepes with banana pieces; drizzle with caramel mixture. Sprinkle with pecans.

PER SERVING 155 calories; 4 g fat (0 g sat.); 3 g protein; 29 g carbohydrate; 2 g fiber; 76 mg sodium; 0 mg cholesterol

Pecan-Apple Custards

Spiced Orange Custards

Pecan-Apple Custards

MAKES 4 servings
PREP 20 minutes **BAKE** 25 minutes **COOL** 15 minutes
OVEN 375°F

- **Nonstick cooking spray**
- **½ cup unsweetened applesauce**
- **⅓ cup fat-free milk**
- **¼ cup refrigerated or frozen egg product, thawed, or 1 egg, lightly beaten**
- **3 tablespoons packed brown sugar**
- **1 tablespoon butter, melted**
- **½ teaspoon vanilla**
- **½ teaspoon maple flavoring**
- **¾ cup chopped cooking apple (1 small)**
- **⅓ cup rolled oats**
- **2 tablespoons chopped pecans, toasted**
- **Powdered sugar (optional)**
- **¼ cup vanilla low-fat or fat-free yogurt (optional)**

1 Preheat oven to 375°F. Lightly coat four 6-ounce custard cups with cooking spray. Place cups in a 15×10×1-inch baking pan; set aside.
2 In a medium bowl stir together applesauce, milk, egg product, brown sugar, melted butter, vanilla, and maple flavoring. Stir in apple and oats. Spoon apple mixture evenly into prepared custard cups.
3 Bake about 25 minutes or until a knife inserted near centers comes out clean. Cool on a wire rack for 15 minutes. Sprinkle custards with pecans and, if desired, powdered sugar. Serve warm. If desired, top with yogurt.

PER SERVING 154 calories; 6 g fat (2 g sat.); 3 g protein; 23 g carbohydrate; 2 g fiber; 63 mg sodium; 8 mg cholesterol

Spiced Orange Custards

MAKES 4 servings
PREP 15 minutes **COOK** 9½ minutes **STAND** 15 minutes

- **1½ cups fat-free milk**
- **3 tablespoons sugar**
- **1 teaspoon vanilla**
- **½ teaspoon finely shredded orange peel**
- **⅛ teaspoon ground nutmeg**
- **¾ cup refrigerated or frozen egg product, thawed, or 3 eggs, beaten**
- **1½ cups water**
- **Finely shredded orange peel (optional)**

1 In a microwave-safe 4-cup glass measure combine milk, sugar, vanilla, the ½ teaspoon orange peel, and the nutmeg, stirring to dissolve sugar. Microwave, uncovered, on 100-percent power (high) for 2½ to 5 minutes or until steaming and foamy but not boiling* (about 180°F), stirring once.
2 Gradually stir all of the hot mixture into egg product. Pour mixture evenly into four 6-ounce microwave-safe custard cups set in a microwave-safe 2-quart square baking dish.
3 In the same 4-cup glass measure, heat the water, uncovered, on 100-percent power (high) about 3 minutes or until boiling. Pour the boiling water into the baking dish around the custard cups.
4 Microwave custards, uncovered, on 100-percent power (high) for 4 to 7 minutes or until edges are set but centers still quiver, carefully rotating the cups after every minute and removing each custard when edge is set. Remove custards from baking dish.
5 Let stand, uncovered, on a wire rack about 15 minutes or until centers are set. Serve warm or chilled. To serve, if desired, unmold custards onto four dessert plates. If desired, garnish with additional shredded orange peel.
***Note:** Watch closely as the mixture will foam up if it is cooked too long.

PER SERVING 92 calories; 0 g fat (0 g sat.); 8 g protein; 15 g carbohydrate; 0 g fiber; 129 mg sodium; 2 mg cholesterol

Fruit Kabobs with Creamy Dipping Sauce 

MAKES 4 servings
START TO FINISH 15 minutes

- **2** **fresh kiwifruit, peeled and quartered**
- **8** **fresh pineapple chunks**
- **8** **fresh strawberries**
- **16** **large fresh blueberries**
- **1** **6-ounce carton strawberry or blueberry low-fat yogurt**
- **½** **cup light dairy sour cream**
- **2** **tablespoons strawberry or blueberry spreadable fruit**

1 Alternately thread fruit evenly on eight 6-inch skewers; set aside. For sauce, in a small bowl stir together yogurt, sour cream, and spreadable fruit. Serve kabobs with yogurt sauce for dipping.

PER SERVING 142 calories; 3 g fat (2 g sat.); 3 g protein; 27 g carbohydrate; 2 g fiber; 51 mg sodium; 11 mg cholesterol

Croutons of angel food cake go perfectly with caramely sweet mango. To make: Cut one-fourth of a 15-ounce purchased angel food cake in half horizontally. Brush all sides of each half with cooking oil. Place cake on a grill rack directly over medium coals. Grill, uncovered, for 2 to 3 minutes or until light brown, turning halfway through grilling. Cut into pieces.

Grilled Mango Blossom

Strawberries with Lemon Cream 

MAKES 6 servings
START TO FINISH 10 minutes

- **3 cups halved fresh strawberries**
- **1 cup whipping cream**
- **2 tablespoons powdered sugar**
- **⅛ teaspoon ground cardamom**
- **¼ teaspoon finely shredded lemon peel**
- **1 tablespoon snipped fresh lemon basil or basil**

1 Divide berries among six dessert dishes; set aside.
2 In a chilled medium mixing bowl beat whipping cream, powdered sugar, and cardamom with an electric mixer on medium speed until soft peaks form (tips curl over). Fold in lemon peel.
3 Spoon whipped cream mixture over berries in dishes. Sprinkle each serving with lemon basil.

PER SERVING 168 calories; 15 g fat (9 g sat.); 1 g protein; 8 g carbohydrate; 2 g fiber; 16 mg sodium; 55 mg cholesterol

Grilled Mango Blossom 

MAKES 3 servings
PREP 20 minutes **GRILL** 4 minutes

- **2 medium mangoes, halved and pitted**
- **3 medium kiwifruit, peeled**
- **1 tablespoon molasses**

1 Peel one of the mango halves; set aside remaining three mango halves. Place peeled mango half in a food processor or blender. Cover and process until smooth. Transfer mango puree to a small bowl; cover and chill.
2 Rinse the food processor or blender. Place kiwifruit in food processor or blender. Cover and process until smooth. Transfer kiwi puree to a small bowl; cover and chill.
3 Place the reserved three mango halves on a cutting board, skin sides down. Cut the flesh in a crisscross pattern, being careful not to cut through the skin.
4 For a charcoal grill, place mango halves, cut sides down, on the grill rack directly over medium coals. Grill, uncovered, for 4 to 6 minutes or until light brown and heated through. Brush with molasses during the last 1 minute of grilling. (For a gas grill, preheat grill. Reduce heat to medium. Place mango halves, cut sides down, on grill rack over heat. Cover and grill as above.)
5 To serve, press the skin of the grilled mango halves so the fruit cubes pop outward. Place a mango half into each of three chilled dessert bowls. Drizzle with fruit purees.

PER SERVING 155 calories; 1 g fat (0 g sat.); 2 g protein; 40 g carbohydrate; 5 g fiber; 8 mg sodium; 0 mg cholesterol

Cherry-Wine Poached Apples

Cherry-Wine Poached Apples

MAKES 2 servings
PREP 10 minutes **COOK** 30 minutes

- **2** **medium cooking apples (such as Granny Smith, Braeburn, Pink Lady, or Jonagold)**
- **1** **cup Riesling wine or unsweetened grape juice**
- **1** **cup frozen unsweetened pitted dark sweet cherries**
- **¼** **cup water**
- **1** **3-inch-long sprig fresh rosemary**
- **Fresh mint leaves (optional)**

1 Using a melon baller, remove the apple cores from the bottom of each apple; do not remove stems. Peel apples, leaving stems intact. Place apples in a medium saucepan. Add wine, cherries, the water, and the rosemary. Bring to boiling; reduce heat. Simmer, covered, about 10 minutes or just until apples are tender, turning occasionally to coat apples evenly with liquid.

2 Using a slotted spoon, transfer apples to serving plates. Simmer cooking liquid, uncovered, about 20 minutes or until reduced to 1 cup. Remove from heat; cool slightly. Strain liquid, discarding cherries and rosemary. Spoon liquid over apples on serving plates. Serve warm, or cover and chill for up to 24 hours. If desired, garnish with fresh mint leaves.

PER SERVING 166 calories; 0 g fat; 1 g protein; 23 g carbohydrate; 2 g fiber; 1 mg sodium; 0 mg cholesterol

Blackberry-Lemon Ice

MAKES 6 to 8 servings
PREP 15 minutes **COOK** 2 minutes **FREEZE** 2½ hours

- **1 cup water**
- **½ cup sugar**
- **4 cups fresh blackberries or frozen unsweetened blackberries**
- **¼ cup fresh lemon juice**
- **2 tablespoons finely shredded lemon peel**

1 In a medium saucepan combine the water and the sugar. Bring to boiling, stirring frequently. Boil gently, uncovered, for 2 minutes. Remove from heat and cool slightly.
2 In a blender or food processor combine blackberries, the warm syrup, and lemon juice. Cover and blend until almost smooth. Strain berry mixture through a fine-mesh sieve; discard seeds. Stir in 1 teaspoon of the lemon peel.
3 Transfer the berry mixture to a 3-quart rectangular baking dish or a 13×9×2-inch baking pan. Place in the freezer, uncovered, for 1½ hours or until almost solid.
4 Remove berry ice from freezer. Using a fork, break up the ice into a somewhat smooth mixture. Freeze for 1 hour more.* Break up the ice with a fork and serve in cups. Top each serving with remaining lemon peel.
***Note:** If mixture is frozen longer than the final hour, let it stand at room temperature about 20 minutes before breaking it up with a fork and serving.

PER SERVING 115 calories; 0 g fat; 1 g protein; 29 g carbohydrate; 5 g fiber; 2 mg sodium; 0 mg cholesterol

Meyer Lemon Sorbet

MAKES 10 (⅓-cup) servings
PREP 10 minutes **STAND** 5 minutes **CHILL** overnight
FREEZE per manufacturer's directions; 4 hours

- **1½ cups sugar**
- **1½ cups water**
- **1 tablespoon finely shredded Meyer lemon peel or lemon peel**
- **1 cup Meyer lemon juice or lemon juice**
- **Finely shredded Meyer lemon peel or lemon peel (optional)**

1 In a small saucepan bring sugar and the water to boiling, stirring to dissolve sugar. Cover and chill overnight or place saucepan in a bowl of ice water and stir until sugar syrup is completely chilled.
2 Stir the 1 tablespoon lemon peel and the lemon juice into sugar syrup. Pour lemon mixture into a 1-quart ice cream freezer.* Freeze according to the manufacturer's directions.
3 Transfer sorbet to an airtight container; let sorbet ripen in the freezer for 4 hours. Before serving, let sorbet stand at room temperature for 5 minutes. If desired, garnish servings with additional lemon peel.
***Note:** If you don't have an ice cream freezer, pour mixture into a 2-quart square baking dish. Cover; freeze for 5 to 6 hours or until almost firm. Break frozen mixture into chunks. Transfer to a chilled bowl. Beat with an electric mixer on medium speed until fluffy but not melted. Return to baking dish. Cover and freeze for at least 1 hour.

PER SERVING 118 calories; 0 g fat; 0 g protein; 31 g carbohydrate; 0 g fiber; 1 mg sodium; 0 mg cholesterol

Meyer Lemon Sorbet

Sherbet Pops

Sherbet Pops

MAKES 10 to 12 pops
PREP 20 minutes **FREEZE** overnight

- **10 to twelve 5-ounce paper or plastic cups**
- **1 cup chopped, peeled kiwifruit (3 medium)**
- **1 tablespoon sugar**
- **1 quart raspberry or tangerine sherbet**
- **3 tablespoons orange juice**
- **10 to 12 flat wooden craft sticks**

1 Arrange cups in a baking pan. In a small bowl stir together kiwifruit and sugar; divide among cups. In a large mixing bowl combine sherbet and orange juice. Beat with an electric mixer on low speed until combined. Spoon sherbet mixture over kiwi, filling cups about three-quarters full.
2 Cover each cup with a square of foil. Use a butter knife to make a small hole in the center of each foil square. Slide a wooden craft stick through each hole and into the fruit mixture in the cup. Freeze overnight.
3 To serve, remove the foil and carefully tear paper cups away from pops. Serve immediately.

PER POP 129 calories; 2 g fat (1 g sat.); 1 g protein; 28 g carbohydrate; 3 g fiber; 36 mg sodium; 0 mg cholesterol

Cherry-Berry Ice Cream

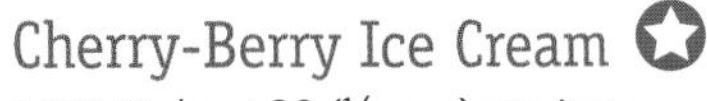

Cherry-Berry Ice Cream

MAKES about 20 (½-cup) servings
PREP 45 minutes **CHILL** 4 to 24 hours
FREEZE per manufacturer's directions

- **¾ cup sugar**
- **1 envelope unflavored gelatin**
- **4 cups whole milk**
- **4 eggs, beaten**
- **1 pound fresh dark sweet cherries, pitted and halved**
- **1 12-ounce package frozen unsweetened red raspberries or 3 cups fresh red raspberries**
- **¼ cup frozen orange juice concentrate, thawed**
- **Sliced fresh strawberries and/or fresh mint leaves (optional)**

1 In a large saucepan combine sugar and gelatin. Stir in milk. Cook and stir over medium heat just until mixture starts to boil. Remove from heat. Whisk about 1 cup of the hot gelatin mixture into beaten eggs; return all to saucepan. Cook and stir for 2 to 3 minutes or until egg mixture coats the back of a clean metal spoon. Do not boil. Stir in cherries, raspberries, and orange juice concentrate. Cover and chill for 4 to 24 hours. (Mixture will be set after chilling.)
2 Transfer the mixture to a 4- or 5-quart ice cream freezer; freeze according to the manufacturer's directions. Serve immediately or, if desired, transfer to an airtight container and let the ice cream ripen in freezer for 4 hours. If desired, garnish with sliced strawberries and/or mint leaves.

PER SERVING 103 calories; 3 g fat (1 g sat.); 4 g protein; 17 g carbohydrate; 1 g fiber; 34 mg sodium; 47 mg cholesterol

Devil's Food Ice Cream Pie

To easily cut through the frozen pie and create smooth straight lines, heat a long sharp knife (such as a chef's knife) under running hot water. Wipe the knife dry with a paper towel and cut through the pie. Reheat the knife between cuts.

Devil's Food Ice Cream Pie 

MAKES 12 servings

PREP 20 minutes **STAND** 10 minutes **FREEZE** 8 hours

- **1 6.75-ounce package fat-free devil's food cookie cakes (12 cookies)**
- **¼ cup peanut butter**
- **¼ cup hot water**
- **1 cup sliced banana (1 large)**
- **4 cups low-fat or light vanilla, chocolate, or desired-flavor ice cream, softened***
- **3 tablespoons fat-free, sugar-free hot fudge-flavored ice cream topping**

1 Coarsely chop cookies. Place pieces in the bottom of an 8-inch springform pan. Set aside. In a small bowl whisk together peanut butter and hot water until smooth. Drizzle evenly over cookie pieces. Top with banana and carefully spoon ice cream evenly over all. Spread ice cream until smooth on top. Cover with plastic wrap and freeze for 8 hours or until firm.

2 Before serving, let stand at room temperature for 10 minutes. Remove the sides of the pan; cut pie into wedges. Drizzle fudge-flavored topping over wedges.

***Note:** To soften ice cream, place ice cream in a large chilled mixing bowl. Stir with a wooden spoon until soft, pressing ice cream against sides of bowl.

PER SERVING 171 calories; 4 g fat (1 g sat.); 4 g protein; 31 g carbohydrate; 1 g fiber; 86 mg sodium; 7 mg cholesterol

Toasted Snowballs 

MAKES 12 servings

PREP 25 minutes **BAKE** 3 minutes **FREEZE** 1 hour **OVEN** 500°F

- **12 graham cracker squares**
- **12 small scoops rocky road or chocolate fudge ice cream (about 1½ cups)**
- **1 7.2-ounce package fluffy white frosting mix**

1 Line a baking sheet with waxed paper. Arrange cracker squares on prepared baking sheet. Use a small ice cream scoop to place scoops of ice cream on each cracker square. Cover and freeze while preparing frosting.

2 Prepare frosting mix according to package directions. Place frosting in a large pastry bag fitted with a large (¼-inch) round tip. Pipe frosting over each ice cream mound to cover. (Or use a spoon to spread frosting over each ice cream scoop, spreading to cover.) Freeze at least 1 hour (cover loosely after frosting is firm).

3 Preheat oven to 500°F. Transfer squares to a greased baking sheet. Bake, uncovered, for 3 to 4 minutes or until frosting is golden brown. Serve immediately.

PER SERVING 120 calories; 2 g fat (1 g sat.); 1 g protein; 25 g carbohydrate; 0 g fiber; 91 mg sodium; 6 mg cholesterol

Toasted Snowballs

Double
Melon Bowls

Double Melon Bowls

MAKES 6 to 8 servings
PREP 25 minutes **STAND** 20 minutes **FREEZE** 2 hours; overnight

- **2 cups cubed, seeded watermelon**
- **1 medium cantaloupe (about 3 pounds), halved and seeded**
- **1 quart vanilla frozen yogurt or vanilla ice cream, softened***
- **Sea salt (optional)**

1 Place watermelon cubes in a single layer on a tray or in a shallow baking pan; freeze for 2 to 3 hours or until firm. Transfer watermelon cubes to a freezer bag or container and freeze until needed.
2 With a large spoon, scoop out flesh from cantaloupe, leaving a 1/4-inch shell; set fruit aside. Cut a thin slice from the bottom of each shell so the shell sits flat. Place shells, upside down, on a paper towel-lined tray; set aside.
3 Place cantaloupe flesh in a food processor or blender; cover and process until smooth. Place pureed cantaloupe in a fine-mesh sieve set over a bowl. Let stand for 5 minutes to remove excess liquid; discard liquid. You should have about 1 cup pulp.
4 In a large bowl gently fold the cantaloupe pulp into the ice cream until just combined. Spoon the ice cream mixture evenly into the cantaloupe shells. Place shells on a baking sheet. Cover and freeze overnight or until very firm.
5 Before serving, let melon bowls stand at room temperature for 20 to 30 minutes to soften slightly. Top with frozen watermelon cubes; if desired, sprinkle watermelon lightly with sea salt. Scoop into serving bowls.
***Note:** To soften ice cream, place ice cream in a large chilled bowl. Stir with a wooden spoon until soft, pressing ice cream against sides of bowl.

PER SERVING 188 calories; 4 g fat (2 g sat.); 4 g protein; 36 g carbohydrate; 1 g fiber; 59 mg sodium; 13 mg cholesterol

Sorbet Melon Parfaits 

MAKES 8 servings
START TO FINISH 15 minutes

- **1½ cups seeded watermelon balls, chilled**
- **1½ cups seeded cantaloupe balls, chilled**
- **1½ cups seeded honeydew melon balls, chilled**
- **2 cups lemon sorbet or mango sorbet**
- **1 cup sweet sparkling wine or sparkling grape juice, chilled**
- **Fresh mint sprigs (optional)**

1 Divide melon balls among eight wine glasses or goblets. Scoop about 1/4 cup sorbet on top of melon in each glass or goblet. Pour about 2 tablespoons sparkling wine over sorbet and melon in each glass or goblet. If desired, garnish with mint. Serve immediately.

PER SERVING 112 calories; 0 g fat; 1 g protein; 24 g carbohydrate; 1 g fiber; 7 mg sodium; 0 mg cholesterol

Sorbet Melon Parfaits

f

g

M

N

O

Q-R

In-a-Pinch Substitutions

It can happen to the best of us: Halfway through a recipe, you find you're completely out of a key ingredient. Here's what to do:

Recipe Calls For:	You May Substitute:
1 square unsweetened chocolate	3 Tbs unsweetened cocoa powder + 1 Tbs butter/margarine
1 cup cake flour	1 cup less 2 Tbs all-purpose flour
2 Tbs flour (for thickening)	1 Tbs cornstarch
1 tsp baking powder	¼ tsp baking soda + ½ tsp cream of tartar + ¼ tsp cornstarch
1 cup corn syrup	1 cup sugar + ¼ cup additional liquid used in recipe
1 cup milk	½ cup evaporated milk + ½ cup water
1 cup buttermilk or sour milk	1 Tbs vinegar or lemon juice + enough milk to make 1 cup
1 cup sour cream (for baking)	1 cup plain yogurt
1 cup firmly packed brown sugar	1 cup sugar + 2 Tbs molasses
1 tsp lemon juice	¼ tsp vinegar (not balsamic)
¼ cup chopped onion	1 Tbs instant minced
1 clove garlic	¼ tsp garlic powder
2 cups tomato sauce	¾ cup tomato paste + 1 cup water
1 Tbs prepared mustard	1 tsp dry mustard + 1 Tbs water

How to Know What You Need

Making a shopping list based on a recipe can be tricky if you don't know how many tomatoes yields 3 cups chopped. Our handy translations:

When the Recipe Calls For:	You Need:
4 cups shredded cabbage	1 small cabbage
1 cup grated raw carrot	1 large carrot
2½ cups sliced carrots	1 pound raw carrots
4 cups cooked cut fresh green beans	1 pound beans
1 cup chopped onion	1 large onion
4 cups sliced raw potatoes	4 medium-size potatoes
1 cup chopped sweet pepper	1 large pepper
1 cup chopped tomato	1 large tomato
2 cups canned tomatoes	16 oz can
4 cups sliced apples	4 medium-size apples
1 cup mashed banana	3 medium-size bananas
1 tsp grated lemon rind	1 medium-size lemon
2 Tbs lemon juice	1 medium-size lemon
4 tsp grated orange rind	1 medium-size orange
1 cup orange juice	3 medium-size oranges
4 cups sliced peaches	8 medium-size peaches
2 cups sliced strawberries	1 pint
1 cup soft bread crumbs	2 slices fresh bread
1 cup bread cubes	2 slices fresh bread
2 cups shredded Swiss or Cheddar cheese	8 oz cheese
1 cup egg whites	6 or 7 large eggs
1 egg white	2 tsp egg white powder + 2 Tbs water
4 cups chopped walnuts or pecans	1 pound shelled